Illustrated Battles of the Continental European Nations 1820-1900
Volume 2

Illustrated Battles of the Continental European Nations 1820-1900
Volume 2

Charles Lowe
A. Hilliard Atteridge
and
John Augustus O'Shea

*Illustrated Battles of the Continental European Nations 1820-1900
Volume 2*
by Charles Lowe
A. Hilliard Atteridge
and
John Augustus O'Shea

First published under the title
Battles of the Nineteenth Century

Leonaur is an imprint of Oakpast Ltd
Copyright in this form © 2017 Oakpast Ltd

ISBN: 978-1-78282-634-7 (hardcover)
ISBN: 978-1-78282-635-4 (softcover)

http://www.leonaur.com

Publisher's Notes

The views expressed in this book are not necessarily those of the publisher.

Contents

The Battle of Brody 1863	7
The Siege of La Puebla May 1863	27
The Storming of the Redoubts of Düppel April 18, 1864	43
The Battle of Königgratz July 3, 1866	63
The Battle of Lissa July 20, 1866	85
The Battle of Custozza June 24, 1866	103
Garibaldi's Defeat at Mentana November 3, 1867	121
The Battle of Wörth August 6, 1870	137
The Battle of Mars-la-Tour August 16, 1870	155
The Battle of Gravelotte (St. Privat) August 18, 1870	181
The Battle of Sedan September 1, 1870	209
The Battle of Saarbrück August 2, 1870	237
The Battle of Champigny November 29-December 2, 1870	249
The Battle of Villersexel January 9-10, 1871	271

The Polish Insurrection
1863

The Battle of Brody 1863

By H. Sutherland Edwards

In England, where fortunately we have known nothing of rebellion for the last 200 years, (as at 1901), popular risings are always attributed to tyrannical government on the part of the rulers. The Polish insurrection, however, of 1863 was due in the first instance to laxity on the part of the rulers. During the Crimean War, when the Russians had Turkey, France, England, Sardinia, and virtually Austria to contend with, the Poles did not move a hand against the government, severe as it had always been, of the Emperor Nicholas. Alexander II., on the other hand, who ruled over Russia and over Poland when the insurrection of 1863 broke out, was a particularly mild sovereign, and though he had introduced no organic reforms into Poland, nevertheless ruled the country with moderation.

The use of the Polish language in the government offices and in the schools, without being formally permitted, was openly tolerated. Several useful institutions—some of them, such as the Agricultural Society, of a national and patriotic character—had been founded without the least opposition on the part of the government. No recruits had been taken for the army since the peace of 1856; and meanwhile the country, without being rendered happy, was growing prosperous and rich. The number of troops maintained in Poland was exceptionally small, and under the new reign there had been no examples of political persecution.

Things were far less quiet in Russia proper, where the emancipation of the serfs had suggested to the landed proprietors that they also ought to be liberated; that they ought to be allowed some voice in the government of the country instead of being treated as the subjects of a pure despotism. Numbers of intelligent but scarcely well-informed men among the Poles looked upon the emancipation of the serfs in Russia as the removal of the keystone on which the whole political edifice rested. They saw at the same time that Italy had been set free by the Emperor of the French, and conceived a hope—not unsupported at the Tuileries—that what Napoleon III. had done for the Italians he would next do for the Poles.

Russia in her disorganised condition would not (they said to themselves) be able to make any formidable resistance to the legions sent against her by the conqueror of Magenta and of Solferino. France, moreover, could without difficulty secure the support of Austria; and the makers of political programmes had already arranged that Austria should give up Galicia towards the formation of a new and enlarged kingdom of Poland, receiving in return for her lost territory the so-called Danubian provinces of Moldavia and Wallachia, now known collectively as Roumania.

This audacious proposition fills one at the present moment with astonishment; but the prosperous future of the two great Hospodarates, soon to be united in one principality and ultimately to be raised to the position of an independent kingdom, could not then be foreseen. France and Austria, in any intervention they might undertake on behalf of Poland, could, it was. thought, count on some measure of support from England—what is called moral support, if nothing more.

Several Polish anniversaries were celebrated by patriotic demonstrations; and these manifestations of national spirit and the spirit of independence assumed at last so serious a character that the Russians forbade them, but without bringing them to an end. At last there was a collision between unresisting, unarmed Polish patriots and Russian troops. There were several victims, and the dead bodies of those who had fallen were exhibited and their photographs circulated among the indignant population of Warsaw. These tragic scenes were repeated. Meanwhile numerous arrests had been made, and soon the prisons of Warsaw were full. Troops, moreover, had been telegraphed for, and the feeble garrison was quickly reinforced.

While repressing public manifestations the government—on the recommendation of the Marquis Wielopolski, a genuine patriot but a hard, unsympathetic man, who was most unpopular with his fellow-countrymen—introduced reforms of considerable importance, which, however, were received not only without gratitude but with ridicule by the Poles, who regarded these concessions as the outcome merely of fear. The emperor sent his brother, the Grand Duke Constantine, to Warsaw in the character of viceroy. But the extreme party— the party of action—were opposed to all attempts at reconciliation. The grand duke and his minister, the before mentioned marquis, were both attacked by assassins, and all possibility of quelling the agitation, which had now become formidable, seemed at an end. Wielopolski's reforms were, however, persisted in. They consisted, briefly, in the exclusion from Poland of all but Polish officials; of the institution of municipal councils and of a university at which richly-salaried chairs were offered to professors from Poland and other Slavonic countries; and, finally, of a regular system of recruitment in lieu of the arbitrary conscription or proscription which had been practised under the Emperor Nicholas.

But before introducing the new system of recruitment, Wielopolski thought it absolutely necessary to get rid of the most irreconcilable enemies of Russia by means of the old one. He knew from the reports of his agents that arms had been secretly introduced into Warsaw, and that a rising was to take place on the night of the 15th of February. He resolved to anticipate this movement, which would be fatal to all his plans for the good of his country, by seizing as recruits, and carrying off to the army, some 2,000 of the most determined of the would-be insurgents. The attempt made on the night of the 14th to execute the conscription in the old proscription style was itself the signal for the rising. The Russians, the Poles of the moderate and so-called aristocratic party, and generally those who knew nothing of the insurrectionary project, thought the next morning that the danger had passed.

But in the evening the Central National Committee—soon to become a government in itself—held a secret meeting, at which it was decided to order a general rising for the 22nd. Couriers were sent out in every direction; and in spite of the great number of persons engaged in preparing the outbreak, the secret was so well kept that on the night of the 22nd it took place simultaneously in all parts of the country. At Warsaw, the soldiers were to have been surprised in the guard-houses and the barracks, and with the arms taken from them the citadel was to have been attacked.

This plan of action was attended with success when tried on a small scale in some of the little country towns. But it was impossible in Warsaw, where in and about the city were some 50,000 troops. The party of action thought with regret of the time, nearly two years before, when they had first proposed to commence the insurrection, and when the Warsaw garrison numbered only 5,000.

The insurrection of 1863 was once described by a Pole as a "patriotic eruption." It broke out over the face of the whole country, and it was difficult to allay; otherwise its symptoms were not very terrible. The Russians always maintained that the movement was not spontaneous, but that it was started and maintained by the "cosmopolitan revolution," with its Polish, Hungarian, and Italian adherents. Revolutionists of all nations did, in fact, join the insurgent bands, but it was the Poles themselves who formed them. Bands of insurgents from 300 or 400 to 3,000 or 4,000 strong soon showed themselves in all parts of Russian Poland, in the so-called kingdom of Poland as formed in 1815, in Lithuania, and in the Polono-Ruthenian provinces of Volhynia, Podolia, and Kiev.

In estimating the forces at the disposal of the Polish National Government it would be a mistake to count those insurgents only who at any time were actually in the field. Everyone who joined a detachment organised by the National Junta became a soldier of the Polish National Army, and had to obey orders, not only as long as his detachment remained in the field (generally only a few hours after its first collision with the enemy), but as long as the insurrection lasted. If the band to which he belonged was driven in, he had to report himself to headquarters, and so hold himself in readiness to start again for the frontier at the shortest notice.

I say "for the frontier," because it was usually within easy reach of the Austrian or Prussian frontier that the engagements between the Polish insurgents and the Russian troops took place. When a detachment of insurgents sought refuge in the Polish province of Posen, its members were usually arrested by the Prussian authorities. The officials, however, in Galicia were better disposed towards the insurgent Poles; or perhaps they wished to give a strong hint to Russia as to what they could do against her. should they ever feel called upon to furnish aid to a Polish insurrection.

The Polish Junta had organised a service of spies and executioners called National Gendarmes. It was their duty to terrify the spies on the Russian side, and to teach patriotism to Polish peasants by hanging them if they declined to join the insurrection. The *Junta* also employed a body of commissioners for collecting taxes and giving and receiving information of various kinds. The war-tax amounted to 10 *per cent*, on clear income, and was, or ought to have been, paid by everyone except the peasants, who were not allowed to pay anything to anybody, and who were so petted by both governments that they would have been quite spoilt had they not already been beyond the possibility of spoiling.

The Russians tried to make the Polish peasant fight against his ancestral master, while the Poles tried to make him fight against the Russian Government. After taking what he could get from both sides, the Polish peasant remained quietly at home, as a rule, doing no work, paying no rent, and enjoying himself after his own fashion. In no instance, however, could the Polish peasant be persuaded to do battle for the Russians; whereas in certain districts and on particular estates he really fought well for his own people.

As an example of the way in which Polish insurgent expeditions were organised in 1863, I may give an account of the rise and fall of one of the most important sent from Galicia across the frontier into Russian territory. It was necessary from time to time to send forth an expedition against the Russians, if only to convince the foreign Powers that the Polish insurrection was not dead; in which case, all idea of intervening on behalf of the Poles would have fallen to the ground.

The preparations made for the seven or eight hours' fighting which took place before the town of Brody and the village of Radzievilov, had occupied the Polish National Junta about four months. Some of the insurgents who were to take part in the expedition had experienced considerable trouble in getting to Cracow, and they found it still more difficult to continue their journey to Lemberg, while the general advance from Lemberg to Brody on the Russo-Volhynian frontier was made on a system of zigzag approaches, almost after the model of siege operations.

Lemberg was so full of insurgents that a circus was opened for their special benefit, when scenes from Mazeppa were performed for the instruction and amusement of men who were themselves bound for the Ukraine, but who never, I may add, had the smallest chance of getting there. Every country house between Lemberg and Brody, for many miles on each side of the main road, served as a halting-place; and many proprietors had from twenty to a hundred insurgents staying in and about their houses and grounds for periods varying from three days to two months.

It was not from any want of kindness on the part of their entertainers that soldiers of the National Army in concealment were sometimes put to sleep in trees. If the words "domiciliary visit" were whispered in the morning or afternoon, everyone was on the look-out for the police in the evening; and as soon as they made their appearance on the one side, the object of their search disappeared on the other. If, when the household retired to rest, the "domiciliary visit" or "revision" had not yet taken place, there was nothing left for the insurgents but to take to the wood by which every manor-house in Eastern Galicia is surrounded.

The scheme for invading Volhynia from Galicia was, in some respects, well-conceived. Wysoçki, with 1,200 men, was to have marched upon Radzievilov in front, while Horodyçki and Minniewski, each with 650, attacked it on the right and left. A day or two afterwards Wisznieswski was to have entered Volhynia farther north than Minniewski, and close to the right bank of the River Bug, while Rozyçki, one of the best leaders who had yet appeared, was to have penetrated into the same province farther south than Horodyçki, and near the frontier of Podolia.

Finally, another officer was to have taken a detachment of cavalry into Podolia itself; and thus from Podolia to Lublin, and along the whole line of the Galician-Volhynian frontier, the Russians would have been attacked; and though some of the detachments were sure to be destroyed, it was thought certain that others would succeed in advancing far into the interior of Volhynia, and that once there, they would either gain the active support of the peasants, or at least show themselves strong enough to ensure their respect and, to a certain extent, their assistance.

The chief appointed to direct the combined movement was General Wysoçki, formerly commander of the Polish Legion in Hungary, and the title given to him by the National Junta was General Commanding in the Province of Lublin and the Ruthenian Provinces

On the day fixed for the commencement of this important movement, in which, had all gone well, some 4,000 men would have been engaged, it was found that only two detachments—those of General Wysoçki and Colonel Horodyçki, his immediate supporter on the right—were ready to start. This unreadiness could be attributed to no want of foresight on the part of the commissaries of the expedition.

Arms had been purchased and confiscated, purchased and confiscated again, for three times the number of men composing the expedition; and although many of these men were arrested and imprisoned, it turned out at the last moment that there were more insurgents than there were arms for them to carry. Fresh seizures of rifles, bayonets, and revolvers were made on the Sunday night and early Monday morning;

THE CASTLE, CRACOW

and on Monday afternoon, when the Wysoçki and Horodyçki detachments were summoned to the wood, it was found impossible to equip for the field more than 1,500 of the former and 450 of the latter.

Insurgents were staying in the houses of the rich as well as of the poor, and were treated with a sort of paternal affection everywhere. Indeed, the kindness and hospitality shown to all classes and conditions of men who called themselves insurgents was, if anything, carried to excess; for many persons received and entertained strangers on the understanding that they belonged to the Volhynian expedition, but without having any positive proof of the fact. Even Austrian officials were in some places touched by this general confidence, and when ordered to institute a "revision," would give a hint beforehand that at such an hour their arrival might be expected. Then the men would go into the woods, the horses would be taken out of the stables and sent into the fields, while the saddles and bridles, were buried in the garden.

I have seen packets of saddles and boxes of arms left at a house without any notification as to where they came from or whither they were to be sent. In such cases the man who took them in put them in a place of safety, and a day or two afterwards would receive a line of writing, or more generally a message by word of mouth, telling him to forward them to some house a few miles nearer the frontier. If the whole country, with the exception of the ignorant peasantry, had not formed one general association for promoting: the interests of Poland, this unbounded trust from Pole to Pole would soon have led to the speedy exposure and frustration of all the national schemes. As it was, they were carried out to a certain point, and never once broke down from any bad faith, or from want of faith, on the part of those called upon to assist in executing them.

The insurgents were from many different lands, but chiefly from the kingdom of Poland and from Galicia. There were a few Hungarians, a few Poles, a Frenchman who had taken part in every kind of insurrection, except an insurrection of Poles, and who told me that he had joined the expedition simply because "this page was wanting to his life." There was a Polish doctor too, himself a revolutionary *dilettante* whom I had met in previous Polish expeditions, and who interested me from the fact of his carrying not only a rifle but also a case of surgical instruments. First, he shot his foe, and then, if life was not extinct, extracted the bullet from the wound, and did his best to cure him.

There were two young ladies, moreover—one of them attired in a tunic and knickerbockers, the other in a grey military uniform. The latter of the two got wounded in the battle. She was shot in the ankle, and when I visited her in hospital, she showed me the bullet that had lamed her, and assured me that she would at the earliest opportunity send it back to its rightful possessors. A certain number of the insurgents were middle-aged men who belonged to what was called the "emigration"—who had emigrated, that is to say, into Poland at the close of the insurrection of 1830, and who since then had been living in Paris or in London, they said:

> The young men here are admirable, sacrificing themselves for a cause which is a very desperate one if they are never to be assisted from abroad. As for us, it does not matter. We are old fellows, and would rather die in Poland than anywhere else; and then we have not led the sort of life which attaches men to this world.

One, an old soldier of the Polish Army of 1830, told me that he had been for thirteen years working at a desk in an insurance office, and that he was not sorry to get a little fresh air and an opportunity of riding on horseback. Another, an officer of the same army, had been keeping a shop, and was making humorous speculations as to how in his absence the business would be carried on. A third saw his native land for the first time, and was saying what nice people the Poles were.

Among the insurgents belonging to Wysoçki's corps was a young lady, described by an eyewitness as "so timid, and so afraid of being looked upon as a wonder, that she kept herself almost in perpetual seclusion," but so brave that on the day of battle she insisted upon being placed in the first line, and greatly distinguished herself in the action fought in the immediate neighbourhood of Brody.

Brody is the last town in Eastern Galicia as one approaches the Russo-Polish province of Volhynia, and the object of the expedition sent from Eastern Galicia into Volhynia was to raise the Volhynian peasantry. They are not of the same religion as the Poles, and they do not seem to have preserved any grateful recollections of the days when Poland was free but the peasantry in Poland enslaved. An endeavour to conciliate them had, however, been made by presenting them with so-called "golden charters," which conveyed to them in fee-simple the ownership of the land which they held, on certain conditions, as of rent-paying or payments in redemption, from the manorial proprietor.

AMONG THE INSURGENTS WAS A YOUNG LADY.

A day or two before the entry into Volhynia I received a message at a country house where I was staying, warning me not to be unprepared if the next morning someone called for me in a carriage in order to drive me into the middle of a neighbouring wood, where I should meet some friends who would enable me to accompany Wysoçki's so-called army on its march towards Radzievilov, the first village in the Russo-Polish province of Volhynia. The person expected came at the appointed time, mentioned my name, and then, instead of taking me to the heart of the forest, drove me through a beautiful woodland country to the house of a neighbouring proprietor, where, besides the host, I found one of the chief promoters of the expedition, and two of the principal officers of the corps commanded by Horodyçki, one of Wysoçki's lieutenants.

One of the officers took out a map of the country about to be entered (it was a photographic print from the private map of the Russian staff), and pointed out to me the place of assembly in the forest, the spot at which the frontier had to be crossed, and the road by which it was intended to advance upon Radzievilov. Discussions on the interminable Polish question, together with pistol-shooting, fencing, and other warlike amusements, filled up the time until dinner, after which the officers went singly to visit our first place of encampment, and came back with the alarming news that an Austrian patrol had been seen hovering about the spot where most of the arms lay buried.

In the evening a "revision" or "domiciliary visit" was announced. The house was cleared of insurgents, and two very suspicious-looking cases were placed where the police were likely to find them. One was empty; the other was labelled "*Vin de Bordeaux*," and contained wine. All through the night messengers were continually arriving, and the first news in the morning was that the arms had been seized, that the labour of three months had been lost, and that the expedition could not start. Ultimately it was discovered that about a hundred rifles had been taken, but that there were still nearly three hundred in a place of comparative safety. The question arose as to whether it would be advisable to postpone the departure of the expedition until more arms could be procured, but it was soon decided not to risk, by further delay, the seizure of the whole stock.

At last, early on Monday afternoon, we got into a cart, built without springs for the same sort of reason for which Highlanders are said not to wear trousers, and went into the wood. Turning from the high- into a cross-road, from the cross-road into a lane, and from the lane into a private path, we came, after many windings, to a little glade, where the long grass had been crushed and flattened as if by a roller. The former presence of human beings in this sequestered spot was indicated by an old boot, which Hoby would have disavowed, and a cask containing gin—from which, as it was not yet empty, it was presumed that the insurgents could not be far distant.

They were so well concealed, however, that although we had good guides (including one of the forest-keepers of the estate), it was not easy to find them. At last we burst upon a band of brothers, who were engaged in the difficult and, to them, evidently novel occupation of trying on boots. The boot so contemptuously abandoned in the first halting-place had apparently been the only one among some thirty men. The major was answering questions on all sorts of subjects from boots upwards, and was at the same time superintending a distribution of pistols, which, being larger than any pistols ever seen before or afterwards out of a pantomime, looked very terrible, and produced (as they were intended to do) a fine and healthy effect on the Ruthenian village population.

The peasants looked a good deal scared as the insurgents marched through the fields, but were soon reassured, or pretended to be, when a few words were spoken to them in kindness. Of attacking or molesting the insurgents in any way there was, of course, no thought, more particularly as the half-detachment, consisting of 200 men, looked in the moonlight, as it straggled along in double file, like a much larger force, and was pronounced by impartial spectators to be at least 1,000 strong. Two peasants, however, were overheard whispering that they had a great mind to go off and tell the Austrians. They were arrested, asked if they wanted to be hanged, and replying in the negative, were told how to avoid that fate so far as it was likely to be inflicted upon them by their Polish compatriots.

They were then put into a cart and driven along after the detachment, and were not liberated until everything had been made ready for crossing the frontier.

We marched during nearly all the first night, passing from the moonlight into the darkness of the dense woods, where nothing but glow-worms, and here and there in the insurgent column the light of a cigar, could be seen, and then again into the moonlight; until at last we came to a river or mountain stream (running down from the Carpathians), and sat down by the side of the waters and supped. It was generally believed to be one of the best suppers they had ever had

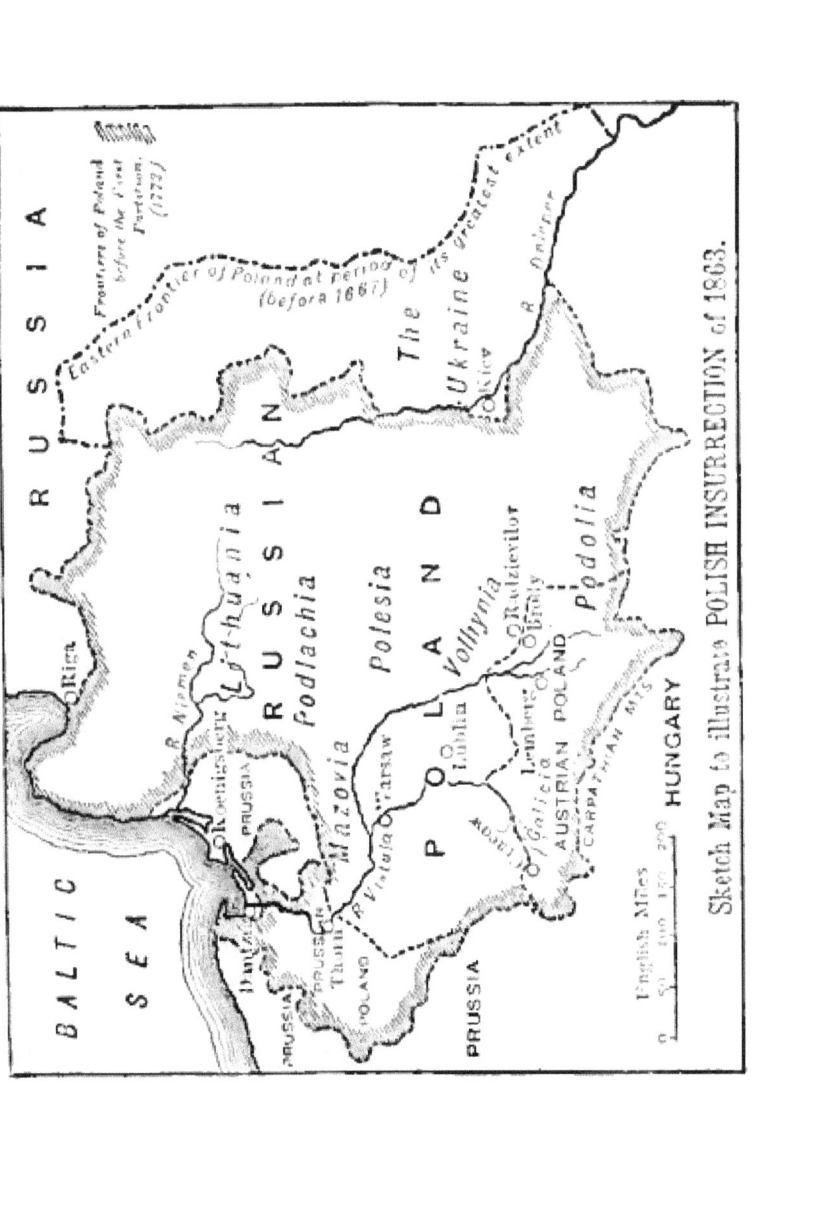

(of many poor fellows it was the last); and the breakfast, to which a select number were invited, was also much admired, especially some tea-soup made in a saucepan and served out in saucepan-lids, wine-glasses, and wooden ladles.

During the halt, of which advantage was taken to eat our hurried breakfast, Horodyçki, the commander of the detachment, joined us, bringing with him 200 infantry, and from forty to fifty cavalry. The rifles, bayonets, and scythes were now disinterred, or pulled out of their hiding places in the brushwood; and I found that this particular batch had all been concealed at about twenty paces distance from the public road running through the middle of the wood. The Austrians had not found them, because they had been hidden where the Austrians would be sure not to look for them.

As the insurgents moved away from the cottage where they had halted for tea, a plain and shrill-voiced woman came out and complained that her husband had deserted her in order to go and fight the Russians. It was impossible not to understand that he had chosen the lesser of two evils. The poor man who preferred his country to his wife and death to his home was in the cavalry, and now galloped to the front and was soon out of sight and, it may be hoped, out of hearing. The great majority of the insurgents, however—especially those in the infantry—could have had nothing to leave: they were men of the vagabond type, the dregs of the Polish towns, who had taken service in the Polish National Army because they were ready to turn their hands to any odd job, especially an exciting one, that might present itself.

The cavalry, on the other hand, was chiefly composed of sons of landed proprietors, large and small; though, with very few exceptions, the sons of the great Polish landowners did not find their way to the insurrection at all. When the family of some great Polish aristocrat was represented among the insurgents, it was usually in the person of some scapegrace scion of the house; so, that if by some strange accident, the national movement were attended by success (as through foreign intervention), the members of the great family might be able to say:

"We also were there, or at least one of us."

The cavalry, with its well-born riders and well-bred steeds, was of very little use, except for the service of the camp and now and then for distant reconnoitring; and it was scarcely ever employed in action. Some of the newcomers, especially among the cavalry, were quite disheartened at the idea of having for comrades such riff-raff as the infantry for the most part consisted of. An officer, noticing this, said to some of the well-to-do insurgents who had just arrived:

> You have come to the camp under the impression that you would find everyone here as good as yourselves; I wish such were the case. But we must do our best, and we shall make soldiers of them all when we get on the other side of the frontier.

As for the officers, they were all men who had seen plenty of service in foreign armies, and who had in many cases taken part in expeditions during the insurrection actually going on. Horodyçki, already mentioned as commanding one of Wysoçki's detachments, dignified by the name of "brigade," had distinguished himself in the Hungarian War of 1848-49 by defending at the head of a battalion of the Polish Legion the bridge and passage of the canal at Temesvar against an overpowering force while the Hungarian army was effecting its retreat.

Major Horodyçki lost half his battalion, but he succeeded in keeping the enemy at bay. He was a simple, straightforward man, a good deal sterner than the majority of Poles, and apparently not much given to seeing visions. He did not believe in any immediate intervention on the behalf of Poland, but felt sure that sooner or later it would come, and that meanwhile it was for the Poles to hasten it. He had never expected any intervention before the spring, and meanwhile the Poles must make such efforts and prove themselves so strong that neither France nor England would refuse them a helping hand. More than this would not be necessary.

Horodyçki did not seem to share the opinion of some of his countrymen as to the goodwill of the peasants towards the insurrection; at least, he turned some of the Ruthenian peasants out of the camp who had come there with the gifts of fresh butter, sheep's milk, cheese, and potted cream. He feared them *et dona ferentes*, and said, when he was asked whether their offering was not a good sign:

> They are with us now we are here; they will be with our enemies when we are gone. I know them, and have sent them away.

A Ruthenian priest and his wife brought something more valuable than butter and cheese. They brought their nephew. This was a proof of sympathy which could not be misunderstood, and the young man was accepted with thanks, and at the proper moment sent across

Polish Peasants

the frontier. Several ladies, too, visited the camp, and so inundated the place with strawberries-and-cream that Horodyçki, fearing, no doubt, that discipline would be relaxed, and the forest of Nakwasha converted into a Capua, gave orders that no more women should be suffered to approach.

The second officer of Horodyçki's detachment—the major commanding the infantry—was Synkiewicz, son of the historian and novelist of that name, and captain in the Italian Army. Synkiewicz, without knowing his country from personal observation, had formed a romantic picture of it in his imagination, and he said that he found the Poles what he had always imagined them to be. Some of them do indeed come up to any ideal which their warmest admirers may have formed of them; and these were the men with whom Synkiewicz habitually associated. It might in other circumstances have been inspiriting, but to those who knew the truth was saddening, to see the delight with which this officer looked forward to the hour fixed for entering Volhynia; for it was certain that he must die there or come back disheartened.

He would not allow that anything was wrong with his detachment. If anyone said that the arms were a little clumsy, he replied that the greatest battles of modern times had been gained with arms not nearly so good. As to the men, they were not prepossessing in appearance, but would know how to fight. As to numbers, if 500 men (of which his battalion consisted) were really determined to cut their way through an opposing force, they could do it, however large that force might be. This officer wore a Garibaldian costume, fearing that if he appeared in the uniform of the Italian regular army, and got taken prisoner, representations might be made to the Italian War Ministry, and his promotion stopped or his commission cancelled.

He was told that the Russians would be sure to pick him off; but he replied that he wished to be conspicuous for the sake of his men, and that the Russians, if they aimed directly at him, would be sure not to hit him. He did them an injustice; for half an hour afterwards they sent a bullet through his long chestnut-coloured beard, just as he was endeavouring at the head of his battalion to dislodge them from Radzievilov.

The first half of Synkiewicz's detachment, consisting of an advance-guard of cavalry and two companies of infantry, had already been taken across the frontier by Captain Tchorszewski, an officer who had served with Horodyçki in Hungary, and who was attached

AS THE REAR-GUARD LEFT THE WOOD IT WAS FIRED UPON BY A PARTY OF COSSACKS

to the British headquarters during the Crimean War. Captain Jagninski, another of Horodyçki's companions in Hungary, took charge of the second half, and was accompanied by Synkiewicz and Horodyçki, chief of the miniature "brigade." The rear-guard of cavalry was under the direction of a Polish officer late of the Russian Army.

The night, which had been beautiful, like the first night of the march, until about ten o'clock, suddenly darkened just as the detachment began to cross the frontier; and the rear-guard passed into Volhynia in the midst of thunder, lightning, and such torrents of rain that, after the lapse of a minute, the dense wood afforded no protection whatever against it. The last man to leave was a Hungarian servant, who had brought nothing into the camp but an old horse with a piece of rope tied round his nose, and who galloped out on a magnificent charger, splendidly equipped, and brandishing a long sabre.

As the rear-guard left the wood it was fired upon by a party of Cossacks, and at the same time a messenger reached us from the Galician side with the news that the Austrians at Podkamin (a town about six miles distant) had found out the position of the camp. General Wysoçki, marching from the other side of Brody, was to have joined Horodyçki and taken the chief command of the combined detachments in front of Radzievilov at daybreak. But Horodyçki arrived at the place of meeting before his time, and attacked the Russians without waiting for Wysoçki, who, as a matter of fact, did not arrive until long after his time.

On entering the town of Radzievilov, Horodyçki at once engaged some 800 Russians who were drawn up in the market-place. Horodyçki had now but 300 men under his command. Of the 450 or 500 infantrymen in the wood, some forty or fifty of the most ill-conditioned had bolted on finding themselves in the presence of the Cossacks, who, as before mentioned, fired into the detachment as it was crossing the frontier. Synkiewicz sent away about an equal number as unfit for the desperate work before them. The rear-guard had been dispersed on crossing the frontier, and the rest of Horodyçki's cavalry could not be employed.

Nearly all the officers of Horodyçki's detachment were killed or wounded. Horodyçki, who throughout the two days' campaign had suffered terribly from acute headache, and wore around his head a bandage constantly moistened, was cured of his complaint by a Russian bullet before he had been many minutes inside Radzievilov. Jagninski and Tchorszewski were also killed. Synkiewicz had to take refuge in a large pond or lake, where he remained for eight hours, while the peasants who had been pursuing him stood on the banks armed with scythes ready to murder him if he ventured to return to dry land. He swam unnoticed to a little island of mud, and there remained concealed amongst rushes and weeds, until he at last thought of taking off his Italian hat and sending it floating along the water. Then the peasants thought their intended victim was drowned, and went home to dinner.

When, after the dispersion and partial destruction of Horodyçki's detachment, Wysoçki's larger corps entered upon the scene, it took up its position in a wood near Radzievilov and sent out companies which fired tranquilly at their assailants from a cornfield not far distant. Of these companies, some showed but little fight, while others behaved with much heroism. The officers in either case got killed. Glisczinski, one of the bravest of the brave, employed on Wysoçki's staff, was actively employed in bringing up and placing the companies until, after having had two horses shot under him, he was struck down by almost the last bullet that was fired. Domogalski, chief of Wysoçki's staff, was mortally wounded, and carried back to Brody to die.

The Battle of Brody, then, was for the Polish insurgents a total and lamentable failure. Instead of making the attack with the combination of several detachments, numbering altogether 4,500 men, they began their brief campaign with only two detachments, which attacked separately and were separately routed. This was the last military operation on anything like an important scale that the directors of the Polish insurrection of 1863 tried to carry out. It was more a political demonstration than a serious military undertaking, and even in the former character it was ineffective. There was never the least chance of the Poles being helped from abroad, unless they first showed that they were really capable of helping themselves.

THE FRANCO-MEXICAN WAR
1861-1867

The Siege of La Puebla
May 1863

By A. Hillard Atteridge

The capture of La Puebla de los Angeles, in 1863, may be said to have been the high-water mark of the fortunes of Napoleon III. It opened the gates of Mexico to his army, and enabled him to pose as the founder of an empire in the New World. Strange to say, it was the defeat of the Confederates at Gettysburg, and the fall of Vicksburg only a few weeks later on in the same year, that decided the fate of this new-made conquest of France, which could only be maintained on condition that the great Republic beyond the Rio Grande was no longer in a position to assert its traditional policy of excluding European interference from the American continent.

But on the day that Puebla fell many of even the shrewdest observers thought that the Southern Confederacy had come to stay, and that thus a power friendly to France was being built up on the frontiers of Mexico. The siege of Puebla is also notable on account of the determined valour with which it was held against the French. The veterans of the Crimea and of Italy, the victors of Sebastopol and Solferino, were held at bay for weeks by a half-irregular force, inspired by the ardent courage of the heroic Ortega.

First a word as to the events which brought the eagles of the Second Empire to the Mexican plateau. In 1861 England, France, and Spain formed an alliance to occupy the city and port of Vera Cruz, in order thus to compel the Republican Government of Mexico to pay the interest on its loans, the bonds of which were chiefly held by the subjects of the three allied governments. At that time, Vera Cruz was the only important port in Mexico, and the allies proceeded to collect the revenues of its custom-house in order to pay their own expenses and make up the default on the Mexican bonds.

There had been no resistance to their landing, but the Republican army held Orizaba and Puebla, on the road to the capital, ready to resist any advance into the interior. The alliance between the three Powers did not last long. Napoleon had entered into relations with the anti-Republican or Conservative party in Mexico, and flattered himself that with their aid he could make himself master of the country. But neither England nor Spain had any such projects in view, nor would they co-operate in them, and their troops and ships were withdrawn from Vera Cruz, leaving the French corps, under General de Lorencez, in sole possession.

After some fruitless negotiations, the French plenipotentiaries issued, on April 16th, 1862, a proclamation of war, not against the Mexican people, but against the Republican Government under President Juarez. Three days later Lorencez began to march towards the highlands, starting from Cordova, to which he had moved up during the negotiations. On the 20th he occupied Orizaba, after a brief skirmish with some Mexican horsemen, the main Republican Army retiring to the pass of the Cumbres, where the road to Puebla and Mexico city ascends the rocky wall of the plateau, by a series of loops and inclines, commanded by strong positions on the upper slopes.

Lorencez marched out of Orizaba on the 27th at the head of 7,500 men, with ten guns. He had a squadron of *Chasseurs d'Afrique* with him, and his infantry was made up of a regiment of the line, a regiment of *Zouaves*, a battalion of *Chasseurs*, and a naval brigade of marines and seamen. On the 28th he drove the Mexicans from their strong position on the Cumbres Pass, General Zaragoca, who commanded there, retreating to Puebla. Lorencez pursued him, and on May 4th the French bivouacked at Amozoc, less than three miles from the eastern side of the city.

La Puebla de los Angeles ("the town of the angels"), to give it its full name (derived from that of an old mission station), was in 1862 the second city of Mexico. It had a population of 74,000 inhabitants. Its streets cross each other at right angles, dividing the solidly built stone houses into square blocks; in several of these blocks there are churches and monasteries, with thick and lofty walls. The French were led to believe by their Mexican friends that it was only the terror inspired by Zaragoca's 10,000 or 12,000 soldiers that prevented the good people of La Puebla from coming out to welcome them and strew their path with flowers. But although there was a French party in the place, the majority of the inhabitants were so loyal to the Republic, that they

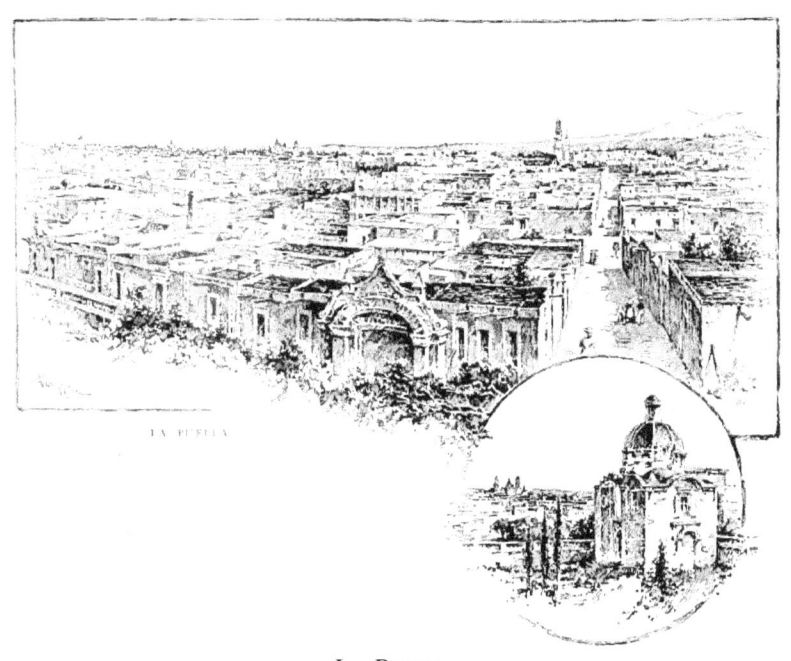

La Puebla

were working night and day to barricade the streets, and to improvise a kind of citadel by linking together, with solid barriers, several large buildings in the centre of the town near the cathedral.

On the south-east side of the city ran the Rio San Francisco. On its further bank rose a bold rocky ridge about 300 feet high and about three-quarters of a mile long. The road from Amozoc crossed it, coming up sharply from a ravine on its eastern side, the ascent being commanded by a large fortified monastery on one side and the fort of Loreto on the other. When the Americans took Puebla in 1846, they had avoided this ridge—locally known as the Cerro de Guadalupe—by a flank march to the south side of the city. But Lorencez had been so easily successful against the Mexicans at the pass of the Cumbres, that he despised the difficulties presented by the Cerro, and resolved to attack Puebla from the eastward. He flattered himself that the capture of the ridge would cost only a short sharp fight, and that, once he had got his guns to the top of it, the city would not offer any further resistance.

At 11 o'clock on the morning of May 5th the French advanced to the attack of the Cerro. It was held by the Mexican general Negrete, with 1.200 men and two batteries. The French guns opened with shell at a range of 2.000 yards, the Mexicans replying from the ridge. The fire of the Mexicans was slow and ineffective, and after about three-quarters of an hour of this artillery duel, Lorencez, supposing that the Mexicans had been sufficiently shaken, gave the signal for the assault of the position. As a matter of fact, the Mexicans had suffered very little loss, and were quite ready to meet the attack. The 2nd regiment of *Zouaves* formed the storming party. A battalion of *Chasseurs* covered their right. A battalion of bluejackets with some mountain-guns was on their left. The marines were to support the sailors. The linesmen were held in reserve.

Negrete had been reinforced from the town, and now had live battalions at his disposal. As the French rushed up the steep slopes they were received with a withering fire, but they came on pluckily, until their further progress was stopped by the ditches of the fort and the fortified monastery. Even here, under a cross-fire from the fort on the right and three rows of loopholes on the left, and with hostile infantry barring the road above them, they tried to struggle across the ditches. Roblot, a bugler of the 2nd battalion of the *Zouaves*, stood for some time on a heap of earth on the edge of the ditch sounding the charge while the bullets whistled round him, yet he escaped untouched.

At last the order was given to retire, just as a terrible thunderstorm burst over the battlefield. The *Chasseurs* on the right were charged by the Mexican cavalry, and two companies had to form square, and were for a few minutes completely surrounded by the rush of horsemen. The French had lost 156 killed and over 300 wounded. The Mexican loss was only 83 killed and 132 wounded. The invaders retired to Amozoc, where they waited for some days, in the hope that Zaragoca would come out and attack them. But the Mexican knew better than to risk the fruits of his victory. The French were suffering from sickness, encumbered with wounded, and unable to collect any supplies from the country, while their Mexican allies had failed to join them. Lorencez at last decided that it was better to retire by the Cumbres to Orizaba, and Zaragoca issued a proclamation to his army, congratulating them on having repulsed "the best soldiers in the world."

The failure at the Cerro de Guadalupe was a stain on the French arms that had to be wiped out at any price. Napoleon determined that next time the march on Puebla should not be attempted by a mere brigade. Thirty thousand picked troops were shipped off as reinforcements for the army of Mexico, and in September General Forey, the victor of Montebello, landed at Vera Cruz to take command. On October 24th, he went up to Orizaba, and proceeded to organise his army for the field. Its effective strength was about 26,000 combatants.

The infantry were organised in two divisions, each about 26,000 strong, under General Bazaine and General Felix Douay. There was, besides, a brigade of marines and colonial troops. The cavalry, 1,500 strong, were commanded by General de Mirandol. The advance upon Puebla was not really begun till the following February. In December, the advanced guard was pushed forward to secure the pass of the Cumbres, but three months in all were given up to collecting supplies and organising a series of posts to secure the communication of the army with Vera Cruz.

At this time Napoleon was in close relations with the Khedive of Egypt, and one curious result was that he was able to obtain the loan of a negro battalion of the Egyptian Army, which arrived at Vera Cruz in February, and was employed to garrison some of the posts in the lowlands between Vera Cruz and the hills the flat *tierras calientes,* or "hot lands," so fatal to Europeans.

When the French again approached Amozoc on March 4th, Zaragoca no longer commanded at La Puebla—he had died during the winter—but the most daring and energetic of his lieutenants.

General Ortega, had taken his place. During the winter the place had been strengthened with an earthwork rampart. Each of the blocks of houses within the city had been converted into an improvised fortress, the forts of the Cerro de Guadalupe had been strengthened, and the fort of San Xavier on the west, between the Mexico and Cholula roads, had been armed and put into a thorough state of defence. The French sympathisers, so far as they were known, had been expelled from the town, and with them went most of the women, children, invalids, and old men. Ortega had resolved that La Puebla should be held against the French, with the same desperate courage and determination that had animated the defenders of Saragossa in the Spanish war of independence.

Strong as he was, Forey would not venture to repeat the tactics of Lorencez by attacking the Cerro de Guadalupe. Halting near Amozoc, he summoned Ortega to surrender, and the reply was a defiance. Then, after some skirmishing with the Mexican cavalry, he pushed Bazaine's division to the north of the place, with orders to barricade the bridges on the road to Mexico and Cholula; for in this direction the Mexican general, Comonfort, was in the field with an army that, although it might not be able to raise the siege, might easily harass the besiegers and cut off their convoys. Douay's division moved round to the south and west. The marines held Amozoc.

Forey established his own headquarters on the north-west near the road to Mexico, in some buildings on a low ridge known as the Cerro de San Juan. The fort of San Xavier was directly opposite to him. But to have effectually closed all the approaches to the place, and made the investment a real blockade, Forey would have required, not 25,000, but at least 60,000 men. This was how it was that, on the night of March 21st, Ortega was able to send out half his cavalry to reinforce Comonfort's army. He had not much further use for them in the defence of the city, and 1,500 of them rode through a gap in the French lines almost without firing a shot or losing a man. Mirandol, Forey's cavalry commander, pushed his force to the northward in pursuit of them, and in the course of the following day. Colonel du Barail, with the Chasseurs d'Afrique, encountered the Mexican horsemen at Cholula and scattered them in a splendid charge.

With the city thus incompletely invested, and with the evidence experimentally obtained the year before at the Cerro de Guadalupe, that mere bombardment was not likely to shake the nerves of Ortega's soldiers, Forey had to make up his mind that if La Puebla was to be taken it must be by sheer hard fighting. He chose as his point of attack the salient formed on the western side by the fort of San Xavier, and proceeded to work his way up to it by a regular system of parallels and saps.

In the darkness of the night of March 23rd the engineers opened the first parallel, the trench being only seven hundred yards from the western angle of San Xavier. There were few guns in the fort, and none of them were of heavy calibre, while to right and left there were no formidable batteries to support it, otherwise the French would have had to begin much further off. Under officers who had learned their business well in the trenches before Sebastopol, the engineers pushed the saps forward so rapidly that in the night of the 25th the heads of the trenches were united by the second parallel at a little less than four hundred yards from the rampart. The siege batteries were established in the parallel, and in the next two days their fire had silenced the guns of the fort, the Mexicans withdrawing the cannon to the barricades in the streets behind it.

The angle of the fort was in ruins, and a mass of the ramparts on both sides of it had been brought down into the ditch. The third parallel was constructed at one hundred and fifty yards from the breach; but in order to still further diminish the distance to be crossed by the storming column, the sappers went to work again, and a fourth parallel was opened only eighty yards from the steep slope of ruined rampart that was to be the way by which the French would rush the town.

The 29th of March, only six days after the opening of the trenches, was the date chosen for the assault. The troops detailed for the storming party were the same regiments which had led the unsuccessful attack upon the Cerro de Guadalupe in the previous month of May. They were given this chance of avenging that defeat. General Douay directed the operations, the *Zouaves* being under the immediate command of Colonel Gastalet, and the *Chasseurs* under Commandant de Courcy. In the afternoon, the stormers were gradually collected in the fourth parallel, while the batteries directed a storm of shells upon San Xavier.

At five o'clock the artillery was suddenly silent, and General Douay gave the signal for the assault. Led by Gastalet, the *Zouaves*, with the fierce yell imitated from the Arabs, sprang over the breastwork of the parallel, poured down into the ditch and up the breach, the *Chasseurs* covering their advance with their rifle fire, and then dashing on to support them. But the Mexicans had rushed to the ramparts and the head of the breach the moment the artillery had ceased firing, and it was only after a fierce bayonet fight that the French cleared the fort. Even then it was seen that it could not be held unless the Mexicans were driven from the neighbouring houses and the streets between them, and until darkness closed in there was a series of desperate combats in the houses and at the barricades. At last the French were in secure possession of San Xavier. Over 600 of the Mexicans had been bayoneted. The victors had lost 230 killed and wounded. General de Laumière, of the artillery, being among the dead.

In most sieges the opening of a practicable breach is followed by a surrender. In nearly every case, once the stormers penetrate the ramparts resistance ceases. But it was not so at La Puebla. The successful assault marked, not the end, but the beginning of the real defence of the place. The French had secured beforehand excellent plans of the city, and on these they had numbered off the blocks of houses. There were 158 in all, each bounded by four streets, and it looked as if each block would cost a little siege of its own. Thus, on March 31st, Blocks Nos. 2 and 9 were stormed by the *Chasseurs*, one of the boundary walls of No. 9 being blown in with gunpowder. Next day an attack on Block No. 26, which was a large barrack, was repulsed.

In the night between the 2nd and 3rd of April an attempt was made to run a mine under its walls, but it was soon stopped by a mass of hard rock. Close by, at Block 24, a section of the engineers were carried off by a vigorous sortie of the Mexicans from the neighbouring barricades. Soldiers and citizens were fighting against the invaders side by side, and this struggle in the streets was a costly business.

On the 7th of April only the houses near San Xavier had been captured, and already more than 500 of the French had fallen. Gunpowder had been so freely used by the engineers that the supply was running short. General Douay gave up for the present the attempt to advance further into the town, and was content to hold his own. Next day Forey, the commander-in-chief, sent down to Vera Cruz a despatch which showed what he thought of the situation. Addressing the naval officer in command of the squadron, he said:

> Write at once to the Minister of War, in my name, that the siege of Puebla is a *serious* operation; and tell him that I beg that he will send us, without loss of time, siege material, men, and munitions of war, with which to replace what are already expended and further provide for the eventualities of the future; and let him take as the basis of his calculations the fact that the

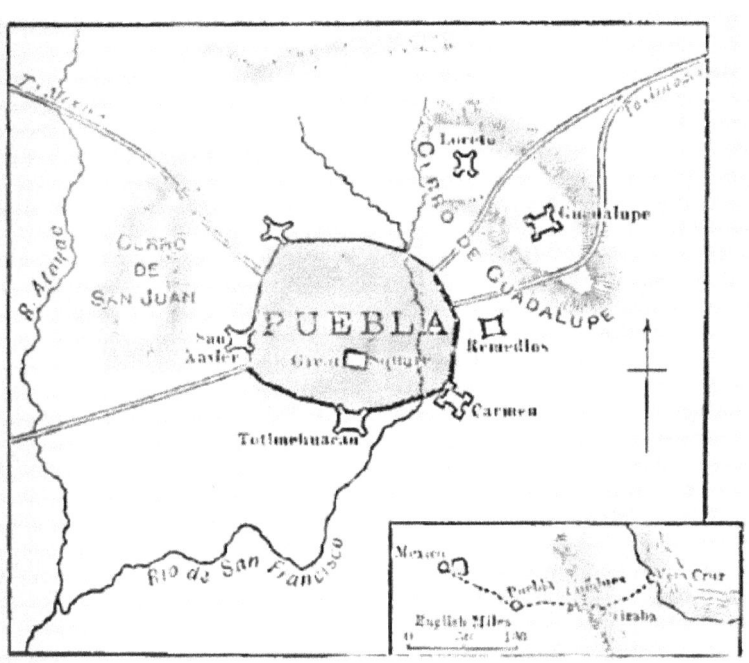

means hitherto put at my disposal are quite insufficient.

This was written ten days after the breach had been stormed, and yet Forey evidently felt that the end was still far off, otherwise he would not have expected supplies to reach him from France in time to be of any use.

Meanwhile, on the south side of the town, Bazaine, with the first division, began a new attack, in the hope that progress might be more rapid in this direction. He had first to deal with the outlying forts of Carmen and Totimehuacan, on the banks of the river below the town. His engineers opened the first and second parallels and began to sap up to the forts. In the second week of April supplies began to run short in the town. Ortega had still 1,500 horsemen with him, and in order to economise his provisions, and in the hope of their bringing in a convoy, he sent them out through the French lines. They got away safely, but when they tried to bring in a convoy the enterprise ended in failure, and they had to gallop off, leaving the waggons to the French.

A sortie from the south side against Bazaine's trenches was repulsed, with considerable loss to the garrison; but they renewed their attacks, and thus delayed the progress of the engineers. Then, a supply of powder having arrived from Vera Cruz, Douay began again the desperate street-fighting near San Xavier. He attacked the monastery of Santa Inez. The massive building was loop-holed, and its walls and those of the adjacent blocks were manned with some 2,000 Mexicans armed with all kinds of weapons, from modern rifles to shot-guns and blunderbusses. The French were repulsed with the loss of 350 killed and wounded, and 130 prisoners. Douay again gave up the attempt to advance, and encouraged by the success at Santa Inez, the Mexicans assumed the offensive and made a fierce attack on the houses and barricades held by the French. This counter-attack failed; and then there was a lull in the street-fighting, both parties being temporarily exhausted.

So, the month of April ended. Bazaine's siege-guns were battering the southern forts, and on the west side Douay held a mere corner of the city. The 5th of May, the anniversary of the French defeat at Cerro de Guadalupe, was approaching, and President Juarez resolved that, if possible, it should be signalised by the relief of La Puebla. He joined Comonfort's army, and sent in word to Ortega that he was to make a vigorous sortie on the morning of the 5th, while Comonfort with the field-army would attack the besiegers from the south-west. The attack was made entirely by the Mexican cavalry, but they were met and dispersed by the better-trained squadrons of the French Chasseurs d'Afrique. At the same time the garrison poured out upon Bazaine's trenches, and within the town attacked Douay's barricades.

Everywhere the French held their own. But Forey felt that it would be dangerous to allow Comonfort to combine a more serious attack with another sortie of the garrison. The Mexican field-army of about 8,000 foot and 2,500 horse was entrenching itself at San Lorenzo, in the Atoyac valley, about seven miles north of La Puebla. Bazaine was ordered to make a night march and break up the Mexican camp. Leaving at midnight the lines before La Puebla, with a small column made up of four battalions of infantry, eight guns, and four squadrons of cavalry, Bazaine marched up the valley, and making a wide sweep to the westward, fell suddenly upon the Mexican position in the grey dawn of the 8th of May. The attack was a complete success, and after a brief struggle the Mexicans dispersed, leaving in the hands of Bazaine 3 standards, 8 guns, 1,000 prisoners, and a large convoy of supplies which Comonfort had hoped to throw into Puebla.

The victory of San Lorenzo sealed the fate of Ortega and his brave garrison. Bazaine was back in his trenches the same morning. On the 12th his batteries had silenced the fire of both Fort Totimehuacan and the fort of Remedies, between the town and the Cerro de Guadalupe. The siege works were pressed forward, and an assault on the south side was being prepared, when on the 17th several loud explosions were heard in the town just before dawn, and when the sun rose, the white flag was seen flying on all the forts. After a defence of sixty-two days, La Puebla was on the point of falling into the hands of the invaders. It had held out for just seven weeks from the storming of San Xavier, which Forey had hoped would put the whole place in his possession.

On the evening of the 16th, General Ortega had decided that further resistance could only last a few hours, and would entail a useless sacrifice of brave men's lives. His provisions were exhausted; his men and the citizens who acted with them were already half-starved. Ammunition was running short: it was doubtful if there were enough rifle cartridges for another day's hard fighting. It was true that the French only held a corner of the town on the western side, but on the south Bazaine's approaches had been pushed close up to the forts, and Ortega thought he saw signs that an assault was being prepared for the early morning of the 17th.

Fell suddenly upon the Mexican position in the grey dawn.

Under these circumstances, he would have been quite justified in capitulating, but the brave soldier was determined that the invaders should obtain as little advantage as might be from his surrender.

Shortly after midnight he issued an order to his officers telling them the end had come, and that further resistance was impossible. The order then went on to direct that, "in order to save the honour and dignity of the army," the hour from 4 to 5 a.m. was to be devoted to a rapid destruction of all the arms in the town. All the cannon mounted on the walls and at the barricades were to be, not simply spiked, but broken up with heavy charges of powder. He said:

> This sacrifice our native land demands of her faithful children, in order that these arms may not be in any way of service to the enemy who has invaded our country.'

This done, the generals commanding divisions and brigades were to declare to their soldiers that the army was disbanded and no longer existed. The men were to be told that after their gallant fight their officers were not going to hand them over as prisoners to the French. There was no complete line of investment round the city, and nothing could prevent a considerable number of them from making their way to the national armies that still kept the field, if they chose to do so.

As they were released from their service, they need not take such a step unless they wished; but as there was no capitulation the laws of war left them free to fight for Mexico again at the first opportunity. The funds in the war-chest of the army were to be divided among the men. Officers and soldiers alike were told that they had reason to be proud of their defence. Only the want of food and other supplies had put an end to it; Ortega wrote:

> For, at this moment, we hold the city and its forts, with the exception only of the one fort of San Xavier and a few blocks of houses in its neighbourhood.

He further announced that the white flag would be hoisted on the forts and at the barricades facing the French near San Xavier at 5 a.m. At the same hour, the officers would assemble in the square before the cathedral, where he would meet them. He would not try to make any terms for them with the conqueror, nor would he bind them in any way: each was free to take whatever line his own honour and conscience prescribed. Those who remained with him would doubtless be made prisoners.

By 4 o'clock the preparations for the destruction of the arms and the burning of all the standards were completed. In the next hour, the work was carried out, the series of explosions giving the French at first an idea that the garrison was attempting a great sortie. By 5 the proclamation dissolving the army of La Puebla had been read, and the disarmed soldiers had broken their ranks with a last cheer for Mexico and for Ortega. The general with his officers, none of whom wore their swords, and most of whom had broken the blades, were assembled before the old cathedral. There was to be no laying down of their arms at the feet of the conqueror. An *aide-de-camp* had ridden out with a flag of truce to Forey's headquarters on the west of the town. He handed the French general the following letter:—

La Puebla de Los Angeles,
May 17th, 1863.

Monsieur le Général,—As it is no longer possible for me to continue to defend this place, through the want of ammunition and provisions, I have disbanded the army placed under my orders, after having destroyed its armament, including the artillery.

The place is therefore at your disposal, and you can proceed to occupy it, taking, if you judge fit, such steps as prudence may dictate to avoid those evils which might result from a sudden and forcible occupation, for which there is now no reason.

The generals and officers of the army are now assembled on the Plaza del Gobierno. These individuals will become your prisoners. I cannot. Monsieur le General, prolong the defence. If I could, you may take my word for it that I would.

Ortega.

It was not till early on the 19th that Forey rode in triumph into the captured town. The 17th and 18th were devoted to quietly taking possession of the forts and walls, and then searching the blocks of houses one after another for arms. It was not till this had been thoroughly done that the victors felt safe. They made prisoners of all whom they could identify as having taken part in the defence in the ranks of the regular army. In all they thus captured 26 generals, 1,432 officers of lower rank, and about 11,000 soldiers.

The generals and other officers refused to give any kind of parole, and more than half of them succeeded in escaping cither from Puebla or from Orizaba, or other points on the road to Vera Cruz, down to which they were marched in order to be sent to France. Of the Mexican officers 530 were actually shipped across the Atlantic to Brest, but 650 escaped, most of them rejoining the national army, where some thousands of the defenders of La Puebla had preceded them. Amongst those who thus regained their liberty was the brave Ortega.

Juarez, having lost Puebla, made no attempt to defend the capital against the French. He retired to San Luis de Potosi, and on June 10th, three weeks after the fall of La Puebla, Forey entered the city of Mexico. The capture of La Puebla, and the occupation of the old capital of the Aztec monarchy, won Forey his marshal's baton. But the honours of the fight were really with the Mexican general, who had made of Puebla another Saragossa. Perhaps the most striking testimony to his merits is the fact that a French soldier who saw his first campaigns in Mexico, and who now commands an army corps on the eastern frontier of France, has told the story of Ortega's gallantry, and set forth the very words of his last order to the garrison of La Puebla as an example to French soldiers of what a brave man should do when fortune is no longer on his side.

In his great work on the art of war, General Pierron cites a series of "Heroic examples to be imitated rather than surrender," and he groups together "Ortega at Puebla" and "Taillant at Phalsbourg," as types of the iron courage and determination which refuse to leave to the victor any advantage of his success that can be wrested from him, even in the depths of defeat.

City of Mexico

THE SECOND SCHLESWIG WAR
1864

The Storming of the Redoubts of Düppel
April 18, 1864
Charles Lowe

Schleswig-Holstein, the cradle of the Anglo-Saxon race, was the beautiful and interesting province which formed the bone of bloody contention between the Prussians and the Danes in the year 1864, just a year after the Prince of Wales had wedded the Danish "sea-king's daughter from over the sea," and made all Englishmen take the very deepest interest in the hopeless struggle of her undaunted countrymen against an overwhelming foe.

The cause of quarrel was one of the most complicated questions which ever vexed the minds of statesmen, and seemed so incapable of solution that an irreverent Frenchman once declared it would remain after the heavens and the earth had passed away. But on the death of Frederick VII. of Denmark, in November, 1863, Herr von Bismarck, who had the year before become Prussian Premier, determined that the difficulty should now be settled by "blood and iron." Briefly put, the new King of Denmark, Christian IX., father of the Princess of Wales, wanted to rule over the Elbe Duchies, as Schleswig-Holstein was called, in a way, as was thought at Berlin, unfavourable to the rights and aspirations of their German population; while, on the other hand, the Germanic *Diet*, or Council of German Sovereigns at Frankfort, was resolved that this should not be so. And rather than that this should be so, it decreed "execution" on the King of Denmark, who had a seat in the *diet* as for the duchies, and selected two of its members, Hanover and Saxony, to enforce its decision.

But not content with this, Austria and Prussia, the leading members of the *diet*, also resolved to take the field, as executive bailiffs, so to speak, of the judgment of the German Court; and this they did at the beginning of 1864 with a united force of about 45.000 men. That was not so very large a force, considering the size of modern armies, but it was much larger than that opposed to it by the valiant Danes, about 36,000 in number, who were commanded by General de Meza. The Austrians were commanded by Field-Marshal von Gablenz, and the Prussians by their own Prince Frederick Charles, surnamed the "Red Prince," from the scarlet uniform of his favourite regiment, the Zieten Hussars.

The commander of the combined Austro-Prussian Army was the Prussian Field-Marshal von Wrangel—"old Papa Wrangel," as he was fondly called—who looked, and spoke, and acted like a survival from the time of the Thirty Years' or the Seven Years' War. He was a grim old *beau sabreur*, who, in his later days, used to grind his teeth (what of them were left) and scatter *groschen* among the street arabs of Berlin, under the impression that he was sowing a crop of bullets that would yet spring up and prove the death of all democrats and other nefarious characters dangerous to military monarchy and the rule of the sword in the civil state.

"*In Gottes Namen drauf!*"—"Forward in God's name!"—"Papa" Wrangel had wired to the various contingents of his forces on the 1st February, when at last the Danes had replied to his demands with an emphatic "No!" and then the combined Austro-Prussian Army swept over the Eider amid a blinding storm of snow.

The Prussians took the right, the Austrians the left of the advance into the duchies; and after one or two preliminary actions of no great moment, the invaders reached the Danewerk, a very strong line of earthworks which had taken the place of the bulwark thrown up by the Danes in ancient times against the incursions of the Germans. Here the Prussians prepared for a stubborn resistance, but what was their surprise and their delight, on the morning of the 6th February, to find that the Danes had evacuated overnight this first bulwark line of theirs, leaving 154 guns and large quantities of stores and ammunition a prey to their enemies! Caution, not cowardice, had been the motive of this retreat of theirs, for they saw that, if they had remained, they would have run the risk of being outflanked and outnumbered; so they determined, from reasons of military policy, to retire further northward and take up their dogged stand behind their second line

Field-Marshal von Wrangel.

Field-Marshal von Wrangel

of entrenchments at Düppel, there to await the assault of their overwhelming foes.

Sending on the Austrians on the left into Jutland to dispose of the Danes in that quarter, "Papa" Wrangel selected the "Red Prince" and his Prussians to crack the nuts which had been thrown in their way in the shape of the redoubts of Düppel. Prince Frederick Charles was one of the best and bravest soldiers that had been produced by the fighting family of the Hohenzollerns since the time of Frederick the Great. A man about the middle height, strongly built, broad-shouldered, florid-faced, sandy-bearded, bull-necked, rough in manner and speech, and homely in all his ways—he was just the sort of leader to command the affections and stimulate the courage of the Prussian soldier. There was much of the bulldog in the "Red Prince," so he was the very man to entrust with such a task as that of hanging on to the Danes at Düppel.

Yet this task was one of exceeding difficulty, for the redoubts of Düppel formed such a formidable line of defence as had rarely, if ever, before opposed the advance of an invading army in the open field. All the natural advantages of ground, with its happy configuration of land and water, were on the side of the Danes, whose main object it was to prevent their foes from setting foot on the Schleswig island of Alsen, forming a stepping-stone, so to speak, to Denmark itself, much in the same way as the island of Anglesey does to Ireland. To continue the comparison, the Menai Strait corresponds to the Alsen-Sund which separates the mainland of Schleswig from the island of Alsen. Of this island the chief town is Sonderburg, which was connected by the mainland, into which it looks over, by two pontoon bridges, at the end of which the Danes threw up a *tête-du-pont*, or bridge-head entrenchment, to defend the approach and passage; while about a couple of miles further inland they had constructed a chain of no fewer than ten heavy forts, or redoubts, all connected by lesser earthworks and entrenchments.

This line of redoubts, about three miles long, ran right across the neck of a peninsula of the mainland, called the Sundewitt, one end resting on the Alsen-Sund and the other on a gulf, or bay, of the Baltic, called the Wenningbund. The redoubts were placed along the brow of a ridge which overlooked and commanded all the undulating country for miles in front, while in the rear again the ground dipped away gently down towards the Alsen-Sund and its bridge-head, affording fine shelter and camping-ground to the Danes. A lovelier or more romantic-looking region, with its winding bays and silver-glancing straits, its picturesque blending of wood and water, could scarcely be imagined.

Such a position as that which the Danes had taken up would have been of no value whatever against foes like the English, seeing that the latter might have gone with their warships and shelled the Danes clean out of their line of redoubts without ever so much as landing a single man, for, as already explained, the line of forts rested on the sea at both ends. But at this time, fortunately for the Danes, the Prussians had little or nothing of a navy, so that they must needs essay on land what they could not attempt by sea; while the Danes, on the other hand, though weaker on land, were decidedly superior to their foes on water. In particular, they had one warship, or monitor, the *Rolf Krake*, which gained immortal fame by the bold and devil-may-care manner in which it worried, and harassed, and damaged, and kept the Prussians perpetually awake. It lurked like a corsair in the corners of the bays, and creeks, and winding sea-arms of that amphibious region, and darted out upon occasion to shell and molest the Prussians in their trenches before the Düppel lines.

For the Prussians had soon come to see that it would be quite impossible for them to capture the Düppel redoubts save by regular process of sap and siege. The redoubts proved to be far more formidable than they ever fancied; and it would have involved an enormous sacrifice of life on the part of the Prussians to rush for them at once. The pretty certain result of such impetuosity would have been that not a soul almost of the stormers would have lived to tell the tale. For three whole years the Danes had been at work on these redoubts, and what it takes three years to construct cannot by any possibility be captured in as many days. Much had to be done by the Prussians, then, before sitting down before the redoubts.

If a simile may be borrowed from the game of football, the "forwards" of the Danes had first to be disposed of. For not only did they occupy the redoubts, but likewise all the strong points in the country for two or three miles in front of them, just as modern ironclads hang out nets to guard their hulls from the impact of torpedoes. In a similar manner the Danes had thrown out a network of men to fend off all hostile approach to their forts and prevent the Prussians from settling down near enough to them for the purposes of sap and siege.

While, therefore, the Prussians were busy bringing to the front their heavy guns and other siege-material, others of them were set to the work of sweeping clean, as with a broom of bayonets, the open positions in front of the redoubts held by their defenders. But this sweeping process was by no means either an easy or a bloodless task. For while the Danes numbered 22,000 troops, the "Red Prince" in front of them disposed at this time (though later he was reinforced) of no more than 16,000 men, and there was always the danger that the Danes, assuming the offensive, would sally out of their lines and seek to overwhelm their numerically weaker foes. Consequently the Prussians had recourse to the spade in order to supplement the defensive power of their rifles, and thus they first of all took up an entrenched position running in a long semicircle from Broacker on their right to Satrup on the left, at a distance of about three miles or more from the real object of their ambition—the line of Danish redoubts.

Two positions in front of these redoubts—the villages of Düppel and Rackebüll—were fiercely contested by the Danes; but on the 17th of March, after fighting in a manner which gave their foes a very high opinion of their courage, they retired behind their earthworks with the loss of 676 men, while the Prussians, on their part, had to pay for their victory by only 138 lives. This disparity in loss was doubtless due to the fact that, while the Danes were only armed with the old smooth-bore muzzle-loading musket, the Prussians had adopted the new Zündnadelgewehr, or needle-gun, the parent of all modern breech-loading and repeating rifles, which gave them a tremendous advantage over their opponents.

In one of the preliminary encounters above referred to, a party of Danes, against whom a superior force of Prussian light-infantry (*Jäger*) was advancing, threw down their arms in token of submission; but as the Prussians came forward, they snatched them up again, fired a volley, and rushed on with the bayonet. The Prussians let them come to within twenty-yards' distance, and then, raising their deadly needle-guns, shot them down to a man. The treacherous conduct of the Danes above referred to caused great bitterness among the Prussians; but, even after death, the latter showed their foes the respect which brave men owe to one another, and in West Düppel they raised a cross with this inscription:—

Here lie twenty-five brave Danes, who died the hero's death, 17th February, 1864.

The result of these preliminary tussles was that the Danes attempted no more outfalls, and from the 17th to the 28th of March one might almost have concluded that an armistice had been agreed to but for an occasional sputtering and spitting of rifle-fire between the foreposts, who thus employed their time when not exchanging other courtesies in the form of pipe-lights, tobacco-pouches, and spirit-flasks. But now the time was come when it behoved the Prussians to get as close to the redoubts as possible, for the purpose of opening their siege-trenches, and General von Raven's Brigade was selected to sweep the ground in front of the Danish position of ail its outposts. It was an early Easter this year, and just when the preachers were proclaiming to their congregations that the season of peace and goodwill to all men had now again come round, the Danes and Prussians were fighting like fiends under cover of the darkness.

The 18th Prussian Fusiliers had crept forward as far nearly as the wire-fencing and palisades in front of the redoubts, when the dawn suddenly revealed them to the Danes; and just at this moment, too, what should appear upon the scene but the ubiquitous *Rolf Krake*, which, at a distance of about five hundred yards, opened upon the advancing Prussians such a shower of shell and grape-shot as forced them to retire, causing these baffled fusiliers to curse the very name of the ship-builder who had ever laid the keel of such a bold and bothersome vessel.

At length, during the night of the 30th March, the Prussians managed to open their first parallel at a distance of about eight hundred paces from the line of the redoubts, and now, so to speak, they had reached the beginning of the end. The men on duty in this parallel, or shelter-trench (about eight feet deep), were relieved at first every forty-eight hours, and then every twenty-four, the former period having been found to be too great a strain on the soldiers, who, in consequence, had soon as many as ten *per cent,* on the sick list. For nothing could have been more trying to the constitution than this trench-life, with its cold nights, and rain, and mud, and manifold wretchedness.

Yet the Prussian soldiers, who were all very young fellows—mere boys some of them—kept up their spirits in the most wonderful manner, and indulged in all kinds of fun—mounting a gas-pipe on a couple of cart-wheels, and thus drawing the fire of the Danes, who imagined it to be a cannon; making sentries out of clay, and otherwise indulging in the thousand-and-one humours of a camp. They were also cheered by frequent visits from their commander, the "Red Prince," who—although housed in most comfortable, not to say luxurious, quarters at the *schloss,* or *château,* of Gravenstein, about six miles to the rear—

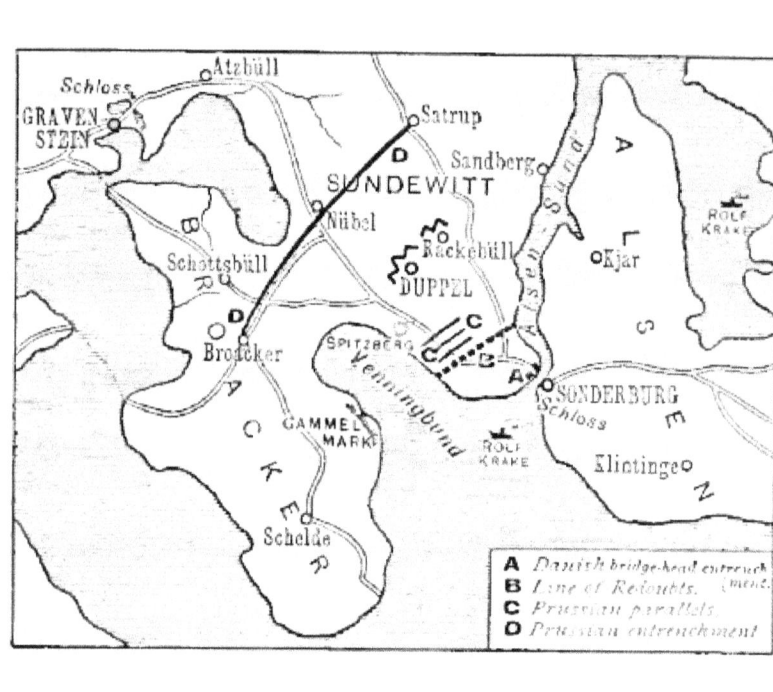

failed not to ride to the front every day and acquaint himself with all that was going on. With such a commander soldiers will do anything, and hence the whole Prussian force in front of the Danish redoubts began to burn with a fighting ardour which neither cold, nor wet, nor knee-deep mud could in the least degree damp or depress.

On the other hand, the Danes, though better off for shelter in their block-houses, wooden barracks, and casemates, were not in such good spirits. One of the few things, apparently, that cheered their hearts was the sight of the numerous English tourists—"T. G's," or "travelling gents," as they used to be called in the Crimea, and *kriegs-bummler,* or war-loafers, as they are dubbed in Germany—who, arrayed in suits of a most fearful and wonderful make, streamed over to the Cimbrian Peninsula in quest of sensation and adventure, exposing themselves on parapet and sky-line to the shells of the Prussians with a devil-me-care coolness which proved a source of new inspiration to the Danskés.

Simultaneously with the pushing on of their parallel work, the Prussians kept up a tremendous fire on the forts, but the Danes showed their good sense by lying quietly in their casemates and scarcely noticing the storm of missiles directed against them. These missiles did them and their earthworks very little harm, and they were not to be terrified by mere noise. Before the Prussians had settled down to their trench-work, their batteries over the bay at Gammelmark firing day and night had in the course of a fortnight thrown about 7,500 shot and shell into the Danish redoubts, yet not more than seventy-five officers and men had been killed or disabled by all this roaring volcano of heavy guns; and, indeed, it was computed about this time that the Prussians were purchasing the lives of their enemies at about 500 cannon-shots per head. "The huge earthen mounds or humps (of forts)," wrote a correspondent, "might have marked the graves of an extinct race, or been the result of some gigantic mole's obscure toil," for all the signs of life which the Prussian bombardment drew from the redoubts.

One night a curious thing happened to a company of the 60th Prussian regiment. In the course of some skirmishing it got too far forward, and, when day broke, it found itself in a slight hollow of the ground so near to Forts 1 and 2 that, had it tried to return to its own lines, it must have been annihilated by the grape-shot of the Danes. The shelter afforded it by the nature of the ground was so trifling that the men were forced to lie down flat upon their bellies to avoid being shot. In this unpleasant position they lay the whole day, for the

Prince Frederick Charles

Danes, strange to say, did not seek to sally out and capture them; and it was not till late in the evening that the company, under cover of the darkness, was able to rejoin their friends. They had eaten nothing in the interval, for, though they had provisions in their pockets, or haversacks, the least movement they made to get at this provender exposed them to the enemy's fire.

The first parallel had been opened on the 30th of March, and the second was accomplished in the night of the 10th of April. It was now expected that the "Red Prince," without more ado, would make a rush for the forts and be done with them—the more so as there now began to be whisperings of a political conference of the Powers which might meet and baulk the Prussian soldier of the final reward of all his toil. But still Prince Frederick Charles gave not the signal for the assault, and then it oozed out that this delay was simply due to the command of his royal uncle, King (afterward *Kaiser*) William, a very humane monarch, who, wishing to spare as much as possible the blood of his brave soldiers, had directed that still another—a third—parallel should be made, so as to shorten the distance across which the stormers would have to rush before reaching the redoubts.

Meanwhile the Prussians prepared themselves for the assault, among other things by getting up sham works in imitation of those they had to attack, where the battalions destined for the purpose were practised in breaking down palisades and using scaling-ladders, as well as in disposing of *chevaux de frise* and other impediments usual in the defence of forts. The Danish redoubts were known to the Prussians as Nos. 1, 2, 3, 4, 5, 6, 7, 8, 9, and 10, beginning from their—the Prussian—right on the sea, and their foremost parallel fronted this line of forts from 1 to 6. Against these forts the Prussians had thrown up twenty-four batteries mounting ninety-four guns, and now at last these guns were to give voice in a chorus such as had not rent the sky since the fall of Sebastopol.

But just as every storm is preceded by a strange delusive silence, so the day before the assault on the Düppel redoubts—the 17th of April—was a beautifully calm, sunny Sunday, with earth and sky embracing in a common joy over the birth of spring, and the encircling sea smooth as glass—a lovely day, and the last but one that many a brave man was doomed to see. For the order had gone forth from Prince Frederick Charles that at 10 o'clock precisely on the following (Monday) morning the redoubts should at last be stormed. At dawn of day the whole line of Prussian batteries should open fire on the forts, pouring upon them one continuous cataract of shot and shell till 10 o'clock, when the storming columns would start out of their trenches and "go for" the redoubts with might and main.

At 2 o'clock a.m. these columns—six in number, drawn by lot from the various brigades so that all might have an impartial share in the honour of the day—emerged from the Büffell-Koppel wood well in the rear, and silently marched in the darkness to the parallels. Each of these six columns was thus composed:—First of all a company of infantry with orders to take extended front about 150 paces from its particular redoubt, and open fire on the besieged. Following these sharpshooters, pioneers and engineers with spades, axes, ladders, and all other storming gear, including bags of blasting powder, and after them, at 100 paces distance, the storming column itself, followed at 150 paces by a reserve of equal strength, together with a score of artillerists for manning the captured guns of the Danes.

The Danes, in the darkness of the night, knew nothing whatever of all these preparations, and it was only when the first streaks of dawn began to chequer the eastern sky that they were aroused out of their sleep by such an infernal outburst of cannon-thunder all along their front as had never before, in lieu of the twittering and chirping of birds, greeted the advent of a beautiful day in spring. For six long mortal hours did the Prussians continue this terrific cannonade, of which the violence and intensity may be inferred from the fact that during this time no fewer than 11,500 shot and shell were hurled at and into the Danish redoubts. The material damage done to these redoubts was less, perhaps, than the demoralisation thereby caused to their defenders; but the latter was the result which the Prussians, perhaps, aimed at and valued most.

Shortly before ten the awful cannonade suddenly ceased, and was followed by a few minutes' painful silence. During this brief interval the field-preachers, who had given the Sacrament to all the stormers the night before, now again addressed to them a few fervid words of religious encouragement, and then at the "*Nun, Kinder, in Gottes Namen!*" ("Now, my children, away with you in God's name!") of their commanders, the six storming columns, raising a loud and simultaneous cheer, dashed out of their trenches and across to their respective redoubts to the stirring music of the *Preussenlied* played by the bands of three regiments—"*Ich bin ein Preussc; kennt Ihr meine Färbe?*" ("I am a Prussian: know ye then my colours?")

For a few seconds the Danes seem to be taken aback by this sudden

The German soldiers making sentries out of clay

onrush of their foes, and then they recognise that this is no mere outpost affair such as caused them some time before to boast that they had repulsed a Prussian attack all along their line. They look and comprehend; and by the time their Prussian assailants have half covered the distance between the trenches and the forts, their parapets are fringed with the smoke of sharp-crackling volleys of musketry, for, strange to say, they do not use their guns and dose their assailants with destructive rounds of grape. The Prussians rush forward, and many of them fall. Their pioneers cut down the wires, hack and blow up the palisades, tug, strain, and open up a passage for the stormers, who swarm down into the ditch and up the formidable face of the breastwork.

The crown prince, at the side of "Papa" Wrangel, is looking on from the Gammelmark height on the opposite side of the bay, while his cousin, the "Red Prince," and his staff have taken their stand on the Spitzberg, well to the rear of the line of zigzags. The stormers swarm up the breastworks like ants, and some of them fall back upon the heads of their comrades mortally struck by Danish bullets. At last they reach the top of the parapets and see the whites of their enemies' eyes, and a short but desperate hand-to-hand encounter ensues. Many of the Danes, seeing the foe thus upon them, throw down their arms and surrender, but many will not give in, and are shot or struck down with bullet, bayonet, and butt.

At Fort 2 the Prussians cannot force their way through the palisades, and are consequently slaughtered as they stand. "Better one of us than ten!" cries a pioneer, Klinké by name (for a monument now stands to his memory on the exact scene of his heroism), who rushes forward with a bag of powder and blows at once the palisades and his own person into atoms—sacrificing himself to save his comrades, and thus secure himself a golden register in the annals of the Prussian Army. The stormers now dash on and up, and presently the black-and-white flag of Prussia is seen waving on the parapets of the redoubt. It sinks again, but is once more raised to remain, and in less than a quarter of an hour from the time that the stormers sprang out of their trenches they are masters of six redoubts. It was all done, so to speak, in the twinkling of an eye—short, sharp, and decisive. From the six redoubts thus so swiftly rushed, the Prussians made a sweep to the rear of the others, and captured them in much the same manner, though one fort spared them the necessity of fighting for it by surrendering.

As it was at Fort 2 where the highest act of individual heroism had been performed on the side of the Prussians by brave pioneer Klinké, so it was also within this redoubt that Danish courage found its most brilliant exponent in the person of Lieutenant Anker. The Prussians were quite aware that a man of more than usual bravery was posted here, for they had admired the stubborn valour with which the redoubt had always been defended. And when at last they had stormed their way behind its parapets, they beheld the man himself whose acts had hitherto moved their admiration. He had spiked some of his guns, and was in the act of firing another when a Prussian officer sprang upon him, and, clapping a revolver to his breast, cried, "If you fire, I fire!" Anker hesitated, and finally desisted. But just afterwards he took up a lighted match and was making for the powder magazine, when the Prussian officer cut him over the head with his sword, only just in time to prevent him from blowing up himself and a considerable number of his foes. He was then taken prisoner, and his lifelike figure may now be seen on the fine bronze bas-relief of the Storming of the Düppel Redoubts, which adorns the Victory Column in Berlin.

The Danes had been defeated—not so much because the Prussians were braver men, which they were not, as because the latter were armed with better guns and rifles, and more expert at handling them; but, above all things, because they had taken their foes by surprise. For it cannot be doubted that this was the fact. Said a Danish officer who was taken prisoner:—

> We waited all morning, thinking the assault might still be given, although we had expected that it would take place still sooner; we waited under the terrific cannonade kept up against us, while hour after hour passed slowly away. At last we said to ourselves that we must have been misinformed, or that the Prussians had changed their minds, and the reserves were withdrawn. It was past nine o'clock when I left the forts and went back to breakfast. While thus engaged, I heard somebody utter an exclamation of dismay. 'What is that? The Prussian flag floats over Fort 4!' And so it was—the forts were lost.

But there was still another and a better reason for concluding that the Danes had not yet awhile expected the Prussian assault, and that was the circumstance that the *Rolf Krake*, most daring and deviceful of warships, did not immediately appear upon the scene to pour its volleys of shell and shrapnel into the flanks of the storming columns. True, it was lying at the entrance to the bay (Wenningbund), like an ever-vigilant watch-dog; but by the time it had got its steam up and come to where it was most wanted, the Prussians were already within the Danish redoubts, and, after firing a few ineffectual rounds, the monitor had to retire again well battered with Prussian cannon-balls, but by no means beaten yet like the battalions which had held the forts.

Yet even these battalions, when beaten out of the redoubts, continued to cling tenaciously to the ground behind them, and once or twice they even made a counter-attack with the object of recovering their lost positions. But Prussian ardour proved too much for Danish obstinacy; and at last the Danes in the country behind the forts, after several hours' fighting, were all swept back to the bridge-head in their rear, and then over into the island of Alsen, leaving their foes undisputed masters of all the field.

This latter phase of the fight was well described by a correspondent with the Danes, who wrote:—

> Düppel was lost, but the battle was by no means at an end. Indeed, as we watched the terrible cannonade from 12 at noon till 3 or 4 p.m., the violence of the fire seemed to increase at every moment. Anything more sublime than that sight and sound no effort of imagination can conjure up, and we stood spellbound, entranced, rooted to the spot, in a state that partook of wild excitement and dumb amazement — a state of being which spread equally to the dull hinds, ploughmen, woodmen, and the foresters, and their families of wives and children, as they emerged from fields, woods, and huts, and clustered in awestruck, dumbfounded groups around us. The flashes of the heavy artillery outsped the rapidity of the glance that strove to watch them; the reports were far more frequent than the pulsations in our arteries, and the reverberation of the thunder throughout the vast spreading forest lengthened out and perpetuated the roar with a solemn cadence that was the grandest of all music to the dullest ear.
>
> The air seemed all alive with these angry shells. I have witnessed fearful thunderstorms in my day in southern and in tropical climates; but here the crash and rattle of all the tempests that ever were seemed to be summed up in the tornado of an hour. Nor was all that noise by any means deafening or stunning. It came to us lingering far and wide in the still air, softened and mellowed by the vastness of space, every note blending admirably

and harmonising with the general concert—the greatest treat that the most consummate pyrotechnic art could possibly contrive for the delight of the eye and ear.

Many of the Danes surrendered, but many more were taken prisoners; and as they came along the Prussian soldiers shook them good-naturedly by the hand and tried to cheer them up. Few of the men seemed to want cheering up, being only too glad, apparently, to have escaped with their lives, though their officers looked gloomy enough over their defeat. The Prussians found these captive Danes "sturdy fellows, but by no means soldierly-looking," with their "rich sandy hair reaching far below the nape of their necks." And, to tell the truth, their victors, no less than their admirers throughout Europe, expected that they would have made a far more vigorous defence; for desperate a defence could scarcely have been called which resulted in the capture of their chief redoubts within the brief space of about ten minutes.

The Prussians had won a glorious victory, but a dear one; for in dead they had lost 16 officers and 213 men, and in wounded 54 officers and 1,118 men. Among the officers who were wounded—mortally, as afterwards proved—was the brave General von Raven, who, as he was being borne to the rear, exclaimed:—

> It is high time that a Prussian general should again show how to die for his king.

On the other side General du Plat was also killed, while in dead and wounded officers and men and prisoners the Danish loss otherwise amounted to about 5,500. Among the trophies of victory which fell into the hands of the Prussians were 118 guns and 40 colours.

On being informed of all this. King William telegraphed from Berlin—

> To Prince Frederick Charles. Next to the Lord of Hosts. I have to thank my splendid army under thy leadership for today's glorious victory. Pray convey to the troops the expression of my highest acknowledgment and my kingly thanks for what they have done."

On seeing that victory was his, the "Red Prince" had bared his head and muttered a prayer of thanksgiving to the Lord of Hosts, while some massed bands played a kind of *Te Deum*.

Dr. Russell wrote:—

The Prussians attacking the Danish breastworks.

In the broad ditch to the rear of Fort No. 4 the bands of four regiments had established themselves, and while the cannon were firing close behind them, they played a chorale, or song of thanksgiving, for the day's success. The effect was striking, and the grouping of the troops and of the musicians, with their smart uniforms and bright instruments, standing in the deep trench against the shell-battered earthwork, and by palisades riven and shattered and shivered by shot, was most picturesque.'

But King William was not content with telegraphing to his troops, through his nephew Prince Frederick Charles, his acknowledgment of their bravery. Following hard on his telegram his Majesty himself hurried to the seat of war, with his "blood-and-iron" Minister, Bismarck, at his side, and passed in review the troops who had so stoutly stormed the redoubts of the Danes. These troops appeared on parade in the dress and equipment they had worn on the day of their great feat, and in the course of their march past jumped a broad drain to show his Majesty how nimbly they had stormed in upon the Danes. A fortnight later a select number of the Düppel stormers escorted into Berlin the guns more than a hundred in number which they had captured from the Danes, and were received with tremendous enthusiasm.

But this popular jubilation grew louder still when a few weeks later the war was ended altogether by the storming of the island of Alsen, into which the Danes had retired after their defeat at Düppel and entrenched themselves down to the water's edge. In the deep darkness of a summer night (June 29th) the Prussians, in 160 boats, crossed the channel—about eight hundred yards broad—between the mainland and the island, though not without the usual amount of harassing opposition from the *Rolf Krake,* and under a murderous fire jumped ashore and made themselves master of the position in a manner which made some observers describe the affair as a mere "skirmish and a scamper."

But all the same it was a feat which recalled the "Island of the Scots," as sung by Ayton, and will always live in military history as a splendid feat of arms.

Lieutenant Anker taken prisoner

THE AUSTRO-PRUSSIAN WAR
1866

The Battle of Königgratz
July 3, 1866
By Charles Lowe

Not since the "*Völkerschlacht*," or Armageddon of the nations at Leipzig, in 1813, when the allies overthrew the hosts of Napoleon, had Europe witnessed such a stupendous conflict as was fought near Königgratz, on the Upper Elbe, in Bohemia, on the 3rd July, 1866. This battle was called of Königgratz by the Prussians, of Sadowa by the Austrians; and, as a matter of topographical fact, the latter was the more correct title, just as the field of Waterloo is known as Mont Saint Jean to the French, and Belle Alliance to the Prussians—in both cases with more justice. At Leipzig about 430,000 men had mingled in fight, while at Königgratz, as we shall call it in complement to our ancient and honoured allies the Prussians, the total number of combatants was about 435,000, or close on half a million of men.

What had called these armed hosts into the field? Briefly put, it was the question which was to be the leading power among the German-speaking peoples—Austria or Prussia. For centuries the former had asserted this position of proud pre-eminence, but there came a time when this claim of the Hapsburgs was no longer allowed by the great and growing monarchy of the Hohenzollerns. Austria wanted to have everything in Germany done after her particular way of thinking, and Prussia began to find it quite incompatible with her honour and her self-respect to be thus lorded over by a State which in many respects she deemed to be her inferior in point of light and leading.

Thus it came to pass that these two rival powers began to lead a very cat-and-dog life at the council-board of the Germanic Confederation of States; and Bismarck, who was the rising statesman of his time, prophesied that this condition of things could go on no longer, and that the only remedy for this eternal quarrelling between the two was a policy of "blood and iron" on the part of Prussia.

Once, however, they seemed to have suddenly become the best of friends. This was when they joined their forces, in 1864, to snatch Schleswig-Holstein, or the Elbe Duchies, as they were called, from the rule of the Danes. Bismarck was the great champion of "Germany for the Germans," and he thought it scandalous and unreasonable that a foreign people like the Danes should continue to domineer over the Teutons in the Elbe Duchies. Prussia and Austria, therefore, at his far-seeing instigation, combined to oust the Danes from the Duchies, and this they finally did after storming the Danish redoubts at Düppel.

But the worst of it was that the conquerors could not agree as to their spoil. Prussia wanted to do one thing with the Duchies, and Austria another. It is a common enough thing for thieves to fall out over the distribution of their booty, and this was precisely what the rival German Powers did with regard to Schleswig-Holstein. Bismarck, the long-headed statesman that he was, clearly foresaw that they must and would do so, and this was the very thing he wanted. He wished to have a good pretext for going to war with Austria, in order that this Power might be altogether excluded from the German family of nations, and that Prussia, taking her place, might inaugurate a new and better era for the Teutonic peoples.

Austria had fallen into the trap which he had laid for her, and she had no choice but to fight. Each, of course, claimed to be the injured party, and the old game of the wolf and the lamb was played over again to the amusement of all Europe. Some of the other German States sided with Austria, and some with Prussia, but the former were soon defeated and disarmed and then Prussia was free to direct her whole strength against the Austrians.

It was known that the latter were collecting all their strength in Bohemia, and King William, who had General von Moltke, the greatest soldier of his time, for his chief of the staff, or principal counsellor in affairs of war, resolved to make a dash into this province before its Austrian defenders knew where they were, and smite them, as David did the Philistines, hip and thigh. Accordingly, he divided the forces of his kingdom into three main armies, each composed of several army corps. The command of the First, or Centre, Army, numbering about 93,000, was entrusted to the king's nephew, Prince Frederick Charles, called by his soldiers the "Red Prince," from the scarlet uniform of the Zieten Hussars which he generally wore; the Second, or left-hand

Army, totalling 100,000 men, was given to the king's high-souled and chivalrous son, the crown prince, Queen Victoria's son-in-law; while the Third, or right-hand host, called of the Elbe, fell to General Herwarth von Bittenfeld, who fought throughout the campaign with a courage worthy of "Hereward, the last of the English."

But these three huge armies did not invade Bohemia in one overwhelming mass. Moltke, the great "battle-thinker," the "Silent One in Seven Languages," as his friends fondly called him, knew a trick worth two of that. His maxim was, "march separately, strike combined"; and yet it behoved him to keep the Austrians in perfect ignorance of where he meant to strike. The crown prince, on the left, started with his army from Silesia; the Red Prince set out from Lusatia, while Herwarth's point of departure was Thuringia.

Did Moltke himself also take the field? No, not at once; for it meanwhile sufficed this great military chess-player, this mathematical planner of victory, to sit quietly among his maps and papers at the offices of the Grand General Staff in Berlin, with his hand on the telegraph wire, and direct the movements of the three armies of invasion. Take the following description that was penned by an English witness of the crossing of the frontier by the army of the Red Prince:—

> It was here (at a toll-house gate) that Prince Frederick Charles took his stand to watch his troops march over the border. He had hardly arrived there before he gave the necessary orders, and in a few moments the *Uhlans*, or lancers, who formed the advance guard of the regiments, were over the frontier. Then followed the infantry. As the leading ranks. of each battalion arrived at the first point on the road from which they caught sight of the Austrian colours that showed the frontier, they raised a cheer, which was quickly caught up by those in the rear, and repeated again, and again till, when the men came up to the toll-house and saw their soldier-prince standing on the border line, it swelled into a rapturous roar of delight, which only ceased to be replaced by a martial song that was caught up by each battalion as it poured into Bohemia. The chief himself stood calm and collected; but he gazed proudly on the passing sections, and never did an army cross an enemy's frontier better equipped, better cared for, or with a higher courage than that which marched out of Saxony that day.

Over the picturesque hills of Saxony, over the Giant Mountains into the fertile plains of Bohemia, swiftly sped the three superbly-organised armies like huge and shining serpents; and ever nearer did they converge on the point which, with mathematical accuracy, had been selected as the place where they would have to coil and deliver their fatal sting of fire. Hard did the Austrians try to block the path of the triune hosts and crush them in detail; but the terribly destructive needle-gun, with the forceful lance of the lunging *Uhlan* and the circling sabre of the ponderous *cuirassier*, ever cleared the way, and a series of preliminary triumphs marked the progress of the three armies towards junction and final victory. By the 29th the Red Prince had reached Gitschin, the objective point of the invasion, while his cousin the crown prince lay at Königinhof, on the left, a long day's march distant. Meanwhile the Austrians had all retired under the shelter of the guns of Königgratz, a strongly fortressed town on the left bank of the Upper Elbe, there to take their final stand, with their backs, as 'twere, to the wall.

The Austrians were commanded by Feldzeugmeister Benedek, and their army had been reinforced by the troops of the King of Saxony, who had sided with the foes of Prussia in the impending conflict, and were sure to give a good account of themselves. An equally stubborn resistance was to be expected from the Hungarian subjects of the Emperor Francis Joseph, who were second to none in all his polyglot dominions in respect of that ancient valour and other chivalrous qualities which had caused this gallant people to be called the "English of the East." Finer horsemen than the Hungarians existed in no army in all the world; and in this campaign, as in every other in which they had ever been engaged, the Austrians were particularly strong in cavalry. But, on the other hand, the Prussians were known to be armed with the lately-invented breech-loading needle-gun, while the Austrians still clung to the older-fashioned muzzle-loader, and professed to make light of their opponents' new-fangled rifle. They were soon to be shown convincingly which was the better weapon.

It was not till June 30th that King William and his *paladins*, Moltke, Bismarck, and von Roon, left Berlin by rail for the seat of war. They had scorned to witness the preliminary heats, so to speak, and only wanted to be present at the grand final. On July 2nd, after reaching Gitschin, which was near the headquarters of the Red Prince, Bismarck wrote to his wife:

Just arrived from Sichrow. The field of battle there is still cov-

Konniggratz

ered with corpses, horses, and arms. Our victories (so far) are greater than we thought. It appears that we have over 15,000 prisoners, while the loss on the Austrian side is still greater in dead and wounded, being no less than 20,000. Two of the Army Corps are utterly scattered, and some of the regiments are wiped out to the last man. I have, indeed, up till now seen more Austrian prisoners than Prussian soldiers.

On the night of the same day (2nd July) King William, now in his seventieth year, had retired to rest in a little room of the "Golden Lion", which overlooks the market-place of Gitschin—a quaint little old town nestling among the hills of Northern Bohemia, on the southern side of the Giant Mountains. Wearied out with the fatigues of the day, he had hardly closed his eyes in sleep when he was unceremoniously woke up. His Majesty opened his eyes, and found Moltke standing by his bedside, the bearer of most important news, which General Voigts-Rhetz had just brought in from the Red Prince, whose headquarters were some six miles further to the east, at the chateau of Kamenitz on the Königgratz road. Voigts-Rhetz had first of all carried his momentous news to Moltke, who lodged on the opposite side of the square, and who was the real ruler of Prussia's battles, now and after in the French war. The king did nothing without consulting Moltke, nor did His Majesty ever issue an order that was not based on the well-thought-out advice of his chief of the staff.

The message of the Red Prince was of the very highest importance, for it upset all the resolutions which had previously been taken at the Prussian headquarters. Early in the day the exact whereabouts of the Austrians was unknown. It was *supposed* that they were on the left, or eastern, side of the Elbe, furthest from the Prussians, with their right and left flanks resting on two strong fortresses—Josephstadt and Königgratz, respectively—a position which it would have been terribly difficult, if not impossible, for their adversaries to assail; so that, pending the discovery of their real whereabouts, it had been resolved to let the Prussian troops rest on the 3rd, as they had been wearied out by their incredible feats of marching and fighting. Presently, however, "from information received," this resolution was revoked and replaced by another which deprived the fagged-out Prussians of the prospect of their much-needed day's rest; and a bold and rapid rider—Lieutenant von Norman—was despatched across country to the crown prince at Königinhof to ensure his cooperation with the Red Prince in a particular manner on the morrow.

But von Norman had barely started on his long and perilous ride when, lo and behold! another officer, Major von Ungar, came spurring in to the quarters of the Red Prince with a great piece of news. Attended by only a few dragoons, this officer had gone out scouting in the direction of Königgratz, and discovered that the bulls of the Austrian Army was without doubt on the right, or Prussian, side of the Elbe, holding a strong position on the further bank of the Bistritz brook, which ran very nearly parallel with the Elbe at a distance from it of some four miles.

MAJOR VON UNGAR CAME SPURRING IN WITH A GREAT PIECE OF NEWS

The position was strong, but not half so much so as the dreaded one beyond the Elbe, and the hearts of the Prussians jumped for joy. It seemed to them as if God had already delivered the Austrians into their hands, as Cromwell avowed of the Scots when they left their high ground at Dunbar and descended to meet his Ironsides on the plain. After gleaning this priceless intelligence, Von Norman had to ride for his life. A squadron of Austrian cavalry made a dash to catch him, but he rode like an English foxhunter, and only left behind him, as a souvenir of his audacious visit to the enemy's lines, a part of his tunic which had been carried away by an Austrian lance-thrust.

This, then, was the news which Voigts-Rhetz had brought to Moltke and the king at Gitschin, and then the situation underwent an immediate and final change. It was resolved to assail the Austrian position early on the morrow with the whole force of the united Prussian armies, and another message to this effect, cancelling all previous ones, as a codicil does a will, was at midnight despatched to the crown prince on one hand and Herwarth on the other, informing them of the altered state of things, and desiring them on the morrow to assail the flanks of the Austrians as fast and furiously as ever they could; while the Red Prince would apply his batteringrams to their elevated and strongly entrenched centre. This urgent message was entrusted to Colonel von Finckenstein, who, after a very dark and dangerous ride of twenty miles, reached the crown prince's quarters about four o'clock on the morning of the 3rd July.

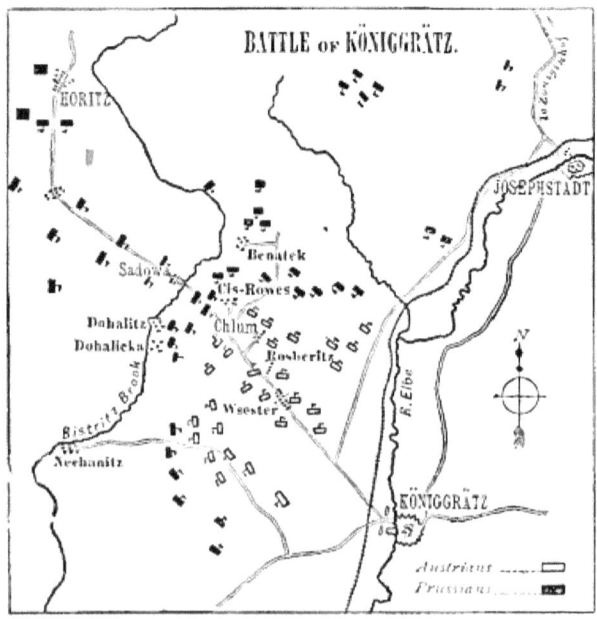

That fateful morning was a very wet and raw one, pretty similar to that which, after a rainy night, had dawned upon the English at Waterloo. Long before midnight the troops had all been in motion to the front. The moon occasionally blinked out, but was mostly hidden behind clouds, and then could be distinctly seen the decaying bivouac fires in the places which had been occupied by the troops along the road from Gitschin to Sadowa and Königgrätz. These fires looked like large will-o'-the-wisps as their flames flickered about in the wind and stretched for many a mile, for the bivouacs of so large a force as that of the Red Prince's army of nearly 100,000 men spread over a wide extent of country. With the first signs of dawn a drizzling rain came on, which lasted until late in the afternoon. The wind increased and blew coldly upon the soldiers, and they were short of both sleep and food, while frequent gusts bore down the water-laden corn on both sides of the ground along the way.

Moltke and his staff had left Gitschin by four o'clock, driving to Horitz, where, mounting their horses, they rode on to Dub and joined Prince Frederick Charles. For this was the centre point of assembly. The *Times* correspondent wrote:

> A few short words passed from the commander of the First Army to his chief of the staff; a few *aides-de-camp*, mounting silently, rode away; and, as it were, by the utterance of a magician's spell, one hundred thousand armed Prussian warriors, springing into sight as if from the bowels of the earth, swept over the southern edge of the Milowitz ravine towards the hill of Dub.

About eight o'clock, King William, with Bismarck and others of his great men, arrived upon the scene. Behind the king, besides his staff, were his royal guests, with their numerous retinues of adjutants and equerries, grooms and horses, in number equal unto about a couple of squadrons—making a fine mark for the shells of the Austrians. Before mounting his good mare "Fenella"—thenceforth to be called "Sadowa"—the king had got into his great-coat and put on galoshes over his boots. A wrong pair of spurs had been brought from Gitschin and would not fit. A groom whipped his off, and strapped them on over the royal galoshes; and thus equipped, with a field-glass slung round his neck by a long strap, the king rode away to view the course of the terrific fight, being everywhere received with tremendous cheering by his enthusiastic troops. For it touched their hearts to see so hoary a king come forth at the head of his "*Volk in Waffen*," or people in arms, to do strenuous battle with the alien. No *roi fainéant*, or stay-at-home monarch he, but one of the good old sort, like our own royal Edwards and Harries, under whose personal leadership the French were "beaten, bobbed, and thumped" at Crécy and at Agincourt.

It had been thought incredible by the Prussian leaders that the Austrians should have waived the advantages of a position behind the Elbe, and come forward several miles on its hither bank so as to meet their adversaries on the terms of the latter. But a closer inspection of their line of battle showed that it had been singularly well chosen. Along their front ran the boggy Bistritz brook, its banks dotted with farmsteads, villages, and clumps of wood, forming fine cover for infantry; while beyond this the ground rose in gentle undulations till it finally assumed the appearance of a commanding swell or ridge, from which Benedek's batteries could pour down death and destruction on the advancing Prussians over the heads of his own infantry when engaging the helmeted wielders of the needle-gun.

GENERAL BENEDEK

From the top of the slight elevation whereon stands the village of Dub the ground slopes gently down to the Bistritz, which the road crosses at the village of Sadowa, a mile and a quarter from Dub. From Sadowa the ground again rises beyond the Bistritz to the little village of Chlum (mark that village!), conspicuous by its church-tower crowning the gentle hill, a mile and a half beyond Sadowa—a beautiful bit of country not unlike some parts of England with its hill and dale, clustering cottages, peeping *châteaux*, hedgerows, groves, and waving grain-fields. Profiting to the full by the defensive advantages of this terraced terrain, the Austrians had seamed it with entrenched batteries, and palisaded their approaches with felled trees and intertwisted branches, making of the whole a natural fortress formidable to their assailants.

But nothing could daunt the hearts of the Prussians. They had got to beat Benedek and his 220,000 men, and the sooner the better. The Red Prince was afraid that, after all, Benedek might seek to retire behind the Elbe, and this had to be prevented at all costs and hazards. The prince might not be able to beat him off-hand, but he could at least fasten on Benedek like a bulldog and hold him fast there till the arrival of the crown prince, when the bull could be altogether felled and laid upon its back. *Bang*, therefore, went the Prussian batteries, and presently the whole sinuous line of battle, extending about five miles from Cistowes (opposite Chlum) on the Prussian left, to Nechanitz on the right, began to be wrapped in wreathed cannon smoke. The Austrians returned shot for shot, and neither side either gained or lost ground. In the centre the Prussians pushed battery after battery into action, and kept up a tremendous fire on the Austrian guns; but these returned it with interest, knowing the ground well, and every shell fell true, heaping the ground with dead and wounded men and horses.

While this furious cannonade was going on, columns of Prussian infantry were moved down towards the Bistritz, with intent to storm the line of villages—Sadowa, Dohalitz, and Dohalicka—on the further side. Shortly before their preparations were complete, the village of Benatek, on the Austrian right, caught fire, and the 7th Prussian Division made a dash to secure it; yet the Austrians were not driven out by the flames, and here, for the first time in the battle, it came to desperate hand-to-hand fighting.

But the bloody *mêlée* here was nothing to what was now mixing up the combatants in the wood of Sadowa, and converting it into a perfect slaughterhouse and hell upon earth. Boldly the Prussians advanced upon this village and its wood, plying the rapid needle-gun with awful effect upon the wood's defenders. But nothing could have exceeded the splendid courage with which the Austrian battalions clung to their cover, and their volleys, supplemented as they were by a truly infernal fire from the batteries behind and above, seemed to mow down whole ranks of their assailants.

The Prussians Pushed Battery after Battery into Action

But neither bullets nor shells could decide the fierce struggle; the bayonet had to be called in to do this. And now ensued most horrible scenes of carnage, which ended, however, before eleven o'clock, in the capture by the Prussians of the aforesaid villages. And no wonder that the Austrians chose to call the tremendous battle after the village and wood where they had made so glorious but ineffectual a stand.

Moltke himself afterwards related that, while he was watching the progress of events in front of Sadowa wood some roe-deer, startled from their leafy glades by the infernal pother around them, came bounding out and past him: and also how, when he and his suite rode forward a little way along the Lissa road to reconnoitre the Austrian position, he encountered an ownerless ox plodding along, serenely indifferent to the shells that were bursting all around it. Opposite the Sadowa wood on the Lissa heights, the Austrians had planted a most formidable entrenched line of guns, and Moltke afterwards told how he succeeded in getting the king to counter-order a command to storm these entrenched batteries from the front, which could only have ended in the bloodiest of disasters to their assailants.

About this time Bismarck, seeing how little headway the Prussians were making, began to be rather apprehensive as to the general result, fearing even that, if the crown prince came not up soon, they might, after all, be beaten. But one little incident gave him fresh hope. Taking out his cigar-case he offered a weed to Moltke, who deliberately chose the best of the lot. "Oh," thought Bismarck to himself, "if Moltke is calm enough to do that, we need have no fear after all."

The coming of the crown prince, with his additional hundred thousand men, had been as anxiously looked for as the arrival of Blücher on the field of Waterloo, and in truth the two situations were closely alike. Suddenly Bismarck, who had been looking intently in the crown prince's direction, lowered his glass and pointed to certain lines in the far distance, but these the others pronounced to be furrows.

"No," said Bismarck, looking again, "the spaces are not equal: they are advancing lines." And so they were; and by eleven o'clock the smoke of some Austrian batteries furnished a convincing proof that their fire was directed, not against the Red Prince's, but "Unser Fritz's" army; and the words "The crown prince is coming!" passed from lip to lip. But, sometime before his advance had thus been signalised, Moltke made answer to the king, who had been questioning him as to the prospects of the fight:

BOLDLY THE PRUSSIANS ADVANCED UPON THIS VILLAGE AND ITS WOOD

Today your Majesty will win, not only the battle, but also the campaign.

A correspondent with the Austrians wrote:

> The Prussian reserves were once more called upon; and from half-past twelve till nearly one o'clock there was an artillery fire from centre to left for six miles or more, which could not well have been exceeded by any action of which history makes mention. The battle was assuming a more awful and tremendous aspect, and the faint rays of sunshine which shot at intervals through the lifting clouds only gave the scene a greater terror.

About this time, also:

> Benedek and his staff passed through the 6th Corps, which was in reserve. As the green plumes were seen rapidly advancing, the bands broke forth into the National Anthem, and the men cheered their commander with no uncertain note. Faces broke into broad smiles; *Jäger* hats were thrown into the air; all seemed joyous in the anticipation of an approaching triumph. Benedek, however, waved to them to cease shouting, saying, in his peculiar tone of voice, 'Not now, my children: wait till tomorrow.'

And it was wise advice; for by this time Benedek had begun to suspect that he and his men would soon all have a very different song to sing.

The storm and stress of battle were now beginning to tell heavily on the Austrians. They were, it is true, still holding their own, or something like it, on the line of the Bistritz; but what is that which suddenly attracts the attention of Benedek and his staff behind the village of Chlum? They gallop away thither to inquire into the cause of all this new turmoil, and are greeted with a destructive volley from the needle-guns of "Unser Fritz," who had by this time, after a forced march of frightful difficulty across the sodden country from Königinhof, come upon the scene with his Guards, and not only turned the flank, but positively fastened on the rear of the Austrian fighting line, at which he was now hammering away with might and main. But his path, so far, had been encumbered with corpses and mutilated bodies in sickening masses, he wrote in his *Diary*:

> Around us lay or hobbled about so many of. the well-known

figures of the Potsdam and Berlin garrisons. A shocking appearance was presented by those who were using their rifles as crutches, or were being led up the heights by some other unwounded comrades. The most horrid spectacle, however, was that of an Austrian battery, of which all the men and horses had been shot down. . . . It is a shocking thing to ride over a battlefield, and it is impossible to describe the hideous mutilations which present themselves. War is really something frightful, and those who create it with a stroke of the pen, sitting at a green-baize table, little dream of what horrors they are conjuring up. . . . In Rosberitz, where the fight must have been frightfully bitter, to judge from the masses of dead and wounded, I found my kinsman. Prince Antony of Hohenzollern, who had been shot in the leg by three balls. (He died of his wounds soon after).

With the turning of the Austrian right by the crown prince, the battle was virtually won. On the extreme left, Herwarth had played similar havoc with the Saxons, in spite of the heroic desperation with which they fought; and by four o'clock the Prussian line of attack resembled a huge semi-circle hemming in the masses of battered and broken Austrian troops. Half an hour later the latter, perceiving that victory had at last been snatched from their grasp, began to give way all along their line; and then, with drums beating and colours flying, the Red Prince's men, with one accord, rose from their positions and began a general advance. Perceiving his opportunity, the king now gallantly placed himself at the head of the whole cavalry reserve of the First Army, which "charged and completely overthrew," to quote His Majesty's own words, a similar mass of Austrian horsemen.

The nature of the ground had hitherto prevented the cavalry of either army from acting in masses, but the country was more open on the line of retreat to Königgratz, and it now became the scene of several splendid lance and sabre conflicts. As the squadrons of the 3rd Prussian Dragoons were rushing forward to charge some Austrian battalions near the village of Wrester, an Austrian *Cuirassier* brigade, led by an Englishman of the name of Beales, charged them in flank. They drove the Prussians back, and, smiting them heavily with their ponderous swords, nearly destroyed the dragoons; but Hohenlohe's Prussian *Uhlans*, seeing their comrades worsted, charged with their lances couched against the Austrian flanks, and compelled them to retire. Pressed by the lancers they fell back, fighting hard, but then the scarlet Zieten Hussars charged them in turn in the rear. A fierce combat ensued, and the gallant Beales himself was borne wounded to the ground.

But all would not avail. The Austrians were in full flight towards the fortress of Königgratz, pursued by cavalry, volleyed at by infantry, and exposed to ever-increasing showers of shell-fire. Yet from some positions of advantage they continued to retaliate in kind; and it was while standing watching the pursuit that King William and his suite became exposed to a terrific counter-fire of shells. Bismarck, who was still with him, ventured to chide His Majesty for thus exposing his precious person so unnecessarily.

"Does your Majesty, then, think they are swallows?" asked Bismarck, on the king affecting to make light of the *whizzing* of shells and bullets.

Bismarck wrote to his wife:

> No one would have ventured to speak to the king as I did, when a whole mass of ten troopers and fifteen horses of a *Cuirassier* regiment lay wallowing in their blood close to us, and the shells whizzed in unpleasant proximity to the king, who remained just as quiet and composed as if he had been on the parade-ground at Berlin.

In spite of all remonstrances the king would not budge, so, edging up on his dark chestnut behind the king's mare, Bismarck gave her a good sly kick with the point of his boot, and made her bound forward with her royal rider out of the zone of fire.

On coming up with the troops of the crown prince, the king had been nearly swallowed up by them for sheer joy. At sight of the venerable monarch, who had been exposing his person throughout the bloody fray like the most dutiful of his soldiers, battalion after battalion—some the mere shadows of their former selves—burst into frenzied cheering and rushed forward, officers and men, to kiss the hand, the boot, the stirrup of their beloved leader. But presently a scene more touching still was presented to the victorious Prussian troops, when the heroic crown prince rode up and met his father.

The crown prince wrote:

> I reported to the king the presence of my army on the battlefield, and kissed his hand, on which he embraced me. Neither of us could speak for a time. He was the first to find words, and then he said he was pleased that I had been successful, and had

GRAVESTONES ERECTED ON THE BATTLEFIELD IN MEMORY OF THE FALLEN.

proved my capacity for command, handing me at the same time the order '*Pour le mérite*' (highest of Prussian war decorations) for my previous victories.

Earlier in the day "Unser Fritz" had met his cousin the Red Prince.

We waved our caps to one another from afar, and then fell into one another's arms amid the cheering of the troops of my extreme right and his extreme left wing . . . . Two years ago I embraced him as victor at Düppel; today we were both victors: for, after the stubborn stand made by his troops, I had come to decide the day with my army.

The battle had been won, but at what a terrible cost! Even the victors shuddered at the sight of the multitudes of bodies which heaped the bloody field. By superior arms, superior numbers, and superior strategy, Prussia, at the cost of 10,000 of her bravest sons, had won a crowning victory over her Austrian rival, who lost 40,000 men (including 18,000 prisoners), 11 standards, and 174 guns.

"I have lost all," exclaimed the defeated Benedek, "except, alas! my life!"

The highest proportion of the Prussian loss of 10,000 had fallen on Franzecky's Division, whereof 2,000, out of 15,000, had bitten the Bohemian dust. But "*Franzecky vor!*" ("Franzecky to the front!") will always live in the Prussian soldier's song as a memory of the ever-ready leader who bore the brunt of the awful struggle on the line of the Bistritz.

That same night the king slept at Horitz—not upon a bed, but on his carriage cushions spread out on a sofa. Bismarck's couch was at first formed by a wisp of straw under the open colonnade of the same townlet, though afterwards he was invited to share the wretched room of the Grand Duke of Mecklenburg. Moltke rode back to Gitschin, a distance of about twenty miles from the battlefield, where a cup of weak tea was all the refreshment that could be got for him; and then, in a fever of fatigue, he threw himself down to sleep in his clothes, as he had to be up betimes and return to Horitz to procure the king's sanction for his further plans.

It was he, the "Great Silent One," who had won the greatest and most momentous battle of modern times.

It had taken Frederick the Great seven long years to humble the pride of Austria; it took William the Victorious, with Moltke as his "battle-thinker," but seven short days to achieve the same result. The

THE CROWN PRINCE RODE UP AND MET HIS FATHER

Prussian soldier preferred to call the battle which he had just helped to win, Königgratz, because this name sounded to his ears as but a pun on the words "*Dem könig geräths*" ("The king will win"). But the king had only won by acting on the sage advice of his all-calculating Moltke, whose motto was "*Erst wägen, dann wagen*"—that is, "*First weigh, then away!*"

The Battle of Lissa
July 20, 1866
By A. Hilliard Atteridge

"Give me iron in the men, and I shall not mind much about the iron in the ships," said the American admiral, Farragut, when some of his officers were discussing the changes that would be introduced into naval warfare by the new ironclad navies. And Farragut was right in holding that, whatever the ships might be made of, the most important thing was to have enough "iron in the men" who worked and fought them. We are sometimes too apt to think that the power of rival fleets can be estimated by setting off their weight of guns and thickness of armour in two parallel columns, and striking a balance, as if it were an account in a ledger. But all naval history goes to prove that, within certain wide limits, the power of navies depends chiefly upon an element that can only be tested by the stress of storm and battle—namely, the courage, the nerve, and the "grit" of their officers and men.

No more striking proof of this was ever given than that which is afforded by the sea-fight of Lissa, the only battle between ironclads that has yet taken place in European waters. In ships, in guns, in armour the Italian fleet was superior to the Austrian. On paper, there could be no doubt on which side lay the power that would secure, in event of war, the command of the Adriatic. The war came, and its grim reality showed how fallacious was the comparison made beforehand. The object of the Italians in 1866 was to drive the Austrians out of Venetia, by attacking them there while they were occupied elsewhere by the struggle with Prussia.

The Italian plan of campaign was to march against the Austrians in northern Italy, and, after defeating their land army, besiege Venice by sea and land. The fleet was to crush the Austrians at sea, in the early days of the war, so to be ready to co-operate in the operations against Venice. It all worked out beautifully on paper. But the plan was never reduced to practice. War was declared on June 20th, and four day's later the Italian field army was defeated by the Austrians at Custozza.

Nearly a month before war was declared, Count Persano had been placed in command of the Italian fleet, and ordered to prepare it for active operations in the Adriatic, making Ancona his headquarters. On June 20th, the day of the declaration of war, eight ships (including two ironclads) were at Ancona. Persano with the main body of the fleet, consisting of ten wooden ships and nine ironclads, was still at the naval arsenal of Taranto.

Admiral Tegethoff, the Austrian commander, was getting his fleet ready for sea at Fasana and Pola, at the head of the Adriatic. He had taken command on the 9th of May, and ever since had been hard at work fitting out his ships and training his crews. The only effective portion of the fleet was a squadron of seven ironclads, broadside ships, with thin armour, and no guns of really heavy calibre. At first, the Austrian Admiralty suggested that the fleet should consist only of these ironclads and a few light steamers to act as scouts and despatch-vessels. But there were lying in the dockyard at Pola and in the port of Trieste an old wooden screw line of battle-ship, the *Kaiser*, and six wooden frigates.

Tegethoff asked for these to be added to his command. "Give me every ship you have," he said: "you may depend on it I will find good use for them."

He was given a free hand, and he organised his fleet in three divisions. The first was composed of seven ironclads. The second, under his friend Commodore Petz, consisted of the seven wooden ships. The third was made up of gunboats, paddle-steamers, and other light craft. The crews were rapidly recruited among the fishing population of the Dalmatian coast, and the sailors of Trieste and Pola.

So new were many of them to work on board a man-of-war that they were not even uniformed when the fleet sailed, and they still wore at Lissa the clothes in which they enlisted. But they were brave and hardy seamen to begin with, and Tegethoff had given them some weeks of training in which the crews were busy from morning to night at target practice, the captains of the guns being taught to lay a whole broadside so as to converge on a single mark; and there was also practice in manoeuvring under steam, in which great stress was laid on the importance of rapid turning so as to avoid the enemy's rams,

From this point Tegethoff kept on the bridge

and use the same weapon successfully against them. The result was that even the newly-enlisted men learned confidence in themselves and in the brave and skilful leader who commanded them.

As soon as war was declared, Tegethoff sent one of his steamers out with orders to reconnoitre the Italian coast from Ancona southwards as far as Bari. On June 23rd, she returned to the admiral's headquarters at Fasana, and reported that there were only a few ships at Ancona, and no sign yet of the enemy's main fleet coming up the coast. Tegethoff, on this, resolved to see if it was possible to make a rapid attack on Ancona, and on the 26th he put to sea with thirteen ships, including six of his ironclads. He arrived off Ancona next day, and saw for himself that in the meantime Persano had collected his entire force in the harbour. But the Italians showed no signs of coming out to meet him, and he had no intention of fighting both their forts and their ironclads at one and the same time. So, he steamed back to Fasana.

Persano's orders were "to clear the Adriatic of the enemy's fleet by destroying it or blockading it in its harbours." But though he had on his side superior numbers, heavier guns, and thicker armour, he seemed very reluctant to begin.

★★★★★★

Note:—The heavier armament of most of the Austrian ships consisted of smooth-bore 48-pounders. New rifled guns of larger calibre were being made for the Austrian fleet by Krupp at Essen, but when war became probable the Prussian Government stopped the delivery of them. On the other hand, one of the Italian ships carried 300-pounder Armstrong guns, mounted in a turret, and some of the other ironclads had 150-pounders in their armament.

★★★★★★

The fact is, he had not much confidence either in his own powers or in his officers and men. He remained at Ancona till July 8th, and only put out to sea on that day because he had received a telegram from the government bidding him to look for the Austrian fleet, and blockade it if it was still at Pola. But even then, all he did was to steam across to the Dalmatian coast and come back to Ancona on the 13th, after practising some fleet manoeuvres. The appearance of his fleet off the island of Grossa was telegraphed to Tegethoff, who, however, refused to sail from Fasana till he knew clearly what were the plans and destination of the enemy.

Two days after the Italian fleet returned to Ancona its admiral re-

ceived a peremptory message from his government informing him that, after the great hopes that had been built upon the fleet, everyone was disappointed with his inactivity, and that if he did not do something at once he would be removed from the command. It was suggested that he should attempt to capture by a *coup-de-main* the fortified island of Lissa on the Dalmatian coast, and several battalions were placed at his disposal to act as a landing party in case he decided to adopt this plan.

Persano was thus driven to venture upon what has always been recognised as one of the most dangerous of naval operations. He was to escort a fleet of transports across the Adriatic, and co-operate with the troops embarked in them in an attack upon a maritime fortress, having all the time a hostile fleet watching for the opportunity to fall upon him, while he was engaged in the siege. True, the Austrian fleet was supposed to be inferior to that which he commanded; but, if this was so, the sound course for him was to blockade it in its harbours or crush it if it tried to come out. The enemy's fleet ought to have been dealt with before anything else was attempted.

If he was not strong enough to do this, he could not hope to reduce Lissa and keep Tegethoff at bay at the same time. But the fact is, he was not acting on any sound principle of naval war. He was merely trying to "do something" to satisfy public opinion; and there was just the chance that he might reduce Lissa before the Austrians arrived, or that Tegethoff might shrink from attacking him; or, if there was a battle, he might still hope that numbers and weight of metal would give Italy the victory over Austria.

Lissa is an island about thirty miles from the Dalmatian coast, and one hundred and thirty from Ancona. As the nearest of the Dalmatian Islands to Italy, it has always been a naval station of some importance when a war has been in progress in the Adriatic; and in our last war with France its waters were the scene of a brilliant frigate action in which our sailors defeated a much superior French force. In 1866 the chief harbour of Lissa, that of San Giorgio, and the neighbouring inlet of Porto Carober were protected by strong batteries. There were also batteries on the high rocks at Porto Comisa and at Manego. The signal station on Monte Hum, the highest point in the island (about 1,600 feet above the sea), commanded in clear weather a view of both sides of the Adriatic, and the island was connected by a submarine cable with the neighbouring island of Lesina and the Dalmatian coast. The garrison of Lissa consisted of 1,800 men, with eighty-eight guns, commanded by Colonel Urs de Margina.

On July 17th Persano steamed round the island, reconnoitred its defences, and decided on his plans for the attack. Next day Admiral Vacca, with three of the Italian ironclads and one wooden ship, attacked the batteries of Porta Comisa. The main body of the fleet closed in upon the harbour batteries of San Giorgio, in order to keep the garrison there as much occupied as possible while Admiral Albini, with another squadron, brought six large screw steamers crowded with troops into the bay at Porto Manego in order to effect a landing there. At Porto Comisa, Vacca found he could not elevate his guns sufficiently to do any serious damage to the high batteries, and he was driven off by their shells.

At Porto Manego, a heavy surf on the beach and the fire of the Austrians from the shore made the landing impossible. At San Giorgio, Persano silenced the low-lying batteries at the harbour mouth, blowing up two of their magazines, but the inner batteries prevented his ships from entering the port. During the day one of his steamers had gone in to the neighbouring island of Lesina and cut the telegraph cable there.

While the Italians were in possession of the telegraph station at Lesina, a message from Tegethoff came through. It was addressed to Colonel de Margina, and told him to hold out to the last, promising that the fleet would come to rescue him. Persano tried to persuade himself that this message was intended to fall into his hands, and was a piece of mere "bluff" on the part of his opponent.

On the following day, he renewed the attack on Lissa, but again failed to force his way into the harbour, while an attempt to land troops at Porto Carober was repulsed with heavy loss. On this same day, July 19th, Tegethoff put to sea with every ship he could muster. His last order to his captains was to close with the enemy before Lissa, and once the battle began, to "Ram everything painted grey." This was the colour of the Italian ships. He gave his own hulls a coat of black paint before they started, in order to make it easier to distinguish friends from foes in the coming melee.

On the evening of the 19th Persano was undecided what to do next day. He had been two days in action, and though his ships had received only slight injuries, his supply both of coal and ammunition was running short. Yet if he went back to Ancona without having obtained a decided success he would be deprived of his command. So, he at last resolved to capture Lissa by a combined attack by land and

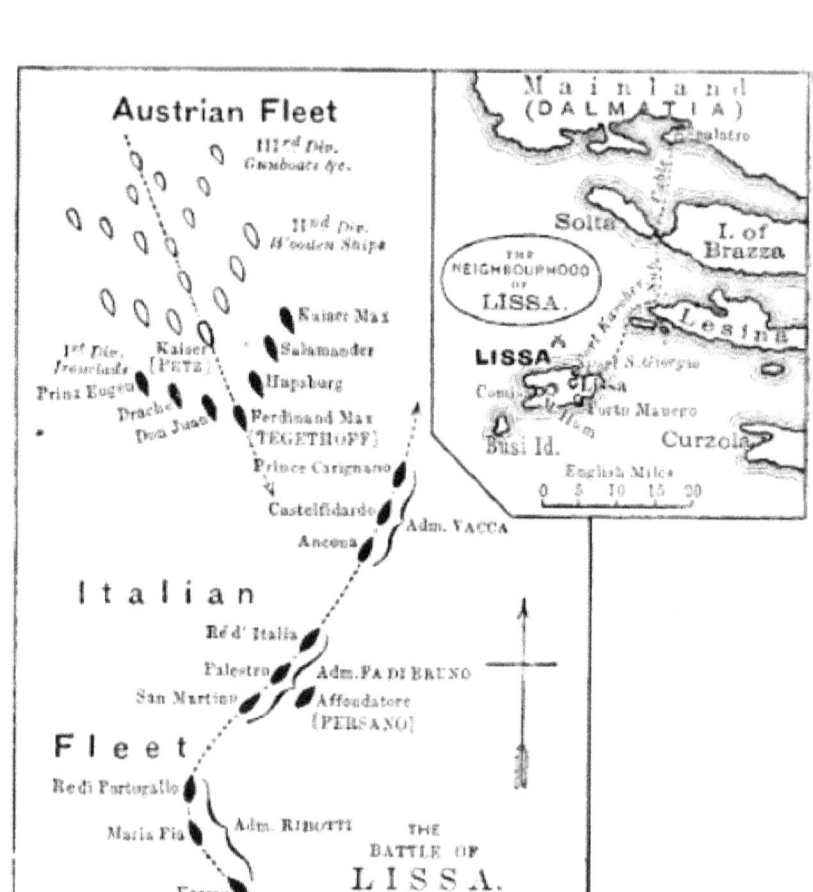

sea. Early next day he signalled to his colleague Albini to prepare for the landing. It was a fine morning, with a good deal of white haze on the sea shutting off the distant view.

Albini was getting the soldiers into the boats, and two of his frigates were standing in towards the creek of Carober to clear the way for the landing. A hospital ship had joined the fleet and was taking its wounded on board. The ironclads had assembled, and were getting up anchor for the attack on San Giorgio. It was eight o'clock: the attack was to begin at nine; but suddenly out of the haze to the north-westward appeared the frigate *Esploratore*, which had been scouting in the offing. She was steaming her fastest, and as she came nearer, Persano was able to read the signal she was flying.

"Suspicious-looking ships are in sight."

He knew at once that he had to deal with the Austrian fleet.

Tegethoff's fleet had been steaming all night in three lines, the ironclads leading, the wooden ships and gunboats following. The despatch-boat *Stadion* was out ahead, and at seven a.m., long before Persano knew what was coming, six of his ships were sighted by the keen eyes of the look-out at the masthead of the leading Austrian ship. She signalled to her consorts:

"Six steamers in sight."

Then the haze closed down ahead, and Tegethoff slackened speed in hopes it would clear, for in such thick weather he did not care to venture into the narrow waters between Lissa and Lesina. He formed for battle, each of his lines throwing forward its centre so as to assume the shape of a flattened wedge.

He led the first line in the *Ferdinand Max*, with three ironclads on either beam. The second line also consisted of seven ships, Petz in the *Kaiser* leading, with three frigates on each side. Thus, the squadron moved towards Lissa under easy steam. The haze was breaking up: it was a hot summer day, and a little before ten o'clock the sky was bright, the air clear, and the sea smooth; and close ahead the Austrians saw the forts of Lissa with the imperial flag still waving over them, and in front of the harbour mouth the mass of wooden ships, transports, and small craft, interrupted in their preparations for the landing, and nearer still the Italian ironclads steaming out in one long line ready for battle.

Persano, regarding his wooden ships as useless, had decided to take

Trieste Harbour.

only his ten ironclads with him, believing that they would be able to deal with the seven which Tegethoff was bringing against him. He formed his ironclads in three divisions, each of three ships, with the turret ship and ram *Affondatore*, then the most powerful vessel in the Adriatic, on the starboard side of the central division.

✶✶✶✶✶✶

Note:—The *Affondatore* was a new ship built in the Thames just before the war. A correspondent of the *Times* who saw her at Cherbourg, where she called on her way down Channel, wrote that she looked sufficiently formidable to destroy the whole Austrian ironclad fleet singlehanded.

✶✶✶✶✶✶

The *Affondatore*, with her ram and her heavy turret guns (two 300-pounders), was to come to the help of whichever of the three divisions was in need of succour. At the last moment, he himself went on board of her—an unfortunate move, which led to much confusion during the battle, as his captains were mostly unaware that the *Ré d'Iltalia*, a large broadside ship, which had till then been flagship, no longer carried the admiral.

When the haze cleared, the Italian fleet was steaming across the Austrian front. Tegethoff had already signalled to clear for action. He now signalled to open fire with the bow guns, and the distant shots from the leading Austrian ships were answered by the broadsides of Admiral Vacca's division, which led that of Italy. But the range was fully two miles, and these "long bowls" did no harm. The fleets were wrapped in drifting clouds of smoke, and geysers of foam shot up here and there from the blue water in the space between.

"Full steam ahead," signalled Tegethoff. The fleets were closing, the Italians still keeping their broadsides to the advancing foe. The fire was closer, and now spars and ropes were cut away, boats and wooden fittings were knocked to splinters, and signalmen and others who had not yet got under cover were wounded or killed by bursting shells. "Ironclads will ram and sink the enemy," signalled Tegethoff, the last order he gave till the battle was won. From this point, he kept on the bridge of the *Ferdinand Max*, regardless of personal danger, and led his fleet by showing his consorts what a well-handled battle-ship could do. Two of his captains, Molb of the ironclad *Drache*, and Klint of the *Novara*, were killed as the fleets came to close quarters. Molb being struck down by the first Italian shot that fell on board his ship.

The two lines of ironclads closed amid thick clouds of smoke. The

THE RAM CRUSHED IN HER IRON SIDE.

Austrian ships broke into the gap between Vacca's three ironclads and the rest of the Italian fleet, and Petz, with the wooden ships coming up on their right, co-operated with them in their attack on the Italian centre. In a moment, all order was lost, and the battle became a melee. The *Ferdinand Max* twice rammed a grey ironclad without succeeding in sinking her, when suddenly up out of the smoke loomed the tall masts of the *Ré d'Italia,* which came up to the rescue of her consort. Tegethoff, thinking he was dealing with the Italian flagship, charged her full speed and struck her fairly amidships.

This time he had succeeded: the ram crushed in her iron side, and the tall masts toppled over as the ironclad went down with her crew of 600 men. The *Ferdinand Max* had reversed her screw to clear the wreck, when another Italian vessel, the name of which could not be made out by the Austrians, came bearing down upon her trying to ram. The Austrian flagship just avoided the collision, and the two ships grazed past each other almost touching.

As she thus ranged up alongside, the Italian ship fired a broadside. What followed would be incredible, only for the clear evidence which supports the Austrian record. So close were the muzzles of the Italian guns to the side of the Austrian flagship that the smoke of the broadside poured in through the open portholes of the *Ferdinand Max* and made her gun-deck for the moment dark as night. But neither the ship nor the men were injured, for in their hurry and confusion the Italian gunners had fired *a broadside of blank cartridge!*

Admiral Ribotti, with the rearward division of the Italian fleet, as he came into the fight encountered only the wooden squadron of Commodore Petz. Ribotti ought to have sunk them one by one, but the Austrians evaded his attempts at ramming, and Petz in the *Kaiser* boldly drove the oaken bows of his battle-ship against the iron sides of his adversaries. He was not able to do them much damage. He hit the *Ré di Portogallo*, Ribotti's own ship, one good blow, that left its mark on her armour, but in doing so his own ship was disabled. The bowsprit was carried away, the foremast fell across the funnel, and the wreck of mast and spars took fire.

The *Kaiser*, her crew working hard at cutting away the debris and putting out the fire, steamed through the Italian fleet and stood in to the harbour of Lissa, exchanging shots with some of the Italian wooden vessels. Cheered by the garrison, she passed the harbour mouth and anchored under the guns of the forts, the first of the relieving squadron to arrive at San Giorgio.

Meanwhile the *mêlée* continued. While Tegethoff was in the thick of the fight, Persano made the great ram *Affondatore* nearly useless by persisting in keeping on the outskirts of the conflict. If he had ventured in with her it is very likely he would have been sunk by the better-handled Austrian ships. The *Palestro*, which had gone into action immediately astern of the *Ré d'Italia*, had been almost as severely handled as her leader. She had been rammed. Her steering gear and rudder had been knocked to pieces, and her gun-decks were on fire. She drew out of the fight, her commander getting his steam hose to work to drown the magazine. The Austrian ships were now clearing the Italian line, and steering for Lissa.

The *mêlée*, which had lasted for rather more than half-an-hour, was over. The position of the two fleets was reversed. The Austrians with their left near Lissa, were forming up in line across the channel between that island and Lesina. Everyone of their ironclads was still m good condition, and even the disabled *Kaiser*, which had gone into the harbour with her foremast burning and her decks strewed with nearly two hundred killed and wounded, was again clearing for action. The Italian wooden ships were assembling off the western end of the island.

To the northward, the ironclads were scattered here and there, on the waters that had just been the scene of the fight. As the smoke cleared, Persano signalled to the nearest ship—"Where is the *Ré d'Italia?*" and got for answer, "Sunk to the bottom." Close astern of the *Affondatore* lay the *Palestro*, the black smoke pouring from hatchway and porthole. Her crew believed that the magazine had been successfully drowned, and that they were getting the fire under. As they recognised Persano on the bridge of the *Affondatore*, they gave him a cheer. His own crew were answering it when there was a burst of flame and a volume of dense smoke from the *Palestro*, and an explosion louder than all the din of battle went echoing over sea and shore. It was the death-knell of 400 men, for the *Palestro* had blown up with all on board.

Admiral Vacca, thinking that Persano had gone down with the *Ré d'Italia*, had signalled to the fleet to re-form in line of battle. The same signal from the *Affondatore* showed him where his commander was. And the ironclads, now, reduced from ten to eight, reformed in line It was noon on a blazing hot day, and for some time the two fleets watched each other across the sunny space of open water that divided them. Persano had still the advantage of numbers, and everyone expected that he would signal to renew the attack.

But if he had very little confidence in his fleet before the battle, he was now reduced to a condition of something like despair. Even the wooden ships of the Austrian squadron had passed in safety through his line, while their ironclads had destroyed two of his ships and more than a thousand of his men. It must be added that he had now been three times in action, and his stock of both coals for his engines and ammunition for his guns must have run very low. In this state of affairs, he persuaded himself that he need not actually attack the Austrians; all that honour demanded of him was to give them the opportunity of renewing the trial of strength if they wished. So, for another hour he remained in line of battle, just out of long range of his enemy's guns.

But Tegethoff had accomplished the task assigned to his fleet. He had relieved Lissa, by bringing the guns, the men, and the supplies of his fleet to the help of its brave little garrison He had done this, too, not by slipping past the Italians in the morning fog, but by fighting his way through their most powerful squadron, making them pay dearly for their attempt to intercept him. Why should he renew the fight when there was nothing more to be gained for the moment?

Persano at last decided that he, too, had done enough for honour. He signalled to the fleet to steam away to the north-west, and shortly after altered his course for Ancona. He anchored there next day, and added to all his previous blunders the final folly of sending to his government, and wiring all over Italy, the report that he had fought a pitched battle with the Austrians, and won a victory over them in the waters of Lissa. That night Florence (then the capital) was illuminated in honour of his "triumph."

Next day the facts began to be known. It was impossible to deny that the Austrian fleet was intact; that the Italians had lost two ships, and had been forced to raise the siege of Lissa. It was in vain that Persano argued that he was the victor because he had remained in possession of the waters in which the battle had been fought, and that he had for a whole hour dared the Austrians to come on again. There was the obvious reply that a naval battle is not fought for the possession of a stretch of open water; that Persano had tried to prevent the Austrians reaching Lissa, that they had gone there in spite of him; and that they would have been fools to come back in order to show twice over that they were not afraid to fight him.

There was a wild outburst of indignation against the unfortunate admiral; there were riots at Florence, and a royal decree removed him from the command of the fleet. As if to add to the general collapse of the Italian navy, the *Affondatore*, supposed to be its most powerful ship, whether through injuries received at Lissa, or through mere defects in her structure, sank at her anchors in the harbour of Ancona.

On the side of Austria, there were rejoicings in which the name of Tegethoff was celebrated as that of an heroic sailor who had given his country the consolation of a naval victory at a time when her fortunes on land were at the lowest. He had won his great victory with comparatively little loss. The *Kaiser* was the only ship that suffered at all heavily. In some of the ironclads there were only a few wounded, and every one of the ships was in a position to continue the fight when the Italian fleet retired. The battle was the first that had been fought by ironclad fleets in European waters, and the impression it made upon naval experts was that the ram would be the chief weapon of future battles on the sea.

Yet, though we have by no means clear or full accounts of what happened in the *mêlée* while the two fleets were passing through each other's lines, it is certain that the number of attempts to ram made by the Austrians was out of all proportion to their two successful attacks. All the attempts of the Italians to ram ended in failure. It must be remembered that since Lissa a great change has come over naval tactics, through the development of the torpedo and the quick-firing gun, and it is now generally recognised by naval men that to attempt to ram an adversary till he is disabled by gunfire or otherwise is to invite failure and disaster. Tegethoff regarded the ram as his chief weapon. Nowadays it is looked upon as the means of giving the *coup de grace* and completing a victory that is already half won.

The victor of Lissa was rightly honoured by his sovereign and his countrymen, while Admiral Persano was put on his trial on the charge of having lost the battle through cowardice and incompetence. He was acquitted of the charge of cowardice, but found guilty of having sacrificed his fleet through his incompetent conduct at Lissa, and he was deprived of all rank and dismissed from the navy. There is no doubt that although he alone was condemned, he was not the only officer of the Italian fleet who was responsible for the defeat of Lissa. Throughout there was a lamentable want of energy, pluck, and decision. Otherwise the Austrians would not have achieved their victory with so slight a loss. Albini's conduct in looking on idly with his frigates while Petz on the Austrian side was leading his wooden squadron against Ribotti's ironclads, is a good instance of this.

Indeed, the Battle of Lissa, considered in its details, shows that success on the sea, as well as on land, is primarily a question of brave and competent leadership. Good officers are the first condition of naval success; well-trained and disciplined crews the second; powerful ships are the third. Public opinion is often so ill informed as to put in the first place what really stands last; but none of these elements of naval power can be safely neglected by a maritime State, and one which claims the Empire of the Sea must spare no effort to possess all three, and to possess them in abundance.

WARS OF ITALIAN UNIFICATION

The Battle of Custozza
June 24, 1866
By A. Hilliard Atteridge

When Nicholas Nickleby suggested to Mr. Vincent Crummles that the "terrific broadsword combat" on his stage would look better if the two adversaries were more of a size, the veteran manager replied that the remark showed how little he knew about the business. What the public really liked to see was the little fellow getting the better of the big one. And Mr. Crummles was right. Most men have a "weakness for the weaker side," and if there is one thing they like better to see than a fair and even fight, it is the spectacle of a victory won by skill and pluck against superior strength. Such was the victory that splendid old soldier the Archduke Albert of Austria won at Custozza during the brief campaign of Northern Italy in 1866.

As it happened, it was—so far as tangible results were concerned—a barren success. The prize that was fought for was the possession of Venice and its territory; and by the course of events this went to Italy at the close of the war, notwithstanding her defeats by land and sea. But for all that, Custozza and Lissa were a solid gain to Austria, for they enabled her to yield to fate without losing heart and hope for the future. Broken as her power was on the wider field of the struggle with Prussia, she could yet trust to sailors of the stamp of Tegethoff, soldiers like the Archduke Albert, to secure for her the respect even of the victors, and to ensure that before long she would again be a factor to be reckoned with in the councils of Europe.

The Archduke Albert was the son of a famous soldier, the Archduke Charles, who was one of the most formidable opponents of the Great Napoleon, and who by the victory of Aspern brought him within sight of ruin many years before Waterloo was fought and won. The Archduke Albert had distinguished himself in the campaigns of

Italy in 1848 and 1840, taking part in more than one hard-fought action on the very ground which he held in 1866. When, in that year, Italy began to prepare to take the field against Austria as the ally of Prussia, the government at Vienna concentrated the bulk of its forces on the northern frontiers of the empire to meet the more formidable attack that was threatened from Berlin, and the archduke was left to hold Venetia against the Italians with very inferior forces. It was this marked inferiority that gave special interest to his successful campaign against the great armies that were marshalled against him.

At the end of the month of May the Italians had concentrated a main army of 140,000 men in Lombardy, and a second force of about 60,000 between Ferrara and Bologna in the Romagna. The army in Lombardy was commanded nominally by the King, Victor Emmanuel; really by his chief of the staff, the veteran General La Marmora, the same who had commanded the Sardinian contingent in the Crimea. The army was divided into three corps under Durando, Cucchiari, and Delia Rocca. The king's eldest son. Prince Humbert, then Crown Prince and now King of Italy, commanded a division in Delia Rocca's corps.

His brother, Prince Amadeo, afterwards King of Spain, commanded a brigade of grenadiers in the first corps. This army was destined to cross the little River Mincio, which formed the boundary between Lombardy and Venetia, thus attacking the Austrians in front; while the second army of 60,000 men under Cialdini would be in a position to cross the lower course of the Po, and fall upon their flank. On the left of the royal army Garibaldi was assembling a third force of between 30,000 and 40,000 men, with which he was to invade the Tyrol.

To meet these three armies—amounting in all to at least 235,000 men—the Archduke Albert had nominally at his disposal a force of 135,000. Thus, he had a majority of 100,000 against him at the very outset, but even this does not represent the whole deficiency. First, he had to detach 12,000 men for the defence of the Tyrol. These were expected to be able to deal with Garibaldi's 30,000 or 40,000 volunteers; 12,000 more were assigned to the defence of Istria and the neighbourhood of Trieste and Pola, where, considering the strength of Italy on the sea, there was supposed to be some danger of a naval descent; 40,000 were employed in the garrisons of the Quadrilateral (Mantua, Verona, Peschiera and Legnago) and in the fortresses of Rovigo and Venice; finally 6,000 had to be left to guard his communications with Austria. This reduced the field army to a little over 60,000 men, and

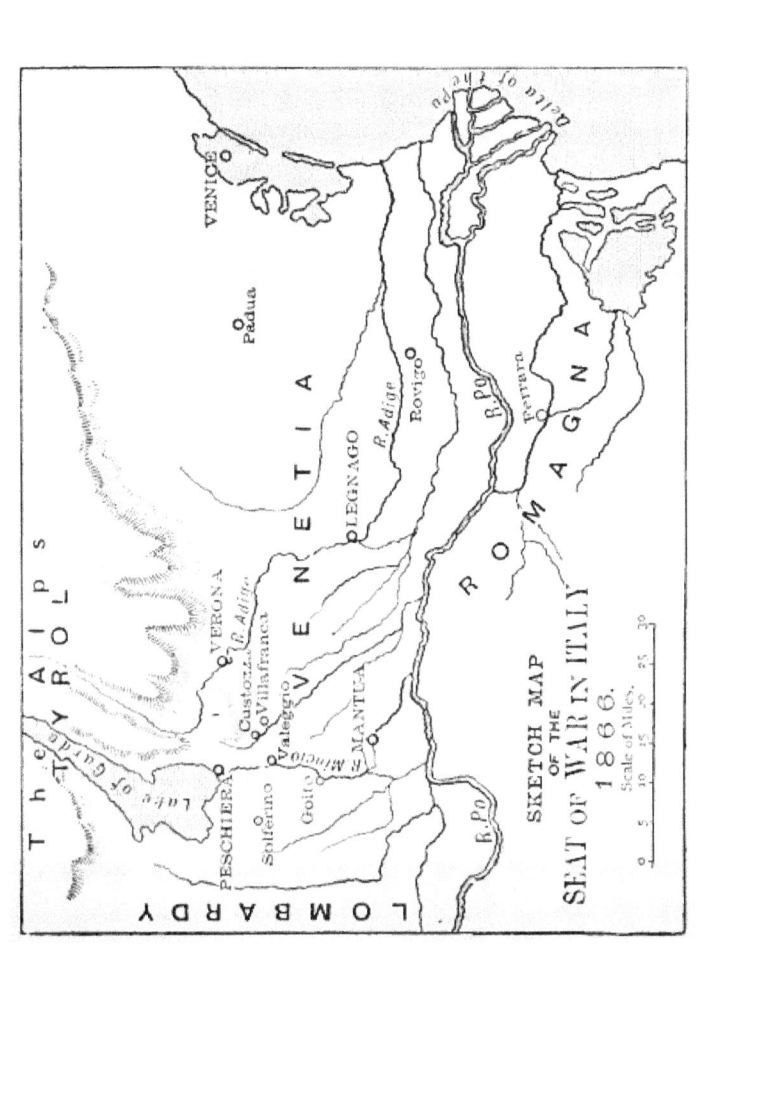

with these he had to meet the 200,000 of Italy.

The Italians had divided their forces, and the archduke saw that his best chance of success would lie in an attempt to deal with one of their armies before the other could come to its assistance. In order to do this, it would be necessary from the very outset to conceal his own position and movements, and be fully informed of those of his opponents. Therefore, concentrating his army in a central position behind the Adige, a little to the east of Verona, a point from which he could move either against the king or against Cialdini, he left only a screen of cavalry outposts along the Mincio, between Peschiera and Mantua, and along the north bank of the Po, opposite Ferrara. Once war was declared they allowed no one to pass the frontier in either direction, and even before that only those few privileged persons who had obtained a special passport from the Austrian military authorities were allowed to cross.

The cavalry scouts and vedettes did their work to perfection. They prevented the Italians from obtaining any information as to the plans or movements of the archduke, and they kept him well informed as to all that was going on upon the Lombard shore of the Mincio. The Archduke had in the last few days before the declaration of war made up his mind to attack the king's army. If Victor Emmanuel crossed the Mincio he would fall upon him on the ground between that river and the Adige; or if the Italians remained in Lombardy he intended himself to cross the Mincio, trusting to be able to defeat them, and then return in time to deal with Cialdini.

In both cases, he would have the advantage of being able to make one or other of the four fortresses of the Quadrilateral the base of his attack. On June 20th, he received notice that war had been declared. On the same day, he had reports from his cavalry outposts to the effect that both the Italian armies were preparing to advance. From the westward, the king's army was closing in upon various points on the Mincio, and to the southward Cialdini was collecting material to construct bridges across the Po at Francolinetto, and had actually occupied an island in the middle of the wide stream at that point. The archduke remained quiet near Verona for nearly two days longer. His plan was to lull his enemy into a false sense of security, and then strike swiftly and sharply.

All the bridges on the Mincio were left standing, and the screen of cavalry posts received orders not to oppose the Italians seriously at any point when they tried to cross. When the invaders entered Venetia,

Verona

the Austrian horsemen were to fall back before them, to do as little fighting as possible, but never to lose sight of them.

On Thursday, June 22nd, the Royal Army of Italy was concentrated on the right or Lombard bank of the Mincio. At Monzambano the engineers were at work constructing bridges. At Valeggio and Goito the cavalry of De Sonnaz was ready to seize the existing bridges as soon as the word was given to advance. In the grey of the early morning of Friday they crossed the river at both points. The Austrian cavalry, under Colonel Pulz, fell back without firing a shot. Avoiding the hills that lie northward towards the Garda lake, Pulz retired across the level ground of the plain of Villafranca. The plain is thickly populated. There are numerous villages and hamlets, and plenty of roads, footpaths, and tracks; but it is difficult country to manoeuvre in, for everywhere the ground is cut up with small watercourses and irrigation channels—hedgerows, orchards, and plantations restrict the view.

Along the course of the streams are swampy rice-fields, and on every stretch of sloping ground there are thickly-planted vineyards. Pulz was able to make the Italians very slow and cautious in their advance. It was the afternoon before he retired from Villafranca, and behind the little country town he made a stand with his horsemen and a battery of artillery; and though he again retreated after a short skirmish, the result was. that the Italian cavalry of De Sonnaz did not push their explorations any further that day. They reported to the royal headquarters that the Austrians had no force between the Adige and the Mincio beyond a couple of regiments of cavalry and a battery of horse artillery; and this confirmed La Marmora in his idea that the archduke would be compelled by his inferior numbers to remain on the defensive near Verona.

All day the Italian army had been pouring across the bridges of the Mincio, and advancing by the hot, sandy roads—the right into the plain of Villafranca, the left towards the low hills that border it on the northward, stretching from the lake of Garda to Custozza and Somma Campagna. General La Marmora was confident of victory. He was occupying the very ground where the allied armies of France and Italy had stayed their onward march in 1859. He was going to take up the work of conquest where Napoleon III. had left off, and he hoped to complete it by entering Venice as a victor. North and south and away to his front lay the famed fortresses of the Quadrilateral, the keys of Northern Italy; but their garrisons were cowering behind the ramparts, and doing nothing to disturb his movements.

On the Saturday night about half the Italian army was across the river, and the rest was close up to the bridges, ready to follow in the morning. The troops were to be moving by 3.30 a.m., and La Marmora had issued orders for an advance upon Verona. The right was to move by the plain of Villafranca to the hills round Somma Campagna; the left was to enter the hill country, more directly marching from Monzambano and Valeggio on Castelnuovo and Sona. The object of the movement was to occupy the mass of hills to the south-east of the lake of Garda, cut off Peschiera from Verona, and threaten the positions held by the Archduke near that fortress.

On the Sunday morning, the Italians were under arms at half-past three, and soon after their columns were on the move. The men had no breakfast before starting, beyond a piece of bread or a biscuit taken from the haversack and eaten as they waited for the order to march off. It was intended to halt later on for breakfast, but the Italian staff was anxious to get the march over as early as possible, as it was expected that it would be a very hot day. So sure were they that the enemy would not be encountered in force that no cavalry were sent out to scout in front. In front of each column there was an advance guard; but so badly was the march arranged, and so loosely was the connection between the advance guards and those that followed them kept up, that the vanguard of Sirtori's division, consisting of some 2,500 men with six guns, took the wrong road, and got in front of the vanguard of Cerale's division; while, by a blunder of the leading portion of Cerale's column, his main body wandered on to the road assigned to General Sirtori. Thus, there was the singular spectacle of two advance guards following each other on one road, while their main bodies calmly marched in long procession along another.

The start had been made shortly before four o'clock. The march had proceeded for a little more than an hour, and five had just struck from the village bell towers, when General La Marmora, who was riding with centre, was surprised at hearing far away to the right, in the direction of Villafranca, the roar of guns in action. The two divisions of the Italian third corps, commanded by the Crown Prince Humbert and by General Bixio, had been attacked by Austrian cavalry and horse-artillery. The Italians behaved well. The infantry formed into squares, and beat off three cavalry charges; the artillery galloped up, unlimbered, and drove away the Austrian guns with a few well-aimed shells.

By six o'clock the fight was over, and the enemy was in retreat. La

Marmora had ridden towards the firing, and when he received the report of what had happened, he at once made up his mind that the affair was of very little importance. He felt sure that the Austrian force consisted only of Pulz's regiments, the same which had been watching the river two days before, and had retired through Villafranca when the Italians advanced on the Saturday.

The divisions of his first corps on the left had now entered the hilly country, and at half-past six, a good half-hour after the last shot had been fired at Villafranca, there was a still more startling incident on the left. Sirtori was marching his division across the deep little valley through which the Tione flows, and the leading regiment was ascending the slope beyond its left bank. Sirtori himself rode near the head of the column. Suddenly a volley was fired at the leading ranks by riflemen lying in ambush among the trees and enclosures of a farmstead at the top of the slope.

Sirtori, pulling up his horse, looked through his field-glasses at the wreaths of smoke that hung in the still, clear morning air; but so well hidden were the riflemen that he could not make out their uniforms. Nevertheless, he felt so sure that the Austrians were not in front of him, and he so little suspected that his vanguard was on another road, that he told those near him that the ambushed foes must be their own comrades of the vanguard firing on them by mistake, and he sent two of his officers galloping forward to stop the fire. They came careering back down the slope to tell him that they had narrowly escaped being killed or captured by a regiment of Austrian *Jägers*, and the next minute the sight of guns unlimbering on the ridge told the startled Italian general that he had come upon a hostile army in battle array. A minute more and the deep voice of the first gun told even La Marmora that he had made a terrible mistake, and that the Austrians were in action on his left as well as his right.

What had happened? The Italian columns working their way into the hills—one by this road, another by that, with no connection between them, with no concerted plan of action, and, what was worse, with the men fasting and unprepared for a long day's battle, were one by one coming into collision with the army drawn up to receive them under the cover of the first ridges of the hills. Late on the Friday the archduke had learned of the Italian advance, and had given orders for the crossing of the Adige, near Verona.

On the Saturday, while the Italians believed he was still inactive behind the river, he had got his whole army across it, and he bivouacked for the night within striking distance of the Royal Army, in which no one, from the king to the youngest soldier, had an idea that 60,000 foes were so close in their front. Considering how densely peopled the whole district is, it is a marvel that none of the inhabitants warned the Italians of their danger. If any of them made an effort to pass the Austrian outposts, the attempt was a failure. At midnight, the archduke received a telegram from General Scudier, who commanded on the lower Po. It informed him that Cialdini's vanguard was crossing the river, and the Austrians were slowly retiring before his advance. But this made no change in the arrangements for next day.

The archduke still counted on smashing up the King's army before the two Italian armies could get near enough to help each other. He believed the king's plan would be to march direct through the plain of Villafranca to the Adige; and his own orders for next day were that the various corps were to face southward and westward, moving from their camps at 2 a.m., gaining the hills, and then sweeping round, so as to descend on the flank of the Italian advance. Although he had not completely divined the plans of the Italians, his own plans were so sound that they met even their altered arrangements.

Instead of falling on their flank, he struck the heads of their ill-connected columns as they strove to gain the hills. His own march

Archduke Albert.

had begun at 2 o'clock, in the darkness of a midsummer night. There was soon enough light to move rapidly and surely. At five the sound of guns engaged in the brief action at Villafranca led the Austrians for a while to believe that the main Italian advance was in the plain; but their scouts soon brought them news of the real direction in which the enemy was moving, and when the Italians entered the hills they blundered into a fight for which they were not prepared, while the Austrians met them with a well-organised battle line, every unit in which worked well with those to the right and left of it, and proved once more that even enormous numbers count for less than discipline and union under one strong will directed by a clear and well-trained mind.

So far as the Italians were concerned, Custozza was a series of detached fights; for the Austrian commander, it was a tremendous struggle, of which he controlled and coordinated all the parts.

Let us return to the fight at the point where it began on the Italian left. As soon as Sirtori found that he had an Austrian force to deal with, he got his division into line on the very unfavourable ground on which its leading battalion stood when the first shots were fired, and made repeated efforts to drive the enemy from the farm and the ridges round Pernisa. Soon he heard firing away to the left and right. The battle was becoming general. To the left, about a mile and a half away, his advanced guard, under General Villahermosa, had come upon the Austrian reserve division holding the slopes of Monte Cricol, a bold ridge over which the Valeggio road runs about two miles to the south of Castelnuovo. The fight here had a very important effect on the fortunes of the day.

Villahermosa, believing that he had the whole of Sirtori's division close behind him, resolved to clear the way for it by driving the Austrians from the hill, and sent forward his riflemen—the famous *Bersaglieri*—whose ordinary marching pace is a smart run. They made a gallant dash at the Monte Cricol, but the attack was a failure. Outnumbered and over-weighted, the Italian riflemen fell back, and then the Austrians came charging down the hill after them, and began to drive Villahermosa and his vanguard along the Valeggio road. More than an hour had passed in this fight in front of Monte Cricol, when again the tide was turned by the arrival of the leading troops of General Cerale's division, which had marched towards the firing. The division consisted of some 12,000 men, with eighteen guns.

First came General Villarey, a Savoyard soldier, with two battalions of *Bersaglieri* as the vanguard. Then came the rest of Villarey's brigade—eight battalions—and behind it the guns and a brigade of eight more battalions under General Dhô. As Cerale brought his division into action he saw not only the victorious Austrians in front, but other white-coated columns moving on the hills to his right, beyond the Tione. These were part of the corps that was attacking his colleague Sirtori, but they brought their guns to bear even upon the Valeggio road, so that Cerale had to turn some of his own artillery upon them. His main force he threw against the Austrians in front, in order to rescue Villahermosa, and for the moment superior force was on the side of the Italians. They cleared the road, captured two guns, and, pushing boldly on, got to the crest of the Monte Cricol, and also turned the enemy out of Mongabia on the right of the road. It looked as if here, on the extreme western edge of the battle, the Italians were winning.

But now came an incident which shows how, even in modern war with tens of thousands in the field, a handful of brave men can change the whole aspect of a battle. Across the Tione, to the right of this portion of the fight, there was a regiment of Austrian cavalry, known as the Sicilian *Uhlans* (lancers, who had formerly had the King of the Two Sicilies for their honorary colonel).

Colonel de Berres, who commanded the lancers, had been watching through his field-glass the fight for the Monte Cricol, and seeing that the Austrian brigade, which was now retiring before the Italians, was hard pressed, he thought he could help his friends by a sudden charge on Cerale's flank. One Italian brigade was in line of battle driving in the Austrians; the other was in a long marching column on the road. Berres called up one of his captains—Bechtoldsheim—and ordered him to take three troops and attack the enemy on the road.

The three troops numbered exactly 103 officers and men. The brigade of General Dhô was at least 5,000 strong, but the hundred without a moment's hesitation trotted off to charge the 5,000. They descended the slope to the Tione, found a ford, got across, and quietly made their way up the hill to the right of the Italians. These seem not to have had the least warning of the coming attack. They were moving slowly forward in column when the handful of splendid horsemen came rushing down the hill like a hurricane. Generals Cerale and Dhô, with their staff, were riding at the head of the column. The *Uhlans*, falling on the flank of the foremost regiment, crashed through it with levelled lances, and then rode for the crowd of officers, and scattered them right and left. The two generals escaped with difficulty.

THE CHARGE OF THE AUSTRIAN LANCERS

Cerale was hit by a revolver bullet in the *mêlée*, and Dhô received three lance wounds. Two guns which were on the road just behind the staff were galloped back to the rear by their teams, and battalion after battalion broke and ran as the lancers dashed down the road cheering and striking right and left with their lances, the retiring guns being now the main object of their charge. At last the frightened gunners cut the traces, and the guns were overturned in the press. But, with the exception of one battalion, Dhô's division was now a panic-stricken mob. On both sides of the road the valley was full of men who had thrown away their arms and were running for their lives.

Two thousand of them did not stop till they had put the bridges of Monzambano and Valeggio between them and the enemy. And yet that enemy consisted only of a handful of lancers. If one company had stood its ground and fired one steady volley the charge would have been stopped. When the lancers at last pulled bridle, and turned to ride back they had not lost a score of their small number. Captain Bechtoldsheim, their brave leader, had had his horse killed under him, but close by an Italian major had just been run through with a lance, and Bechtoldsheim caught the horse of his fallen foe and again put himself at the head of his men. But as they rode back they found the one Italian battalion that had kept together had lined the ditches on both sides of the only possible track. The lancers had to gallop through a sheet of flame from the hostile rifles, and the road was strewn with men and horses.

When Bechtoldsheim regained the hill, there were only sixteen of his brave *Uhlans* beside him. They had left two officers, eighty-four men, and seventy-nine horses in the valley, killed and wounded; but they had done their work, and their charge had decided the fortune of the day. Villarey's brigade was now all that was left of Cerale's division. The Austrians had been reinforced, and they promptly attacked and retook the Monte Cricol, and drove the Italians down the hill and along the same valley which had just witnessed the charge of the lancers. The Italians tried more than once to make a stand, but they were driven from position after position, and their commander, Villarey, was shot dead while forming the 30th Regiment for a counter-attack on the victors.

After his fall, there was nothing but wild confusion on the Italian left. Here and there, however, handfuls of brave men acted in a way that did something to redeem the honour of the Italian arms. A little group of ten officers and thirty men of the 44th Regiment, finding that they were abandoned by their panic-stricken comrades, threw themselves into a farmhouse, taking the flag of the regiment with them. They held it for two hours against the Austrians, and only surrendered it when the building was set on fire. But their flag was not captured. They had cut it into forty pieces, and each of them took a piece. When they came back from Austria after the war the pieces were sewn together, and the flag was restored to the regiment.

The village of Oliosi, between the Valeggio road and the Tione, was held by the Italians, and afforded some protection to their retreat from the disastrous fight before the Monte Cricol. It was stormed by a column of two Austrian regiments under General Piret, which crossed the river, and cleared the village without much difficulty. In one house—the presbytery, near the village church—the Italians held out for nearly two hours. When the house was all but demolished the little garrison surrendered, and five officers and forty-nine men were made prisoners.

What was left of Cerale's division, together with part of Sirtori's vanguard, now rallied on the bold ridge of Monte Vento. To their left General Pianelli's division, which had just crossed the Mincio, was coming up from the bridges of Monzambano, bringing some 12,000 fresh men to support them. The Austrians were pushing in between the hill and the river; and one of their rifle regiments advancing overboldly, was surrounded by Pianelli's troops, and the 700 *Jagers* were all either shot down or captured. The reserve of the Italian 1st corps, consisting chiefly of *Bersaglieri*, was also directed upon Monte Vento. On the possession of this ridge the safety of the whole army depended, for if the Austrians took it they would be in a position to cut off the Italians from the bridges over the Mincio.

So far, the fight on the left had gone by ten o'clock. On the rest of the field it was the same. Everywhere the Italians had come into action piecemeal against solid masses of Austrians, and in every one of the detached fights that was in progress from left to right they were being pushed back. In the Tione valley Sirtori had failed to carry the ridge near Pernisa. He had himself been routed and driven across the river by the advancing Austrians, and had lost three guns. He had rallied his men and crossed the stream a second time, only to be a second time driven back. Still further to the right among the hills towards Custozza Brignone's division had come to grief. The Italians had fought well and lost heavily, Prince Amadeo and General Gozzani both falling severely wounded at the head of their brigades.

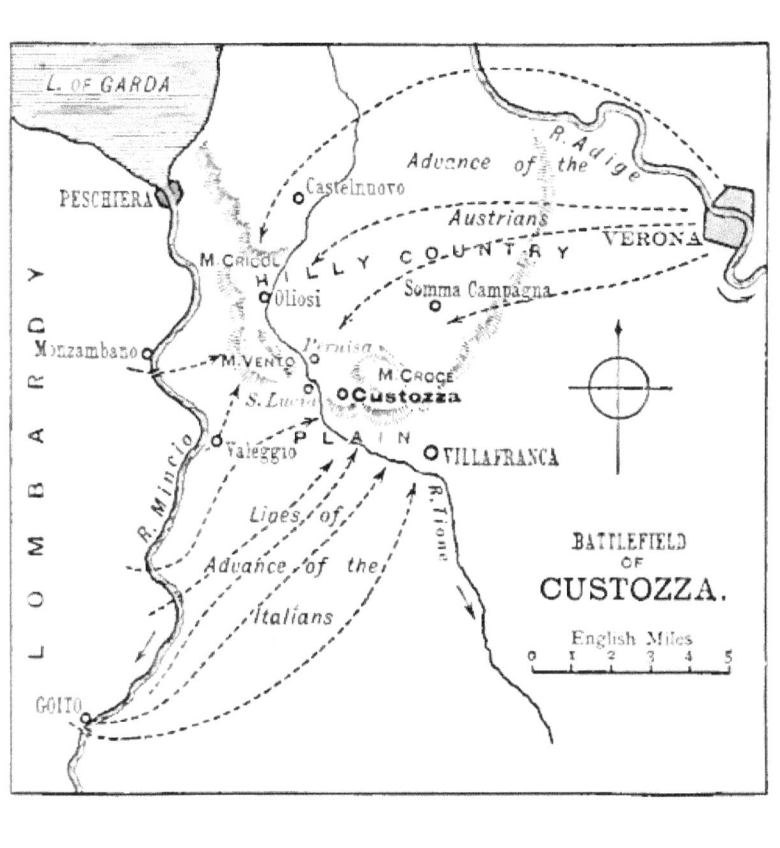

About ten. La Marmora was so alarmed by the reports that reached him from every side that he told the King he thought it was a lost battle, and was on the point of giving the order to retire to the bridges when an encouraging message from Durando, who was bringing the reserves into action on the left, led him to change his mind, and continue the fight. Having made at the outset such a terrible mistake as to the position of the Austrians, he seemed all day to be expecting some new surprise and disaster; and though really there were only Pulz's cavalry in the plain to his extreme right, he was so anxious about a possible attack in that direction that he kept Bixio and Prince Humbert's division inactive all day at Villafranca. They had not fired a shot since the short skirmish with the cavalry, in the early morning, and all through the blazing heat of the day the men sat or lay stretched in the shadows of the trees, listening to the roar of the fight in the hills, while their officers impatiently waited for orders to move.

The only order they got was a message that all was lost, and the moment had come to retreat. But this was some hours later. By eleven o'clock the Austrians had disposed of Sirtori's division, and crossing the river after his retreating battalions, they stormed the strong position of Santa Lucia, thus almost interposing between the Italian left and right. Artillery was massed against Monte Vento, and further westward a column of attack moved forward to attempt to seize the bridges on the Mincio at Monzambano. On the right the two fresh divisions of Cugia and Govone strengthened the Italian line, and delayed for a while the advance of the Austrians, whose object in this quarter was the capture of the village of Custozza, which stands on a bold hill overlooking the plain of Villafranca.

The loss of Santa Lucia made it very difficult for the Italians to hold on to Monte Vento. General Durando was actually discussing the question of retiring when he was shot down, and General Chilini, who had assumed the command in his stead, abandoned the position as soon as the Austrians advanced upon it. This made the defeat of the whole Italian army inevitable, for the Austrians could now advance and seize the ground between Monte Vento and the Mincio, the very ground over which the Italian Army must retire if it was to withdraw to its own territory, and across which it would have to keep up its communications with Lombardy, even if it could maintain itself in Venetia.

On the right the Italians had been driven back upon Custozza. It was near four o'clock. The Austrians had every available man and every gun in action. Their men were weary with the night march and the long fight among the hills under the blazing midsummer sun, which shone in a cloudless sky. But it was worse for the Italians. Most of them had eaten nothing all day, and they had none of the inspiration of success. They had been losing ground all day, and they had lost all confidence in their chiefs and in themselves.

Yet they had still forty thousand men who either had not fired a shot or had not been seriously engaged. These were the two divisions at Villafranca (Bixio's and the crown prince's) and the two reserve divisions of Cucchiari's corps, which were struggling along roads so encumbered with a confused mass of baggage and ammunition waggons that it was only when all was over that they approached the field. It would be difficult to find more striking proof of the hopeless incapacity of La Marmora and his staff.

At five o'clock the village and hill of Custozza were stormed with a fierce rush by the columns on the Austrian left. The hills were now completely in the possession of the archduke. He had driven the last of the Italians on to the low ground, and everywhere they were retiring towards the river, thousands having already streamed across the bridges in a confused and disorderly march. The Austrians were so exhausted with their nineteen hours of marching and fighting that there was no pursuit. If the archduke had had a few thousand fresh troops he might have captured whole masses of the fugitives, who were huddled together along the Mincio, waiting to cross.

Next day the Austrian cavalry pushed into Lombardy, and such was the impression made on the Italian Army by the collapse of Custozza that La Marmora made no effort to stop them, but retired first behind the Chiese and then behind the Oglio, abandoning a considerable part of Lombardy. Meanwhile, the archduke had marched from the scene of his victory back to the Adige, in order to be able to fall on Cialdini if he persisted in his invasion of Venetia. But the lesson of Custozza was enough to make the second Italian Army withdraw into the Romagna.

The Austrians lost in the battle 960 killed, 3,690 wounded, and some hundreds of prisoners, chiefly the *Jagers* captured by Pianelli's division. The Italian loss in killed and wounded was not quite so heavy, the killed being 720 and the wounded 3,112, but they lost in prisoners and missing 4,315 officers and men. On the Italian side, General Villarey was killed, and Generals Dhô, Durando, Gozzani, and Prince Amadoe were wounded. But a mere comparison of losses can give no idea of the effect of the battle on the two armies. The Austrian army was for all practical purposes intact, full of confidence in itself and in its leader. A great part of the Italian Army had degenerated into something like an armed mob, all confidence in the generals was gone, and, instead of talking of a march upon Venice, men were asking themselves if they could hold Northern Italy against an Austrian invasion. Custozza had given one more proof of the fact that victory is not always with the big battalions, and that a skilful leader can bring to nought the onset of less ably handled troops, though they outnumber his own by tens of thousands.

WARS OF ITALIAN UNIFICATION

Garibaldi's Defeat at Mentana November 3, 1867
By Donat Sampson

A sovereign of the House of Savoy is reported to have said that Italy was like an artichoke, which must be devoured leaf by leaf; and the saying became a fact in 1859 and 1860, when Lombardy, Tuscany, the Duchies of Parma and Modena, the greater part of the Papal States, and the kingdom of the Two Sicilies (a very tough leaf this last, which took some time to digest), were one by one absorbed by the little kingdom of Piedmont. After a short interval of rest, the province of Venetia was added to the others in 1866, and to carry out the comparison and devour the last leaf of the artichoke, there remained but to annex Rome.

This was not an easy task, for that city and the provinces which had been left to the Pope after the campaign of Castelfidardo were garrisoned by the soldiers of Napoleon III., who seemed resolved to maintain the independence of the Holy See; but a Convention was signed on September 15th, 1864, by which the emperor agreed to withdraw his troops within two years, while the Italian Government undertook not to invade the Papal territory, and to hinder, even by force, any attack upon that territory, coming from without. Some diplomatic correspondence, however, ensued between the two governments, which left no doubt that if an insurrection were to take place in Rome, Italy would be free to act, and that an attempt might probably be made to bring about that insurrection.

The last French soldiers embarked at Città Vecchia on December 11th, 1866, and to replace them every Catholic nation in Europe, but more especially France, Belgium, and Holland, furnished its contingent of volunteers representing all classes of society, from the noble whose ancestors had fought in the Crusades to the workman and the peasant; and on October 1st, 1867, the Papal army reckoned nearly 13,000 men. Of these, 2,083 were *gendarmes*; 878 artillerymen; 975 *chasseurs*; 1,595 infantry of the line; 442 dragoons, and 625 *squadriglieri*, or armed mountaineers. All these were Papal subjects.

The foreigners were 2,237 *Zouaves*, about two-thirds Dutch and Belgians, the rest French or other nationalities, 1,233 Swiss *Carabiniers*, and 1096 French soldiers, who formed the *Légion d'Antibes*. (Ireland did not send a contingent as in the previous campaign, but was represented in the *Zouaves* by Captain d'Arcy and Captain Delahoyd, who had served in the battalion of St. Patrick in 1860; by Surgeon-Major O'Flynn, who, in the same year, had taken part in the defence of Spoleto under Major O'Reilly; and by several recruits who hastened to enlist under the Papal standard when the Garibaldian invasion began.) The effective force, however, available for fighting did not amount to more than 8,000 men; but their excellent discipline and organisation and, still more, the spirit which animated them, compensated for their deficiency in numbers.

Garibaldi spent the summer of 1867 enrolling volunteers in all parts of Italy for an expedition against Rome, without meeting with much opposition from the Italian Government. They amounted to 30,000 men, and the general's plan was to invade the Papal territory in three divisions. The right wing, under Colonel Acerbi, was to advance from Orvieto towards Viterbo; the centre, under Menotti Garibaldi, from Terni towards Monte Rotondo and Tivoli; the left wing, under Nicotera, from the south towards Velletri. If the Papal troops were dispersed over the country to oppose these bands, Rome would be free to rebel, and if they remained on the defensive in Rome, the three divisions would unite and attack the Eternal City.

The Prime Minister, Ratazzi, feigned to be unaware of these warlike preparations; but at last, fearing an armed intervention on the part of France, he ordered Garibaldi to be arrested at Sinalunga, near Arezzo, on September 23rd, and taken to the fortress of Alessandria, whence a few days later he was brought back to Caprera and set free, though several cruisers apparently maintained a blockade round the island. The enlistment of volunteers still went on; and, before the chiefs were ready to begin the campaign, several small bands crossed the frontier at various points, without orders, on September 28th and the following days, but they were everywhere broken up and repulsed by patrols of Papal troops, though one band of 300 men had a short-

THE ZOUAVES TOOK ONE OF THE BARRICADES
BY A DASHING BAYONET CHARGE

lived success at Acquapendente, where it overcame the little garrison of twenty-seven *gendarmes*.

The first serious encounter was at Bagnorea, a village to the north of Viterbo, strongly situated on a hill surrounded by deep ravines and accessible only at one point by a bridge. It was occupied on October 1st by a body of Garibaldians, who seized the funds of the municipality and plundered the churches. The remnants of the bands defeated elsewhere rallied round them, bringing their numbers up to 500, and, to strengthen their position, they fortified the convent of San Francesco situated outside the walls, raised barricades on the roads leading to the gate, and loop-holed the adjacent houses. Colonel Azzanesi, who commanded the garrison of Viterbo, sent a detachment of 45 soldiers of the line, 20 *Zouaves*, and 4 *gendarmes* to make a reconnaissance; they made instead an attack, and, though the *Zouaves* took one of the barricades by a dashing bayonet charge, the detachment was repulsed with loss when it came under the hail of bullets from the houses.

Two days later, however. Colonel Azzanesi marched against the town with two companies of Zouaves under Captain le Gonidec, four companies of the line under Captain Zanetti, a few dragoons, and two guns—in all 460 men. The Garibaldian advanced posts situated on the rocky heights in front of the town were obstinately defended, but were stormed one after another; the doors of the convent were smashed in and its defenders bayoneted or disarmed, the two barricades were taken, and the Garibaldians driven back into the town. A few cannon-shots soon overcame their resistance, and they fled in disorder through the ravines where the cavalry could not follow them, while the citizens flung open their gates and welcomed their liberators. This victory cost the Papal troops only six men wounded; the loss of the enemy was 96 killed and wounded.

In spite of this defeat the incursions of volunteers did not cease, for the Italian Government granted them free tickets over the railways, allowed them to take the arms of the National Guards, and the troops placed along the frontier to arrest them let them pass. Fighting took place, therefore, every day in many localities, and the most brilliant of these combats is that which occurred on October 13th at Monte Libretti.

This is a walled village, about ten miles to the north of Monte Rotondo, built round an old feudal castle on the summit of a steep and isolated hill, at the foot of which is a street commanded by the castle and leading up to the gate. It was known that Menotti Garibaldi was advancing towards it with a numerous band, and Lieutenant-Colonel de Charette ordered three detachments to march from different points to intercept him. One of these columns coming from Palombara had already been sent in another direction, and did not receive the counter-order in time; another, from Monte Maggiore, came to the point of junction too soon, and, after waiting for a long while, withdrew.

The third column from Monte Rotondo, composed of 90 *Zouaves* under Lieutenant Guillemin, on arriving near Monte Libretti at six in the evening, met the Garibaldian advanced posts, attacked them at once, and drove them back. The lieutenant then sent one section of his men, under Sub-Lieutenant de Quélen, to turn the enemy's position, and at the head of the other dashed through the narrow street, under a heavy fire from the castle and the houses, till he reached the open space before the gate, which was filled with Garibaldians. Here he fell with a bullet through the brain; Sergeant-Major Bach, a Bavarian, took the command, and a furious hand-to-hand fight ensued, in spite of the inequality in numbers.

Major Fazzari, a Garibaldian leader, was wounded and made prisoner; Corporal Alfred Collingridge, of London, surrounded by six Garibaldians, fought desperately till he was mortally wounded; and Peter Yong, a tall and athletic Dutchman, killed sixteen Garibaldians with the butt-end of his rifle, then dropped breathless with fatigue and was immediately bayoneted. The fight had lasted for a quarter of an hour, when the second column came up and drove the Garibaldians into the town, the gate of which they could not completely close.

It was now nearly dark; the *Zouaves* made three attempts to storm the gate, but as they passed through the narrow opening they were met with a hail of bullets from all sides; de Quélen fell pierced with nine wounds, and his men were at last driven back, but the Garibaldians, who, as it has since been ascertained, were nearly 1,200, did not pursue them. The *Zouaves* had lost 17 dead and 18 wounded; Sergeant de la Bégassiere took the command of the survivors and retreated to Monte Maggiore, but Sergeant-Major Bach, who with a few *Zouaves* had become separated from the rest in the darkness, took refuge in a house near the gate, and exchanged shots with the Garibaldians as long as there was moonlight. At four next morning, he, too, retreated to Monte Maggiore, and Menotti Garibaldi, believing that this handful of *Zouaves* were the vanguard of a large body of troops, withdrew in the opposite direction to Nerola.

Lieutenant-Colonel de Charette was ordered to dislodge him from

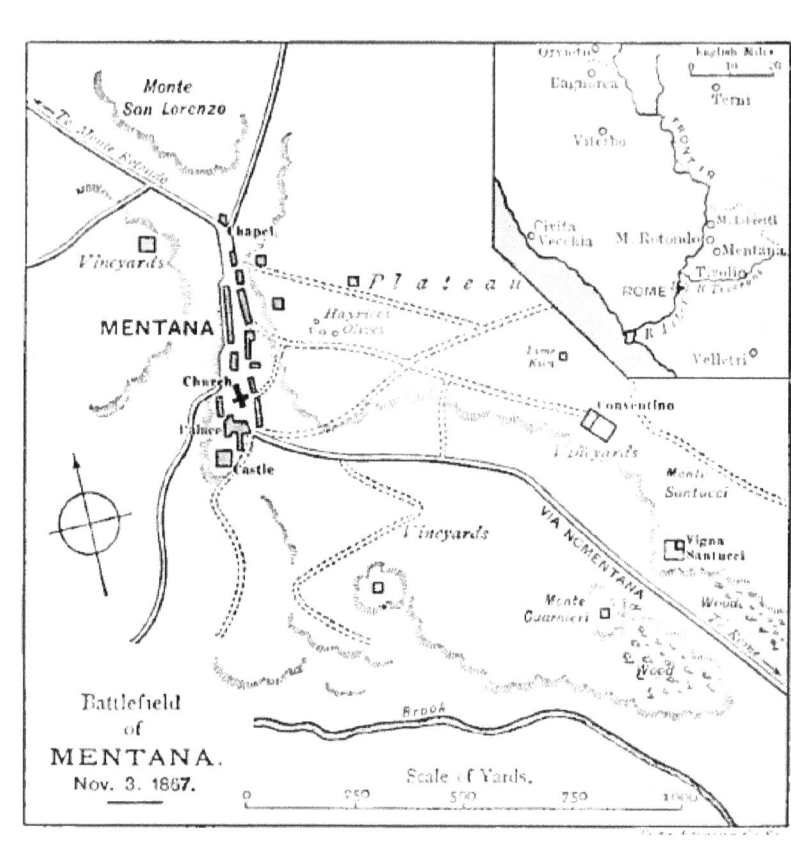

this strong position—a village situated on a high hill with a strongly-built castle on which only artillery could have any effect; and he left Monte Rotondo on the 17th with one gun and about 900 men belonging to the *Zouaves*, the *Légion d'Antibes* and the Swiss Rifles. On their approach the next day, Menotti Garibaldi withdrew to Montorio Romano, leaving a detachment to defend the castle, which capitulated after little more than an hour's firing.

In the meantime, Garibaldian emissaries were actively engaged in preparing an insurrection in Rome, and the government was no less energetic in taking precautions against it. The city was declared to be in a state of siege; most of the gates were closed and barricaded, outside the others earthworks armed with guns were thrown up, artillery was placed in position on the Aventine, the ditches of the Castle of St. Angelo were filled with water, and the guards were strengthened. The writer was then in the depot of the *Zouaves* in the Monastery of St. Callisto, where a few hundred recruits of all nations were being initiated into the mysteries of drill, and as almost all the troops were in campaign, a large share of guard-mounting and patrolling fell to our lot. It was a service which entailed but little of the fatigue or danger, and none of the excitement, of actual warfare; but we were in constant expectation of an attack, and to be ready for any emergency the two companies which formed the depot remained under arms in front of the barracks every night from sunset till past midnight, while advanced posts and sentinels were placed in the neighbouring streets to guard against a surprise.

The insurrection, in which not many Romans took part, began on the evening of October 22nd. The Serristori barracks, not far from St. Peter's, were blown up: the greater part of the men quartered there were luckily absent at the time, but thirty-seven *Zouaves*, eighteen of whom were Italians, were buried beneath the ruins. At the same time an attack was made on the Capitol and repulsed by the Swiss *Carabiniers*; and the guard-house at the gate of St. Paul's was surprised and taken by a band of Garibaldians in order to facilitate the entry of a convoy of arms, which had been hidden in a neighbouring vineyard; but the arms had already been seized by the police, and the Garibaldians were soon dispersed.

Other attacks were made on the gasworks and the military hospital, but without success, and before midnight all was again quiet in Rome. The next day a body of seventy-six Garibaldians, all picked men, led by the two brothers Cairoli, who had hoped to enter Rome with another convoy of arms and take the command of the insurgents, but had failed to arrive in time, was discovered by a patrol, lurking in the grounds of a villa outside the walls, and after a short skirmish in which the Garibaldians fought desperately, the survivors of the band fled back to the frontier.

Just before these events took place. Garibaldi escaped from Caprera, passed over to the mainland, and arrived in Florence on October 20th; Ratazzi took no steps to arrest him till be was out of his reach, and he crossed the frontier at Correse. He immediately ordered all the bands in the neighbourhood to join him, and on the 23rd he was at the head of at least 10,000 men. A large proportion of these were drawn from the populace of the great cities of Italy, and were attracted mainly by the hope of plunder; but there were also many soldiers and officers of the regular army, and many veterans who had fought under Garibaldi in former campaigns: their arms, drill, and organisation were, as a rule, good; but they were, for the most part, shabbily dressed, and very few of them wore the traditional red shirt.

POPE PIUS IX

The road to Rome lay through Monte Rotondo, a small town situated on a height. About one-third of its circuit is defended by a wall in which are three gates, the rest is closed by the walls of the houses which stand on the brow of the steep hill. Near the centre is the palace of the Prince of Piombino—a massive building of three storeys with a tall tower. The garrison, commanded by Captain Costes, of the Antibes Legion, was composed of two companies of the legion, one of Swiss *Carabiniers*, a few *gendarmes*, dragoons, and artillerymen—in all, 323 men with two guns.

Early on the morning of the 25th, three Garibaldian columns were seen marching towards the town and taking up their positions round it; they were under the command of Menotti Garibaldi, his father with the reserves being in the rear. At six, two strong detachments advanced to assault the gates, but they were received with such a heavy fire that after three hours' fighting they fell back discouraged. Garibaldi then took the command: he rallied his men and again surrounded the town, which was assailed at every point; attack followed attack throughout the day, but without success; the Garibaldians were everywhere repulsed, and after eight hours' fighting, their fire gradually slackened and at last ceased.

Garibaldi had not expected this obstinate resistance, and he was furious at having lost a day, during which he might, by a forced march, have surprised Rome; the arrival of reinforcements determined him to renew the assault that night, and a waggon laden with faggots and petroleum was pushed up against one of the gates, under a heavy fire, and lighted. The gate was soon a sheet of flame, but while it was burning, the besieged raised barricades in the streets leading from it, and when the Garibaldians entered the town, it was only after two hours of desperate fighting that the Papal troops, wearied and outnumbered, were driven back, into the castle. There they held out for some time till the Garibaldians began to undermine the walls, when they capitulated, after a defence of twenty-seven hours, which, as Garibaldi confessed, had cost him over 500 killed and wounded.

The outlying detachments of the Papal army in garrison in the provinces were immediately recalled to guard Rome against a sudden attack, and hold it until the arrival of the French troops, which the emperor, after much hesitation and many counter orders, had at last despatched. They landed at Civita Vecchia on the 29th, marched into Rome on the 30th, and Garibaldi, whose troops had advanced as far as the bridges over the Teverone, about three miles from Rome, and exchanged shots with the Papal outposts, retreated to Monte Rotondo.

He intended at first to make a stand there, but considering that Tivoli, equally distant from Rome, was a much stronger position—with a river in front, and a mountainous country, suitable for guerilla warfare, in the rear—he gave orders to march upon that town at daybreak on November 3rd. The necessity of distributing clothes and shoes to his men delayed his departure till eleven, and his vanguard had got only a short distance beyond Mentana when it met the Papal troops.

A large number of Garibaldians had deserted during the retreat from Rome, and the losses at Monte Rotondo had been heavy; but reinforcements had come up during the attack on that town, and, according to the most trustworthy estimates. Garibaldi had still, at least, 10,000 soldiers when he accepted battle at Mentana.

The column which left Rome that morning under the command of General Kanzler, was composed of 2,913 men of the Papal Army, under General de Courten, 1,500 of whom were *Zouaves*, and a little more than 2,000 of the French soldiers just arrived, under General de Polhès—making in all about 5,000 men with ten guns.

The troops were under arms at one on the morning of the 3rd, but it was four o'clock when they marched out of the Porta Pia, the Papal forces leading and the French following at some distance. It was a dark and rainy morning, and the soldiers in heavy marching order and carrying two days' rations in addition to their usual burdens, advanced slowly over the muddy road. After crossing the Ponte Nomentano, about four miles from Rome, Major de Troussures was sent with three companies of *Zouaves* by a road to the left, to gain the valley of the Tiber and march on a line parallel to that followed by the main body, to threaten the right flank, of the Garibaldians.

The remainder of the column went on till it reached the farm of Capobianco, half-way to Mentana, where it halted to let the men get some food and dry their clothes. By this time the rain had ceased, and, as after an hour's rest they again formed their ranks to continue their march, the sun shone brightly in a cloudless sky.

On leaving Capobianco, the road ascends for some distance, crosses a broad tableland, and then winds rising and falling as it passes over the lower slopes of several hills covered with brushwood. It was half-past twelve when the dragoons who preceded the column came upon the Garibaldian outposts commanded by Colonel Missori, occupying a strong position in the woods on each side of the road. They fired their

THEY MADE SOME PRISONERS

carbines and returned at full gallop to give the alarm. The first company of *Zouaves*, under Captain d'Albiousse, and the second, under Captain Thomalé, were immediately extended in skirmishing order to the left and right, the third company, under Captain Alain de Charette, and the fourth, under Captain le Gonidec, following as supports.

The woods were soon cleared of Garibaldians, and the heights scaled; but a Genoese battalion, commanded by Captain Stallo, and another from Leghorn, led by Captain Meyer, held the tableland to the right of the road, and their heavy fire checked the advance of the *Zouaves* till their line was strengthened by the companies of Captain de Moncuit and Captain de Veaux; and Lieutenant-Colonel de Charette, hastening up with the company of Captain Lefebvre, led a furious bayonet-charge, which swept the Garibaldians before it. It was in vain that they tried to rally and re-form behind trees or farmhouses; they were driven from one place of refuge after another, and a long line of killed and wounded marked the track of the *Zouaves* as they drove the shattered battalions back upon the Santucci vineyard.

This strong position—a walled enclosure which had been loopholed, as well as the large farmhouse standing on a height within it—was held by the battalion of Major Ciotti: it commands the approach to Mentana from the east across the tableland above that village, while the approaches from the front and from the west can be swept by a plunging fire from the Castle of Mentana. The approach to the vineyard was protected by a cross-fire from Monte Guarnieri, a wooded height on the opposite side of the road; this had to be carried first, and it was taken by Captain Alain de Charette, whose company climbed the steep slopes and drove the Garibaldian sharpshooters from their shelter among the trees.

A piece of artillery, commanded by Count Bernardini, then opened fire on the Santucci vineyard, while Lieutenant-Colonel de Charette attacked it in front with some companies of *Zouaves*, supported on their right by five companies of Swiss *Carabiniers*. The walls of the enclosure were soon scaled, and the Garibaldians driven back into the farmhouse, where they made a stubborn resistance till the doors were broken in, when they laid down their arms. In this attack, Lieutenant-Colonel de Charette's horse was killed under him. and Captain de Veaux fell, struck by a bullet which drove down into his heart the cross he had won at Castelfidardo.

The Papal troops had been equally successful on the left of the high road, where they had driven the Garibaldians from the woods and come out on the open slopes which descend towards Mentana, from which they could pour a heavy fire on the crowd of fugitives hastening from all directions towards the village. It was then two o'clock; there was a cessation of the fight for a few minutes to pick up and carry away the wounded, and General Kanzler, who had established his headquarters at the Santucci vineyard, prepared to attack Mentana.

The Castle of Mentana, a feudal fortress of the Borghese family, stands upon a rock with precipitous sides advancing from the high road into a deep valley; it was held, along with the adjacent Borghese palace, the village, and the barricade erected at its entrance, by four battalions of Garibaldians, under Lieutenant-Colonel Frigyesi, a Hungarian; the height above the village, where there was a large farm with stacks of hay and corn, was occupied by six battalions, commanded by Colonel Elia and Major Valzania; Major Cantoni, with three battalions, was stationed to the left of the village on the road leading to Monte Rotondo, and the two guns which had been taken at the siege of that town were drawn up on Monte San Lorenzo, a little to the rear.

General Kanzler placed three guns, two of which belonged to the French, on Monte Guarnieri, another on the high road, and two more in the Santucci vineyard, to counteract the fire of the castle and of the Garibaldian artillery; the *Zouaves* advanced from the vineyard in skirmishing order and drove the Garibaldians from a building called the Conventino, beyond which the ground gradually rises towards the height which commands Mentana, where Elia's battalions were posted having their flanks protected by the fire from the castle and the adjacent houses. Five companies of Swiss *Carabiniers* advanced in line with the *Zouaves*.

On arriving in sight of the position held by the Garibaldians, the *Zouaves*, instead of waiting till the fire of the artillery had thrown the ranks of the enemy into disorder, broke away madly from their officers, and charged. Heedless of the voice of their colonel or of the sound of the bugles, they pressed on, driving the Garibaldians from every hedge or clump of trees which they sought to defend, and flung them back into the houses. There the charge was stopped by a hail of bullets from the loop-holed walls, but the *Zouaves* held their ground, sheltered by the haystacks, from behind which they returned the fire of the Garibaldians.

A desperate sortie of the enemy dislodged them, but three companies, led by Major de Lambilly, came to their relief; they regained their positions, and at this spot, which was alternately lost and retaken, the greatest amount of slaughter took place; and the struggle lasted till nightfall.

The front attack having been thus stopped, Garibaldi sent two strong columns to turn the flanks of the Papal army. One of these, of three battalions, marched from the northern end of the village, and nearly succeeded in surrounding and cutting off two companies of Swiss *Carabiniers* on our right. They retired slowly in good order, firing as they went, until being reinforced by two more Swiss companies, and two of the *Légion d'Antibes*, they dashed forward, broke up the Garibaldian column and pursued it as far as the road to Monte Rotondo.

The other column, which marched from the south of the village, was not more successful — it was repulsed by three companies of the *Légion d'Antibes*, who followed it as far as the entrance of the village, where they took a house and made some prisoners, but had to retire in presence of superior numbers.

Just then the detachment under Major de Troussures was seen advancing in the direction of the road to Monte Rotondo. Garibaldi at once perceived that the day was lost, and his line of retreat nearly intercepted, he hastened to provide for his safety and left Mentana, while his staff-officers still continued to defend the village.

They immediately collected all the men still able to fight, to make a last desperate effort to envelope the wings of the Papal army; and when General Kanzler, who had sent forward all his reserves, saw two strong columns of companies issuing in good order from Mentana, he requested General de Polhés, whose infantry had hitherto taken no part in the combat, to bring forward his troops. A French battalion and three companies of *Chasseurs*, under Colonel Fremont, marched at once on the Garibaldian left, deployed into line, and for the first time the "*Chassepot*" was brought into action.

The fight ceased for a moment over all the field of battle, as the soldiers on both sides paused to listen to that deadly fire, rapid and ceaseless as the rolling of a drum, before which the hostile battalions disbanded and fled back into Mentana or Monte Rotondo, in spite of all the efforts of Menotti Garibaldi and his officers to rally them. The column on the right wing met with the same fate: attacked by Lieutenant-Colonel Saussier with a French battalion and the *Zouaves* of Major de Troussures, it broke and dispersed in various directions.

Mentana was now completely surrounded, and it was decided to take it by assault. General de Polhés led a French regiment and a battalion of *Chasseurs* to storm the barricade at the entrance of the village, while the *Zouaves* attacked a neighbouring house.

It was just then, at the end of the fight, that Julian Watts-Russell, an English *Zouave*, and one of the youngest soldiers in the Papal Army, fell, close to the village; his comrades succeeded in taking the house, but the French column, crushed by the heavy fire from the barricade, the houses and the castle, retreated after losing heavily.

Night had fallen, and it would have been impossible to continue the struggle; the troops lit their watch-fires round the village, throwing out strong advanced posts and sentinels, and held themselves in readiness against a surprise. The next morning at dawn. Major Fauchon, with a French battalion, entered Mentana, when some hundreds of Garibaldians laid down their arms. Seven hundred others in the castle capitulated, and were allowed to cross the frontier without arms. They had left 600 dead and 500 wounded on the field; while the loss of the Pontifical troops was 30 killed and 114 wounded, and of the French, 2 killed and 36 wounded. Garibaldi continued his retreat as far as Correse on the evening of the battle, and crossed the frontier the next day with 5,000 men; while 900 others, under Colonel Salomone, escaped into the Abruzzi. The other Garibaldian bands, under Acerbi and Nicotera, which had occupied the provinces of Velletri and Viterbo, and the Italian troops which had followed them, gradually withdrew without offering any resistance, and thus ended the campaign.

BOGNOKIA

THE FRANCO-PRUSSIAN WARS
1870-1871

The Battle of Wörth
August 6, 1870
By Archibald Forbes

When France was whetting her sword in the reckless July days of 1870, it was not in the nature of things—notwithstanding that the emperor had an ignoble grudge against him, and that he had haughtily held aloof from the courtly coteries of Compiègne and Saint-Cloud—that the brilliant soldier who had stormed the Malakoff and had saved the day at Magenta should not hold high command in the impending struggle.

MacMahon was no heaven-born general, indeed, his true place was that of a divisional commander—but he had long and varied experience of war, and France had no more prompt and staunch fighting soldier. He carried with him to his sphere of duty in Alsace the knowledge, which he shared only with Le Bœuf, of the emperor's plan for an offensive campaign, which was destined never even to be begun, but in which, had it taken shape, he was to have led the van. Appointed, meanwhile, to the command of the 1st Corps, in course of concentration about Strasburg, where he arrived on July 22nd, it befell him but too speedily to realise how faint was the prospect that he should head an invasion into the hostile territory on the further bank of the Rhine.

On paper his command was imposing, with its four infantry divisions, its cavalry division three brigades strong, and Bonnemain's reserve cavalry division, consisting of four regiments of *cuirassiers*. But, with the line troops coming in from the eastern departments he had the task of incorporating, as they arrived piecemeal from Algeria, wild regiments of *Zouaves* and battalion on battalion of half-savage Turcos; and he had also to requisition, beg, discover, or invent the mass of materiel and equipment requisite for a campaign. Presently, with the object of giving the marshal unrestricted disposal of all the forces in Alsace, the 7th Corps, whose headquarters were in Belfort, was placed under his orders. This nominally substantial reinforcement proved curiously delusive. An infantry division and a cavalry brigade belonging to this corps were detained at Lyons to quell the seditious population of that turbulent city; another division, garrisoning Belfort, was merely in course of formation; and its third division, gradually filling its ranks at Colmar, was still poorly prepared to take the field.

By the end of July, the offensive intention on the part of the French had been wholly abandoned, and the emperor had ordered MacMahon to close in from Strasburg to the north-west upon De Failly, commanding the 5th Corps in the neighbourhood of Bitche. In doing so, he had to approach the point of the angle where the French frontier on the Lauter struck the Rhine, thus exposing his outward flank to a hostile stroke from beyond the former river, where the German 3rd Army was suspected to be massing. To guard against this, Abel Douay's division was pushed out a day's march to Wissembourg—a feeble and inadequate protection, as the event speedily proved.

On the morning of August 4th, the army of the crown prince crossed the frontier in strength, and surprised Douay's division in the act of breakfasting. Wissembourg was shelled and occupied after several repulses; and the adjacent heights of the Geisberg, which were occupied by the mass of Douay's staunch soldiers, were furiously assailed by a couple of German divisions, supported by a heavy artillery fire. General Douay had early ordered a retreat from the manifestly untenable position, but that retirement was seriously obstructed by the vigour of the German assault on the Geisberg; and the *château* of that name—a very defensible building—was most stubbornly defended by its garrison to cover the movement.

The King's Grenadier Regiment—one of the most famous of the German line—assailed it furiously, but was repulsed with heavy loss; nor did the gallant defenders of the Geisberg surrender until artillery had been dragged up on to the height. The brave Douay fell fighting, 1,200 of his 8,000 men were struck down; and the Germans, who owned to a loss of 91 officers and 1,460 men, made 1,000 unwounded prisoners. The responsibility for the virtual destruction of this fine division does not rest on MacMahon, who had not yet quitted Strasburg, but on Ducrot, who was provisionally in command in the absence of his chief, and who, when Douay complained of his exposed and unsupported position, gave him the peremptory order to accept a combat there.

Stung by this misfortune, and in utter ignorance alike of his enemy's strength and of his line of approach, MacMahon resolved to fight a battle in front of the northern passes of the Vosges. He moved his troops into a position on the undulating spurs which, clad with vineyards and hop-gardens, extend between the Sauerbach and the Eberbach. His front line—from Neehwiller, on the north, to Albrechtshäuser, on the south—had a length of about three-and-a-half miles. During the greater part of this length MacMahon's front was covered by the Sauerbach—a stream very difficult to cross except at the bridges.

The meadow-land, averaging 1,000 paces in breadth, through which it flows, afforded no cover in the approach, so that the French infantry could profit by all the advantages of their superior position and superior weapon. The eastern slope of the valley is commanded at all points from the western. In front of the French centre lay the town of Wörth, with its bridge over the Sauer. That country town, as also the other villages within the position, contains many spacious and well-built houses, capable of being strongly defended. Thickly-planted gardens and vineyards extend up the heights from the western exit of the town.

The village of Fröschwiller formed the crowning feature of the French position. Commanding the ground in all directions, situated at the highest point of the hilly plateau, it constituted with its spacious church and other strong buildings a bastion-like redoubt to the entire line of defence. To the southward, on somewhat lower ground, lay the village of Elsasshausen—a very defensible point. The undulating character of the ground, and the cover it afforded, favoured the employment of a large number of skirmishers, and concealed the position and movements of the reserves from the enemy's view. The French, moreover, had not neglected to strengthen the position by well-placed field entrenchments and other obstacles. Morsbronn, a village south of the extreme right, did not at first form part of the position, but was perfectly commanded. The passages of the Sauer at Gunstett and Dürrenbach, on the enemy's left flank, were within effective cannon-range. Both of the French flanks were somewhat refused.

MacMahon had summoned up from Colmar the 3rd division of the 7th Corps, which reached him on the morning of the 6th; and, having the 5th Corps also placed at his disposition, he called on De Failly, its commander, to make haste to join him—none of whose troops, however, could arrive in time to take part in the battle. The troops actually in the marshal's hand for the impending fight consisted of the four infantry divisions of the 1st Corps and the 3rd division of the 7th Corps, and of the following cavalry: the cavalry division of the 1st Corps, composed of Septeuil's brigade of hussars and *chasseurs*; Michel's *cuirassier* brigade; Nansouty's brigade of lancers and dragoons, employed as divisional cavalry; and Bonnemain's reserve division, consisting of four regiments of *cuirassiers*.

The disposition of MacMahon's forces was as follows:—The 1st Division, commanded by Ducrot, formed the right of the line. It faced almost due north, and, therefore, constituted the defensive flank against Lembach, its left wing resting on the Grosswald, its right wing on the village of Fröschwiller. Beyond its extreme left, the villages of Neehwiller and Jägerthal were each occupied by a company. The 3rd Division, commanded by Raoult, faced due east, its left brigade resting on Fröschwiller, its right on Elsasshausen. The dense forest of the Niederwald made a gap in the line of front; behind the forest was posted in reserve the 2nd Division, now, in consequence of Douay's death on the 4th, commanded by Pellé, and materially weakened by its losses at Wissembourg.

South of the Niederwald stood the 4th Division (Lartigue's), its left brigade facing Gunstett on the opposite bank of the Sauer, its right brigade looking south-east towards Morsbronn. In rear of Pellé's division were the 3rd division of the 7th Corps, just arrived from Colmar, and Michel's *cuirassier* brigade. Further northward, about the sources of the Eberbach and behind Raoult's division, were Bonnemain's reserve cavalry division and Septeuil's brigade of light cavalry. This was the French disposition on the morning of the 6th. The heights eastward of Elsasshausen gave the best *point de vue* of the entire neighbourhood, and it was here that MacMahon remained during the greater part of the battle.

It was a curious coincidence that neither side had intended to engage until the 7th. But MacMahon, standing on the defensive, was ready on the morning of the 6th; and that same morning a subordinate commander of the hostile army, part of which was within striking distance, took the liberty of forcing the hand of the commander-in-chief, with the ultimate result of an unpremeditated battle. Major-General von Walther, commanding a brigade of the 5th German Army Corps, while making a reconnaissance at daylight, remarked an unusual noise and movement in the French camp, which led him to suppose that

MacMahon was evacuating his position.

In quest of information on this point Walther pushed his reconnaissance in force beyond Wörth. He found the bridges destroyed and the town unoccupied; but his skirmishers waded the Sauer and presently found themselves involved in an engagement with very superior forces. Walther therefore broke off the action and withdrew into bivouac. Meanwhile, a French detachment had taken the initiative against Gunstett; but no real attack resulted and the affair was merely an interchange of artillery and musketry fire.

The 2nd Bavarian Corps held the right of the German army. Its 4th Division had been in readiness at Mattstall since daybreak, charged with the specific duty of outflanking the French left and of participating in any action which might take place on the part of the German centre opposite Wörth. Hearing the sound of a cannonade, which covered the withdrawal of Walther's reconnaissance, and regarding that sound as the signal for his advance, General Hartmann, the commander of the 2nd Bavarian Corps, ordered his 4th Division to move forward from Langensulzbach and engage Ducrot's division in position on the extreme left of the French line.

The fighting in this quarter soon became very hot; for a time, the Bavarians seemed to have the best of it but later were able only to maintain a defensive attitude against the French division, and that with difficulty. Meanwhile a French detachment had retaliated by a counter-stroke in the direction of Gunstett against the vanguard of the Prussian 11th Corps, which had come up into position on the German left. The French effort was repulsed; but the cannon-thunder on his right and left inspired General Kirchbach, commanding the 5th Corps, which constituted the German centre, with the conviction that he must strike in vigorously to hinder the enemy from concentrating his strength against one or other of the German flanks.

Kirchbach, therefore, took it upon himself to engage in the serious offensive; and by 10 o'clock a hundred German cannon were in action on the eastern slopes against the French centre behind Wörth, while, after sharp fighting, considerable bodies of German infantry had already gained a foothold beyond the Sauerbach stream and were in occupation of the town of Wörth.

The crown prince, as Kirchbach knew, did not wish to fight a battle until his forces were concentrated, which was far from being the case on the morning of the 6th. Informed that an incipient action was already in progress, the prince sent from his headquarters in Sulz, several miles behind the front, a firm order to General Kirchbach, and also to Hartmann, the Bavarian commander, "not to continue the struggle, and to avoid everything which might bring on a fresh one." Kirchbach then took upon himself an almost unique responsibility. On one hand was the specific command that he should desist from further action.

On the other hand, he recognised that the fighting could not be broken off under existing conditions, without entailing heavy losses to no purpose, and that his withdrawal would give the adversary undisputed right to claim a material victory, involving loss of prestige to the German arms at the outset of a momentous campaign. He considered that with his own corps alone he could expect decisive results, even without co-operation from the force on either flank. Accordingly, after mature consideration, he ordered his troops to continue the offensive, reporting this decision to the crown prince, and desiring the corps on either hand to afford him their co-operation.

Kirchbach had greatly dared; and fortune for a time was only partially propitious. Von Bose, commanding the 11th Corps, reached the front at Gunstett about 11 o'clock. He had been informed of the commander-in-chief's prohibition against continuing the fighting, and presently there came to him Kirchbach's request for cooperation in the continuation of the fighting. Von Bose calmly disregarded the order of the crown prince. He promptly assured Kirchbach that he would not fail to support his comrade; and he proved his comradeship by ordering up his corps artillery, and by sending word to his leading division to cross the stream and assail the right flank of the enemy's position.

Kirchbach, therefore, was at ease as regarded prompt and full co-operation on his left; but he had to undergo a disappointment in respect to the Bavarian Corps, on whose support on his right he had also considered himself entitled to rely. Following on his determination to put aside the order of his superior and to continue the fighting, he had sent to Hartmann, the Bavarian Corps commander on his right, a request for the latter's co-operation. But this request reached Hartmann tardily. Already, at half-past ten, a Prussian staff officer had brought him verbal instructions to suspend the contest and fall back from the positions which he was holding. With great skill and celerity Hartmann conducted the unpalatable duty, and the larger part of his troops were withdrawn out of action by half-past eleven o'clock and were retreating behind Langensulzbach.

THE BATTERIES PRESSED THROUGH THE STREETS
ENCUMBERED WITH TROOPS

But, while those movements were only partially completed, a communication reached him from Kirchbach at a quarter past eleven, intimating that the battle was to be prosecuted vigorously, and that the co-operation of his Bavarians against the French flank was expected. Hartmann replied, not without a little temper, that he had broken off the action by superior orders, but would resume the attack with the least possible delay. But it was not until the afternoon that Hartmann's command was able to make itself again present in the front.

Soon after ten o'clock, when the infantry of the 21st Division were engaged in the action about Gunstett, when the other portions of the 11th Corps were fast coming up, and when the superiority of the German artillery was apparent, Kirchbach considered that the time had come for the advance guard of the 5th Corps to cross the Sauerbach, occupy Wörth, and attempt the seizure of the heights beyond. The leading companies of the 37th Fusiliers crossed the stream on an improvised bridge in lieu of the one previously destroyed, and found Wörth again unoccupied; while other companies waded the stream above and below, the men breast-high in the water and exposed to a heavy musketry and shell-fire.

At first, although suffering from a crushing fire, the companies climbed the heights beyond the town, and met with success until the enemy brought up strong reserves and drove them back into Wörth. The reinforcements sent across lower down took up a position in a hop plantation; but the enemy dislodged them, and they had to incline to the left and connect themselves with the battalions of the 50th Regiment, which had crossed between Wörth and Spachbach. Those battalions fought their way under fire on the Hagenau road, on the upland; and one battalion advanced to the attack of the Elsasshausen heights, but was forced back as far as the Hagenau road.

One company connected itself with the right flank of the 11th Corps, but all the others were driven down on to the road, in the ditches of which the battalions found cover and checked the hostile advance with an effective fire. Several companies of the two gallant regiments of the advanced guard—the 37th Fusiliers and the 50th—held on to Wörth and its vicinity with great difficulty, under the murderous fire and the repeated and violent onslaughts of the enemy. The latter had a firm hold of the slopes beyond the town, whence they were able to baulk the Prussian infantry whenever they tried to advance, and to overwhelm them with withering showers of projectiles.

At no point were the Prussians successful in making any progress beyond Wörth, and their rearward movements were attended with especially heavy loss. Once Major von Sydow gathered all the available men of the Fusiliers in Wörth for an offensive attempt; he succeeded, indeed, in ascending the slopes and advancing some hundred paces beyond, but was promptly hurled back on the town by a powerful counter-attack on the part of the French. Attempt after attempt to do more than hold the town proved futile, and the occupancy of it was maintained with no little difficulty against the pressure of the enemy, notwithstanding that a whole brigade was added to the previous defence of the place. By 12.30 the aspect of affairs became more and more threatening, and a fresh battalion had to be brought up in support.

Of the 11th Corps, the first troops to cross the Sauer were six companies of the 87th Regiment, having first advanced to Spachbach, whence some waded, others scrambling over hastily felled tree-trunks. The enemy's fire was severe, there was no cover at the landing-place, and the officers, with rapid resolution, rallied their men and hurried them across the meadows, over the Hagenau road, and into the Niederwald in pursuit of the French skirmishers who had been holding its fringes. A battalion followed, but halted after having crossed the stream.

The companies of the 87th fared ill in the Niederwald, having encountered very superior hostile detachments; and after strenuous and bloody fighting in which several officers were slain, the dislocated companies were repulsed from the forest, and there occurred a headlong rush back across the Sauer and as far as Spachbach. A later attempt to cross the stream at the Bruch Mill, near Gunstett, was temporarily successful, but ultimately failed, the detachment making it being impetuously attacked and driven back to the left bank, the occupants of which were continually annoyed by the French musketry fire on the other side.

At 1 p.m. the crown prince—who, on his way to the front, had received General Kirchbach's report—reached the high ground opposite to Wörth, his position, which dominated the whole battlefield, being under a tree on a little hill about midway between Spachbach and Gunstett. The prince realised that, independently of the fact that the struggle could not at this advanced stage be now broken off, he could scarcely indulge the expectation of fighting later under more advantageous conditions than now presented themselves. He might well apprehend, on the contrary, that Marshal MacMahon should have recognised the danger which threatened his position, and would evacuate it as soon as there occurred some relaxation of the German attacks.

The crown prince, after a short study of the situation, decided on pressing the battle to a conclusion. Prior to his arrival, Kirchbach had been contented with utilising merely his leading brigade in the fighting about and beyond Wörth, until the whole of the German Army should have come up. The crown prince's first task was to infuse harmony into the attacks of the foremost fighting line, and to direct reinforcements as they arrived to the points where their exertions would be most effective. He gave orders that the 2nd Bavarian Corps should reoccupy its position of the morning, and press on the French left flank so as to gain a position on the latter's flank and rear.

The 1st Bavarian Corps came into line between the 2nd Bavarian and the 5h Corps, while the 11th Corps was directed to cross the stream, turn the French right, and advance by way of Elsasshausen and through the Niederwald upon Fröschwiller, the Würtemberg Division to follow the 11th Corps. Kirchbach was instructed to delay his main attack on the heights beyond Wörth for some time, until the 1st Bavarian Corps and the mass of the 11th Corps should have come up.

The whole of the infantry of the 10th Division of the 5th Corps, with the exception of detachments left in reserve, was already employed in the foremost fighting line beyond Wörth. The 9th Division was brought forward, and of its two brigades the 18th crossed at Spachbach, the 17th at Wörth. The leading regiment of the former advanced across the meadow-land, but its attempts to gain the Elsasshausen heights and the Niederland forest were checked by a forward movement of superior hostile forces. But the repeated offensive movements of the French towards the Hagenau road were nullified by the resolute bearing of the four battalions holding that road, which with great tenacity held the enemy's superior force at bay.

On the arrival in the field of the 1st Bavarian Corps, Kirchbach determined to lead forward the whole of his troops now on the western bank of the Sauer to the attack of the heights in possession of the French. The advance was made in company columns, under the hottest fire from the enemy. The skirmishers succeeded in gaining a firm position on the slopes; but all attacks on the heights were fruitless, until a fortunate diversion was made on the right flank of the broken and jagged line.

A fusilier battalion drove in the enemy's skirmishers lining the slopes, and with a charge reached the heights, where it received a murderous fire at close quarters from two half-moon breastworks. Those were both stormed and occupied, and the gallant fusiliers chased their adversaries at the bayonet-point to the edge of the opposite wood. As the open crest of the heights was everywhere within close musketry range, and the intervening valley was swept by *mitrailleuse* fire, no further progress was at this juncture possible; but the captured breastworks were maintained, and the crest remained in German possession. Successes were also achieved on the other flank, and in the centre the upper edge of the sloping vineyard ground was surrounded by German skirmishers.

In order, however, to maintain the ground gained so dearly against the unceasing and energetic French attacks, Kirchbach found himself compelled to bring up his last reserves from the eastern bank. The whole of his infantry was brought over and drawn into the foremost fighting line. Hitherto his artillery had been in a great measure masked by the advance of his infantry on the western bank. Now the divisional batteries of the 10th Division, and half his corps artillery, crossed the hastily-restored bridge of Wörth, and pressed to the front, through the streets encumbered with troops, dead and wounded men, scared townspeople, and miscellaneous wreck.

The artillery of the 9th Division remained on the eastern bank, opposite to the Wörth position, and was reinforced subsequently by batteries of the 1st Bavarian Corps. Thus, the whole strength of the 5th Army Corps, constituting the German centre, was employed in gaining a firm footing on the western bank of the Sauer, and in occupying the adversary in front until the corps on either flank should attain positions enabling them to operate effectively against the hostile flanks.

It had been only by degrees and by dint of hard lighting and bloody sacrifices that Kirchbach's brave and staunch soldiers made any progress. Their battalions had become mixed; the greater part of the officers had been killed or wounded; while, on the other hand, the enemy brought up fresh reserves unceasingly. The successful attack of the 11th Army Corps against the French right flank, now to be briefly described, was to be the first signal to the sorely-tried 5th Corps of the long-looked-for support.

It has been already told how in the morning the 41st brigade of the 11th Corps had been driven back to the east bank in considerable confusion. Towards the forenoon, the 88th Regiment crossed the Sauer at

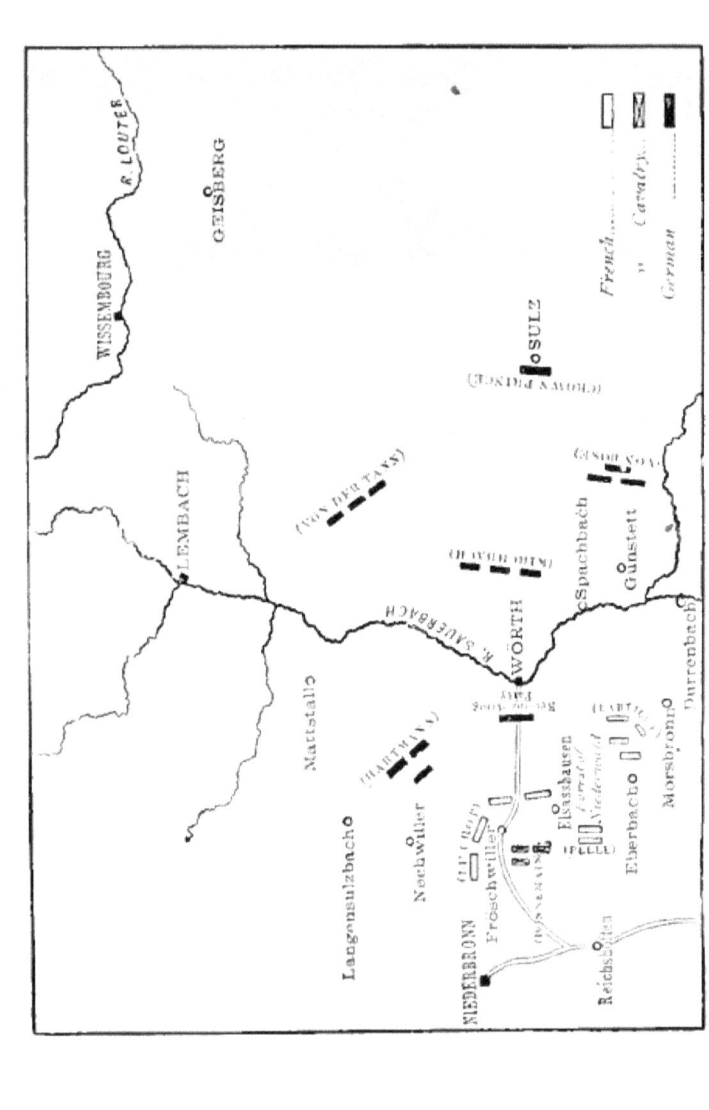

Spachbach, having rallied the companies of the 80th and 87th, which had been driven back into that village; and the united body advanced across the meadows, under a brisk fire of musketry and shrapnel, towards the eastern border of the Niederwald, which was lined by hostile skirmishers. The skirt of the forest was carried, and its northern edge was reached in rather loose order. In the woodland, between the Niederwald and Elsasshausen, retreating detachments of the enemy made a successful stand against the German efforts to expel them.

From the centre of the 11th Corps at Gunstett, six companies of the 95th Regiment crossed the stream by the Bruch Mill, and headed in the direction of Eberbach. The skirmishers, followed by the main body in line, gained the Hagenau road at the first rush. The French of Lartigue's division made an obstinate defence on the heights, the slope from which favoured their free range of fire, while the massive buildings of the Albrechtshaüser-Hof afforded them a strong defence. The German attack, therefore, progressed but slowly; but the left wing, reaching the cover of the hop plantations on the Morsbronn-Fröschwiller road, at length succeeded thence in outflanking the Albrechtshaüser-Hof. The enemy did not evacuate the place until the buildings had been fired by the German artillery, and until a musketry fire at close range had been brought to bear on the stubborn defenders.

From the left of the 11th Corps the 32nd Regiment marched through Dürrenbach, and headed for the village of Morsbronn, an outpost on the extreme right of the French position. The advance against the place was made by the 32nd and 94th Regiments, the left of the movement covered by the 13th Hussars. The village, which was but weakly occupied, was captured at the first rush by a battalion of the 32nd, another battalion of which regiment seized the heights further to the left. Morsbronn and the Albrechtshaüser-Hof thus in German possession, preparations were in progress to move in a north-westerly direction against the Niederwald, into which the French right wing was gradually withdrawing, when the German troops about Morsbronn had suddenly to confront a furious attack on the part of hostile cavalry.

General Lartigue, commanding the French right flank division, recognised that a German advance from Morsbronn would seriously compromise the French position, and had given orders for Michel's *Cuirassier* brigade, which was posted in the bottom eastward of Eberbach, to send forward a regiment against the left flank of the German force about Morsbronn.

MARSHAL MACMAHON

Michel's massive troopers were burning with impatience for the fray, and their officers, the chivalry of France, were yet more ardent than their men. "A regiment" was Lartigue's order; but Michel read "brigade" for "regiment," and acted on his own version of the order. His brigade consisted of the 5th and 9th Cuirassiers; and, whether by intent or by chance, there had linked itself to the Cuirassier brigade the 6th Regiment of Lancers from Nansouty's command.

The ground to be traversed, which had not been reconnoitred in advance, was extremely unfavourable for cavalry. Rows of trees cut down near the ground and deep ditches were calculated to dislocate the movements of large bodies in close formation, whereas the fire of the German infantry had a free range over the gentle slopes of the comparatively bare height

Behind Michel there rode in first line the 8th Cuirassiers in column of squadrons; on their right rear three squadrons of the 9th Cuirassiers in line, the fourth squadron in column of division behind; still further to the right rode the Lancer regiment—in all a serried mass of more than a thousand horsemen. Michel's loud word of command had for response a wild shout of "*Vive l'Empereur!*" and then the massive squadrons, glittering in their steel, swept headlong down, through and over the encumbrances of tree-stumps and ditches. The devoted troopers rode swift and straight to their ruin.

As the avalanche of mail clad riders and straining chargers came thundering on, the German companies halted and braced themselves. Only when the leading cavalry column was in close proximity, when the fierce breath from the nostrils of the war-horses was dimming the sheen of the bayonets, were the lines of infantrymen veiled for the moment in flame and smoke. As the wind wafted the smoke aside, a weltering mass of men and horses was disclosed covering the ground. It was a strange and lurid spectacle. The French infantry were pouring showers of *Chassepot* bullets on the German linesmen; while the latter, disdaining the obsolete order of "form square to prepare for cavalry," stood in open order striking down into the dust the mail-clad French horsemen. Michel's *Cuirassiers* and the lancers were almost utterly destroyed; the losses of the German infantrymen were very inconsiderable.

The devoted charge of Michel's cavalry had enabled Lartigue's infantry of the French right wing to withdraw unmolested towards Eberbach and the contiguous portion of the Niederwald, toward which they were presently followed by the German troops from Morsbronn and its vicinity. This advance was headed by the 32nd Regiment in line. One battalion of the 94th captured the village of Eberbach, but could get no further until later, and its other two battalions followed the road leading from Morsbronn to Fröschwiller.

The line thus constituted encountered no resistance at first, and joined the troops about the Albrechtshaüser-Hof, where, in all, there was a German force of about the strength of a brigade, but in a very mixed-up state owing to constant hard fighting. The final assault of the French on the Albrechtshaüser-Hof position was ultimately repulsed, and MacMahon's troops on the right wing were thrown back into the Niederwald. The foremost fighting line of the German 11th Corps followed, and, to support it, General von Bose threw into the fight his last reserves brought across from Gunstett. and also brought up the whole of his artillery. With stubborn fighting, ground was gradually gained in the Niederwald, until at last its northern edge was attained; but between it and the hamlet of Elsasshausen there was an intervening copse, occupied in strength by the French, with strong reserves between the copse and the village.

The battle hereabouts swayed to and fro with great slaughter. At length von Bose brought up into line seven batteries, whose fire crushed the French guns and overwhelmed the village and its staunch occupants. Elsasshausen was set on fire, yet its defenders still held out. At length, von Bose gave the order, "The whole will advance!" and a dash was made on the village, some detachments of the 5th Corps taking part with troops of the 11th in the attack. The village was carried, but the French promptly made a counter-stroke, which drove the German captors of Elsasshausen back into the shelter of the Niederwald. But there the counter-attack was checked; the German troops were re-formed, and the blazing village finally remained in the possession of von Bose's forces.

From Elsasshausen the advance battalions of the 11th Corps, having in a measure re-formed the dislocation in their ranks, were following up the French withdrawal in the direction of Fröschwiller. As a last resource, MacMahon called on Bonnemain's cavalry division, consisting of four regiments of *cuirassiers*, to stem the tide of French disaster. It was an heroic but forlorn expedient. When the order to attack reached Bonnemain, his division was in a fold of ground somewhat northward of the source of the Eberbach, his 1st Brigade on the right front of the 2nd—both brigades in close column of squadrons.

The ground over which he had to attack was extremely unfavourable, as the numerous ditches and tree-stumps were calculated to impede the movements of bodies of horse. But the gallant horsemen recked not of obstacles. A sudden thunder of horse-hoofs dominated for the moment the roar of the cannon, as the mail-clad squadrons came crashing through the vineyards and hopfields. Shells tore through the serried ranks, and at every stride men and horses went down. Still the squadrons rode straight to their doom, until the belching volleys of case-shot swept down the files in great swaths of dead and dying. Of the four splendid regiments, no single squadron cohered to strike home, so deadly was the file-fire encountered, yet many a trooper who came out from that massacre carried a bloody sword. The division was all but destroyed; while the German infantry did not care to form square, but shot down the horsemen in group-formation, supported by cannon fire.

The end of the long, fierce struggle was not yet. Although MacMahon's valiant soldiers must have realised that the situation was desperate, they were none the less resolute to fight to the bitter end. After several hours of deadly strife, the Germans, with their great preponderance of numerical strength, had succeeded in driving in the French army on the keystone of its position at Fröschwiller, in wrecking the

French cavalry, and in threatening the line of French retreat upon Reichshoffen.

Between three and four o'clock in the afternoon, save for a gap to the westward, the entire German line of battle, from Eberbach and Morsbronn, on the south-east and south-west, round to the Neehwiller heights on the north-west, was engaged in encompassing the French Army in and about Fröschwiller in a ring of German soldiers, with arms in their hands which they were plying vigorously; and in forming an almost entire cincture of batteries from which poured steadily upon the French position a rain of shell-fire; while the French fought on the defensive with a resolute constancy which elicited the admiration of their adversaries.

Many details of the momentous struggle for this final stronghold of the French Army defy all description; for German troops in broken detachments reached and stormed in upon the common goal almost simultaneously, and the convulsive surging of intermingled friend and foe precluded any precision in fixing the hours of events, and in attempting with an accuracy to establish any cohesion of recollection between the various isolated collisions.

Von der Tann and Hartmann, the commanders of the 1st and 2nd Bavarian Corps, on the right centre and right of the German line of battle, carried their respective commands through the broken ground on the slopes stretching upward towards Fröschwiller, to where Ducrot was still showing a resolute front on the partially refused French left flank. At length, by four o'clock, the Bavarians succeeded in overcoming Ducrot's vigorous resistance on the slopes of the Fröschwiller heights, and in forcing him back on the village; and they reached its northern and eastern confines almost simultaneously with the retreating foe.

The French maintained for some time a fierce but hopeless street-fight in the village of Fröschwiller, a part of which was already in German possession. It ended in a general storm on the part of the Germans, as the result of which the French troops who had not been taken prisoners in the village fled in complete disorder along the Reichshoffen and Niederbronn road, in doing which they came under the guns of the German batteries, the fire of which swept that main line of the French retreat.

By five o'clock the obstinate struggle at Fröschwiller was at an end. The prisoners—who amounted to some 9,000—stood downcast and sombre in the village street, many engaged in roughly bandaging their wounds. Dead and severely wounded lay thick, and blood was running in the gutters. Von der Tann came riding in at the head of his 2nd Division, having despatched in pursuit, by way of Niederbronn, artillery, cavalry, and infantry. The Würtemberg infantry halted at the southwestern exit, until they got their orders to intercept the retreat by way of Gundershoffen. But the chief line of retreat was by Niederbronn; and the crown prince, when assured that the issue of the battle was no longer doubtful, gave immediate instructions for a vigorous pursuit in that direction.

The Würtemberg cavalry were early on the track of the rout, and their batteries soon followed. The pursuit presently degenerated into an utter *dêbacle*. The Bavarian cavalry spurred fast in chase of the fugitives. The disintegration of the French Army was complete, and there was no halt in the panic-stricken rout until Saverne was reached. The Prussian 4th Cavalry Division was a march in the rear, and could not, therefore, immediately take part in the pursuit. But after a hard ride from Wörth Prince Albrecht overtook the rear of the fugitives on the evening of August 7th, near Steinberg, at the foot of the Vosges. The sight of his troopers imparted to the panic-stricken fugitives a fresh impulse of flight, and a hasty and scattered retreat on Luneville followed.

The German victory was a decisive one. The prisoners of war were 200 officers and 9,000 men. The trophies were an eagle, 4 standards, 28 guns, 5 *mitrailleuses*, 23 waggonsful of rifles and side-arms, 158 other carriages, and 2,000 horses. The German losses were 489 officers and 10,153 men. Wörth was an unquestionable victory, but scarcely a triumph. MacMahon's strength, at most, was under 50,000; the German strength actually engaged did not fall short of 90,000. MacMahon, it is true, had a commanding position, of which he made the most; but it had serious defects, of which in this their earliest important battle, the Germans did not take full avail. Moltke was not present at Wörth, and Blumenthal, the military adviser of the crown prince, did not appear to advantage. The man who really won the battle was old Kirchbach. In any other service than the German he would have been broke for disobedience to orders.

THE FRANCO-PRUSSIAN WARS
1870-71

The Battle of Mars-la-Tour
August 16, 1870
By Charles Lowe

"Look out for cavalry!" Such was the cry that was raised on the sanguinary field of Vionville-Mars-la-Tour oftener than in any other battle of the Franco-German war.

When France declared war against Germany in July, 1870, she sent all her available troops—numbering about 300,000 men—as fast as ever she could to her eastern frontier, where they formed themselves into what was called the "Army of the Rhine," under the supreme command of the Emperor Napoleon. This "Army of the Rhine" was composed of eight separate Army Corps, or *Corps d'Armée*, commanded by Marshals Bazaine, MacMahon, and Canrobert, and by Generals Bourbaki, Frossard, Ladmirault, Failly, and Félix Douay.

On the other hand, the Germans divided their forces into three main armies—each also consisting of several Army Corps—of which the combined strength was about 384,000 men; and so quickly had the Germans—who are famous for their powers of organisation—done the difficult work of mobilising their forces (that is to say, preparing them to take the field), that, within a fortnight after the order for this process had been issued, no fewer than 300,000 helmeted defenders of the Fatherland stood ranked up and ready along the Rhine.

Old King William of Prussia assumed the nominal command of all this tremendous fighting force; but in reality, the man who directed and controlled its movements was Field-Marshal Count von Moltke, who was perhaps the most studious and scientific soldier the world had ever seen. He had divided all the field strength of Germany into three separate armies—each also composed of several army corps. The First Army, on the right, was commanded by General von Steinmetz; the Second, in the centre, by Prince Frederick Charles, known as the

"Red Prince;" and the Third, on the left, by the crown prince, son-in-law of Queen Victoria.

The crown prince was the first to draw blood, on the 4th August (war had only been formally declared on the 19th July), when he won the great battle of Weissenburg, and on the 6th at Wörth, when he completed the defeat of Marshal MacMahon's army. On this very same day, too, Steinmetz, on the right, had stormed the heights of Spicheren at a very great sacrifice of life, causing Frossard, who held these heights, to fall back on the excessively strong fortress of Metz, which stands in the lovely valley of the Moselle. MacMahon had retreated towards the great training camp—the Aldershot, so to speak, of France—at Chalons; while the rest of the "Army of the Rhine" meanwhile retired on Metz, and thither the Germans now also began to push with might and main.

It was thought probable by Moltke, from all appearances, that the French meant to make a desperate stand in front of Metz. But he met with less resistance there than he expected; and on the 14th August a victory gained by the Germans at Colombey-Nouilly had the effect of making all their opponents in the open field thereabouts withdraw towards the fortressed city. This battle had been fought on the east of Metz, while on the west side ran the high road to Verdun and Paris. On the 15th the Germans came to the conclusion that the French in Metz, not wishing to expose themselves to the risk of being cooped up and rendered useless within their fortress, meant to escape towards Verdun, to join hands with MacMahon's beaten forces, and then give battle to the advancing Germans in the plain.

For the French were confident that they could give a good account of their hitherto victorious foes, could they but meet them on pretty equal terms in the open. The Germans saw very well that the object of the French at Metz was to escape to the west, and they therefore determined to strain every nerve to prevent this. Yet they sadly feared they would not succeed, for they were on the right, or east, bank of the Moselle, while the French were on the left, or west side; and it was necessary for their pursuers to make a wide sweep in order to cross the river and insert themselves in good time between Metz and Paris, so as to have the retreating Frenchmen face to face.

As early as the evening of the 15th a Division of Cavalry—the 5th, under Rheinbaden—had crossed the Moselle, and pressed round and forward with prying intent as far as the village of Mars-la-Tour, on the Verdun road, where it bivouacked for the night. It had seen certain masses of French troops away in the direction of Metz, but was unable to conclude whether this formed the rear-guard of the French Army retreating on Verdun, or only its vanguard. As a matter of fact, this army was still struggling with the difficulties of getting away from Metz.

Early on the morning of the 16th the French Emperor, escorted by two brigades of cavalry, had driven away to Verdun by the Etain road, which was still comparatively safe, leaving the command of the Metz Army to Marshal Bazaine.

All the roads from Metz were blocked by heavy baggage, and the French Army could not get away from the fortress with expedition and method. The left wing of the army was ready to march, but not the right; and so, the left had been sent back to its bivouacs until the afternoon. Thus, Bazaine lost much valuable time, and what he lost the "Red Prince" won. For by 10 a.m. on the morning of the 16th August, the 3rd, or Brandenburg, Army Corps—one of the best and bravest in all Germany—had come within sight of the Verdun road, marked at intervals of about a mile by the successive villages (coming from Metz) of Gravelotte, Rezonville, Vionville, and Mars-la-Tour, which the German soldiers punningly called *Marche-rétour* after the French had been finally beaten back on Metz.

It was an excessively hot day, the sun pouring down its rays on field and wood with almost tropical force; and by the time the brave Brandenburgers of General von Alvensleben, who had crossed the Moselle at Novéant the previous night, and resumed their forced march after a brief snatch of rest—by the time, I say, they had threaded the wooded glen of Gorze, leading right on to the Verdun road, they beheld to their great joy that a French force was in front of them.

After some preliminary skirmishing and wood-fighting, Alvensleben came to the conclusion that he had to deal with the whole, or at least the greater part, of Bazaine's army, which had thus not escaped after all. But before the arrival of Alvensleben's Corps on the scene, the action had been opened by the horse-batteries of Rheinbaden, which, advancing from Mars-la-Tour towards Vionville, opened a destructive shell-fire on Murat's dragoons, who, encamped thereabout, were engaged in cooking. A regular stampede ensued, the dragoons bolting through the camp. But the French infantry were quickly on their guard, and opened so heavy a fire on the audacious German horsemen—who had, of course, followed their guns—that the latter were soon driven to seek shelter in hollows and behind copses.

It was at this time that Alvensleben's Corps made its timely appearance, and began to enter into action, although it could not doubt that it had to contend against desperate odds. But it had been sent forward by its old commander, Prince Frederick Charles—who still wore the scarlet uniform of one of its Hussar (Zieten) regiments, and hence was known as the "Red Prince"—to seek out and hold Bazaine at bay, as a bulldog would a bull, until the arrival of reinforcements; and the doughty Brandenburgers were ready to resist to the very last man, if they must die for it. What would their beloved "Red Prince" say if they allowed the game to escape? Their only chance lay in the hope that Bazaine would not be able to concentrate all his colossal host and hurl it against them at once, and that the 10th Prussian Corps, with other parts of their army which they knew to have been despatched on the same errand as themselves, would meanwhile hurry up to their assistance and save them from complete annihilation.

The infantry part of the battle began on some wooded hills above the village of Gorze, about eight miles south-west of Metz, on a stream running from Mars-la-Tour into the Moselle at Novéant. A correspondent of the *Daily News* said:—

> The Prussians pushed into the woods, gradually, by dint of numbers and sheer hard fighting, driving the French skirmishers from them. What happened in this part of the battle no one knows or can know, as it was entirely in the woods and valleys, and no general view of it could be obtained. The French position here was a most formidable one, and the wonder is, not that it took the Prussians seven hours to take it, but that they ever got it at all.
>
> The woods above Gorze extend to within about two miles of Gravelotte, behind which village the French lay in the morning, as also at Rezonville, another village higher up on the road from Metz to Verdun. Nearly the whole of the Prussian second position was backed by the thick woods they had got possession of in the morning.
>
> The plain on which the battle was fought extends from the woods to the Verdun road, about one mile and a half, and is about three miles in length. On the French right the ground rises gently, and this was the key of the position, as the artillery, which could maintain itself there, swept the whole field. More towards the centre are two small valleys, one of which, being

deep, was most useful to the Prussians in advancing their troops. In the centre of the field is the road from Gorze to Rezonville and Gravelotte, joining the main road to Verdun between the two villages. (*There is a slight inaccuracy here, thee Gorze road runs into the main road to Verdun at Rezonville*). From the woods to Rezonville, on the Verdun road, there is no cover, except one cottage midway on the Gorze road. This cottage was held by a half-battery of French *mitrailleuses*, which did frightful execution in the Prussian ranks as they advanced from the wood.

The Brandenburg Corps consisted of two Divisions, one (the 5th) commanded by Stülpnagel, and the other (the 6th) by Buddenbrock. The latter was on the right of the German line, and it fought its way to the front with desperate courage, but with varying fortune. One regiment in particular—the 52nd—lost heavily in recovering some ground which had been wrested from it by the French. Its first battalion lost every one of its officers, the colours were passed from hand to hand as the bearers were successively shot down by the bullets of the *chassepots*, and the commander of the brigade. General von Döring, fell mortally wounded. General von Stülpnagel rode along the line of fire to encourage the men, while General von Schwerin collected the remnants of the troops bereft of their leaders, and held the most commanding point on the field of battle until reinforced by a portion of the 10th Corps.

But it was Buddenbrock's Division, on the left wing, which began to be so sorely pressed. This division had been ordered to advance on the old Roman road, also leading from Metz to Verdun, on the assumption that Bazaine might choose this as his main line of retreat. But on approaching Tronville, near Mars-la-Tour, it was quick to see how matters stood, and then, wheeling to the right, it advanced with the most death-despising courage against Vionville and Flavigny.

It is impossible in the space at my disposal to describe all the ins and outs of the tremendous conflict which now ensued; I can only give its salient points and incidents. When Bazaine had seen the Germans advance *from the direction of Verdun*, whither he himself was bound, he muttered to himself: "*C'est une reconnaissance*" ("It is only a scouting affair"). But he was quickly undeceived, and saw that he would have to fight and conquer before he could continue his westward march. The position of the French was one of great advantage, their left flank being protected by the fortress of Metz and their right by formidable batteries along the old Roman road, while they also had at their disposal a very strong force of cavalry (three and a-quarter Divisions to two German ones), so that they could thus afford to wait an attack on their centre.

The two Infantry Divisions of the Germans began to get very much mixed; but, by taking advantage of every rise in the ground for cover, the regimental officers got their men steadily forward in spite of the very heavy fire from the French infantry and guns. Flavigny was taken by assault, and one cannon, with a number of prisoners, fell into the hands of the brave Brandenburgers. Slowly, but surely, the Prussians made their way beyond Flavigny and Vionville, and, assisted by a heavy fire from their artillery, compelled the right wing of the 2nd French Corps to retire on Rezonville—a movement which turned into a perfect flight when the French generals Bataille and Valazé had been killed.

To regain the lost ground, the French *Cuirassier* Guards turned resolutely on their Prussian pursuers; but their charge was cut short by the *schnellfeuer* (or rapid fire) of two companies of the 52nd Regiment, drawn up in line (like the 93rd Highlanders at Balaclava), who waited until the rushing horsemen, with their flashing swords and waving plumes, were within 250 yards, and then poured a murderous volley into the teeth of their assailants. The latter, parting to right and left, rushed past and into the fire of more infantry behind, leaving 243 of their horses and riders lying on the plain. These French *Cuirassiers* barely escaped complete annihilation; for scarcely had they turned to retire when they were set upon by Redern's Horse Brigade (of Rheinbaden's Division), consisting of the 11th Black Brunswickers—Prussia's "Death or Glory" boys—and 17th Hussars, who, emerging from a hollow behind Flavigny, dashed straight at the flying foe and cut many more of them out of their saddles.

But their pursuit was presently checked by a French battery in front of Rezonville, which began to blaze away at them; and for this battery, in turn, they went like the wind. Shots and sabre-cuts are exchanged in the wild *mêlée*, the gunners are cut down, and only a knot of mounted French officers remain. One of them—a short. broad shouldered, bull necked man, with drawn sword—is evidently a general of high rank from the richness of his uniform. As a matter of fact, it is Bazaine himself, the commander-in-chief of the French Army, who has placed this battery in position. A knot of the Black Brunswickers make a dash at him, but his Staff surrounds him, parry-

COUNT VON MOLTKE.

MARSHAL BAZAINE

ing the sabre thrusts and cuts of the Hussars, till at last he is rescued by a timely charge of the 5th French Hussars forming his escort, and many of the Brunswickers straightway find death as well as glory.

But now the 6th Cavalry Division of the Prussians—*Cuirassiers*, Lancers, and Hussars—led on by the Duke of Mecklenburg-Schwerin, rushes up in turn to repel this cavalry counterstroke of the French which had the effect of rescuing Bazaine; and then is seen another surging mass of mounted combatants mingling in a "murder grim and great." Presently the eye is diverted from this dust-enveloped spectacle by the sight of the red-tunicked Zieten Hussars—so called after the Great Frederick's greatest horse-captain—emerging from the dust-clouds and dashing themselves with a wild cheer at a line of French infantry—Grenadier Guards—in their front.

But at about 500 paces distance they are received with a truly infernal fire from *chassepot*, field-gun, and *mitrailleuse*, and their colonel—also a Herr von Zieten—falls dead out of the saddle, while Captain von Grimm is mortally wounded, and the horse of the adjutant, Lieutenant von Winterfeldt, is literally torn to pieces by a shell. The bravest men on earth cannot face such a fire; so, the Zieten Hussars wheel round and rush back to their lines, leaving the ground strewn with scarlet uniforms, as if it were an English battlefield. The French fire is too murderous; the Germans must check their advance; the battle for some little time after becomes an artillery duel.

It was now two o'clock. So far, Alvensleben had skilful deceived the enemy, with regard to the slender number of his troops, by incessant assaults. But the battle was now at a standstill, the battalions visibly thinned by four hours of the hardest and bloodiest fighting, while the infantry had almost exhausted their cartridges. There was not a battalion, not a battery, left in reserve all along the exposed line. Nevertheless, the Brandenburgers would not yield a single inch of the ground they had so bravely won.

Presently, however, they were threatened with a new danger. Their left wing at Vionville was very much exposed to the French artillery on the Roman road, and they were threatened with a turning of this weakest flank. At the same time, Marshal Canrobert, our old Crimean ally, discerned from his position in the centre the true moment to make a push for Vionville with ail his forces. Ruin or retreat stared the Germans in the face. It looked as if they were going to be completely overwhelmed in this part of the field. The reinforcements from the 10th Corps, which they were so anxiously awaiting, had not yet made

The Prussians pushed into the woods driving the French skirmishers from them

their appearance, and the French were assuming an ever more threatening attitude. What was to be done?

In a hollow behind Vionville was standing Bredow's heavy Cavalry brigade, consisting of the 7th Magdeburg Cuirassiers (Prince Bismarck's regiment) and 16th Uhlans, or Lancers, both of the Old Mark of Brandenburg. The former was commanded by Colonel Count von Schmettow, the latter by Colonel von der Dollen. The regiments were in a reduced condition, having only three squadrons each instead of five. Before them were the enemy's guns, and behind these, dense masses of infantry, fresh to the front.

"That infantry over there must be broken!" said an *aide-de-camp* to General von Bredow.

"That infantry?" echoed the general, in some surprise, as his eye ranged along its bristling front behind the guns.

"The fate of the day depends upon it," was the brief reply.

That was quite enough. Leading his brigade out of the hollow in column, he quickly formed it into line of squadrons—the *Cuirassiers* on the left and the *Uhlans* on the right, a little thrown back—and then, with a "Forward!" "Trot!" "Charge!" while their thrilling clarions rang out above the din of battle, away dashed the devoted troopers with a loud and long-continued roar more than a cheer.

It is Balaclava over again. In a few moments, they are among the first French guns, sabring and stabbing the gunners; and then, in the teeth of a frightful hail of bullets from cannon, musket, and *mitrailleuse*, they storm across to the next infantry line, with which they play equal havoc. The second infantry line was next broken through by the ponderous horsemen, many of whom had already fallen, and the panic they created by their heroic *Todtenritt*, or ride to death, even spread to the remoter line of batteries, which prepared to limber up. In its excitement, the brigade, like the Scots Greys at Waterloo, rode far beyond its mark, and, like the gallant Greys, it suffered terribly for its excess of ardour.

After charging on thus for about 3,000 paces, it was set upon in the most furious manner by an overwhelming force of French horsemen—the cavalry brigades of Murat and Gramont, and the entire division of Vallabreque. Thinned as Bredow's ranks now were, and exhausted by their exertions so far, how were they to cope with such hordes of horsemen? Yet cope they did with them stoutly and gallantly, like Scarlet's Heavy Brigade at Balaclava, riding in and out of the ranks of their assailants and bearing many of them to the ground.

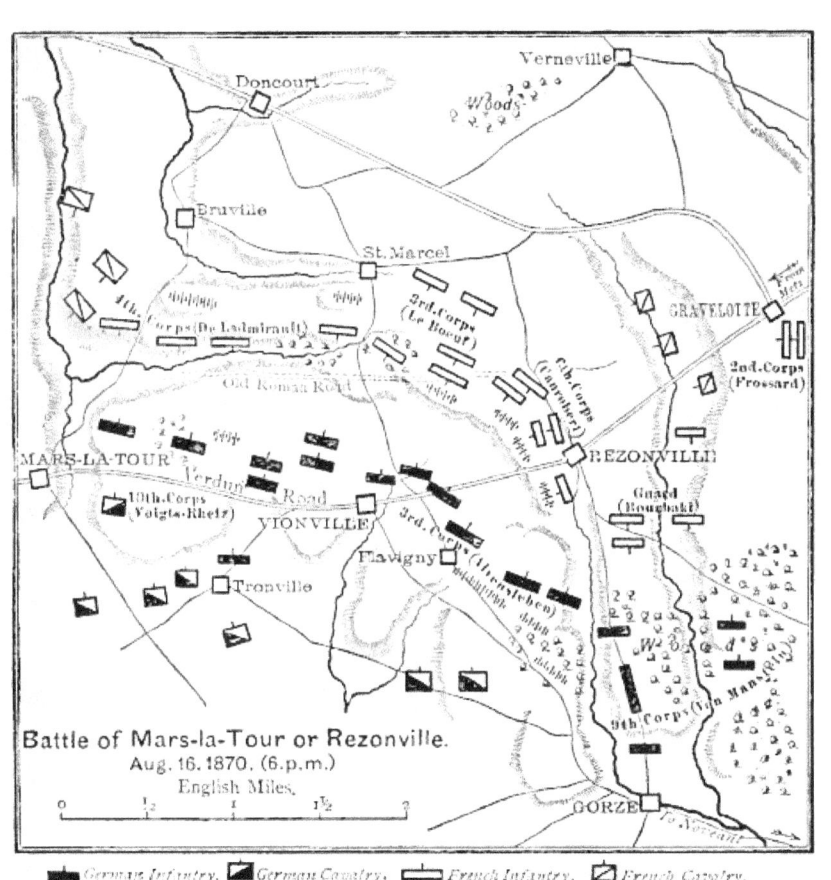

And as "Scotland for Ever!" was the cry of the "Greys," both at Waterloo and Balaclava, so Scotland is also again to the front on this battlefield of Vionville in the person of one of her adventurous sons. This is young Campbell of Craignish, in the shire of Argyll, who is serving as a lieutenant in the Bismarck Cuirassiers, and who, rushing where the fight is thickest, captures a French eagle after cutting down its bearer. Then he is set upon by a crowd of French troopers, who are determined to win this darling badge of honour back. It is the one French standard which has been captured, and at all costs it must be recovered. A pistol-shot shatters Lieutenant Campbell's hand, and he has to relinquish his trophy. But some of his men, hewing their way into the circle of his assailants, succeed in cutting him out of the *mêlée*.

All that the little remnant of the brigade could now do was to rally as well as possible and sabre its way back to its own lines. This it did, pursued by the masses of French horsemen, volleyed at by infantry, and rained upon by *mitrailleuse* bullets, but game to the last. Less than half of the men returned to Flavigny alive, where they were reorganised into two squadrons—two, instead of six. Of 310 *Cuirassiers* who had gone into action, only 104 came out of it; while only 90 *Uhlans* answered to the roll-call. Of our Light Brigade charge at Balaclava, Marshal Canrobert observed that it might be magnificent, but it certainly was not war. But the charge of Bredow's Heavy Brigade at Vionville, which was equally witnessed by Canrobert, was both one and the other, as the gallant Marshal himself must have been the first to admit.

It had been beautiful to look at, and it had entailed a fearful sacrifice of life; but it had achieved its object, which was to save Buddenbrock's infantry division and give it breathing-time. The French had received such a shock from the charge of Bredow's Brigade that, for the present, they abandoned their attempt to encircle the German left and advance on Vionville and Flavigny. The loss of life had been immense, but it had been justified by the result; and, after all, that is the main thing in war.

General Henry, of Canrobert's Corps, afterwards said:—

On taking position with my battery nothing was to be seen of Prussian cavalry. Where in the world had these *Cuirassiers* come from? All of a sudden, they were upon my guns like a whirlwind, and rode or cut down all my men save only one. And this one was saved by Schmettow. The gunner ran towards the *Cuirassiers*, crying "*Je me rends! je me rends!*" But the Prussians, not understanding this, were for despatching him, and were only prevented from doing so by their colonel, Count von Schmettow.

The man lived to tell the tale, and to receive the golden medal. General Henry continued:—

> It was only by the skin of my teeth that I myself escaped as the mass of furious horsemen swept past me, trampling down or sabring the gunners. But it was a magnificent military spectacle, and I could not help exclaiming to my adjutant as we rode away, '*Ah! Quelle attaque magnifique!*'

On the other hand, Count von Schmettow, who commanded the *Cuirassiers*, gave the following account of their "death-ride":—

> Every one of the gunners of the first battery on which the troopers fell were cut down or pierced (the count himself striking down the captain). In approaching the second battery my helmet was pierced by two bullets, and my orderly officer thrown from his horse, wounded in two places. Lieutenant Campbell, the Scottish officer, when the French *Cuirassiers* fell in turn upon us, seized the eagle of the regiment in his left hand, which was at once shattered by a bullet, and he was surrounded by the French horsemen; but some of our own *Cuirassiers* cut their way desperately towards him, and saved him. Never shall I forget the moment when I gave the order to the first trumpeter I met to sound the rally. The trumpet had been shattered by a shot, and produced a sound which pierced us to the quick.

This incident has been immortalised by the great German poet Freiligrath in the following ballad, entitled *The Trumpeter of Mars-la-Tour*—the spirited English version being by his daughter, Kate Freiligrath-Kroeker:—

> *Death and destruction, they belched forth in vain,*
> *We grimly defied their thunder;*
> *Two columns of foot and batteries twain—*
> *We rode and cleft them asunder.*
> *With brandished sabres, with reins all slack.*
> *Raised standards, and low-couched lances.*
> *Thus, we Uhlans and Cuirassiers wildly drove back,*

And hotly repelled their advances.
But the ride was a ride of death and of blood;
With our thrusts, we forced them to sever,
But of two whole regiments, lusty and good.
Out of two men, one rose never.
With breast shot through, with brow gaping wide,
They lay pale and cold in the valley,
Snatched away in their youth, in their manhood's pride—
"Now, Trumpeter, sound to the rally!"
And he took the trumpet, whose angry thrill
Urged us on to the glorious battle.
And he blew a blast—but all silent and still
Was the trump, save a dull hoarse rattle;
Save a voiceless wail, save a cry of woe.
That burst forth in fitful throbbing—
A bullet had pierced its metal through.
For the Dead, the wounded was sobbing!
For the faithful, the brave, for our brethren all,
For the Watch on the Rhine, true-hearted!—
Oh! the sound cut into our inmost soul!—
It brokenly wailed the Departed!
And now fell the night, and we galloped past,
Watch-fires were flaring and flying.
Our chargers snorted, the rain poured fast—
And we thought of the Dead and the Dying!

Then take the following from a correspondent of *The Times*, who was a witness of the battle:—

The want of infantry caused a somewhat serious sacrifice of cavalry, which had repeatedly to charge both infantry and artillery to hold them in check. The men do not ride particularly well to look at, but the manner in which they ride into the jaws of death is really quite à *la* Balaclava. One regiment—the 7th Cuirassiers—was ordered to charge a battery of artillery, and actually got into it, one of the first in, I am proud to say, being a young Englishman, who has taken service in the Prussian army, and has just got his lieutenancy. It went in some 300 strong, and what its loss is I tremble to say. When I next saw it, it scarcely seemed to me a hundred all told.

At 2.30 the reserve artillery was brought up, and the cannonade became heavier than ever. The sun, too, at this moment seemed to have come nearer to us, as if to see this fearful butchery of mankind, and the heat became tremendous. Then, wherever you went, came the pleading cry of 'Water! Water! For pity's sake give me water!' The Krankenträger, or bearers of the sick, had now more than they could do, admirable as the whole machinery of the corps is worked. . . . The positions of both the combative forces were perfectly stationary for about an hour, a sort of duel being carried on between them, which, though at some distance, was quite near enough to have fearful results. I saw a whole string of (French) prisoners brought in of every description. There was the burly giant of *cuirassiers* beside the little French liner, the green-jacketed hussar, and the artilleryman—all chattering away, and seeming to me uncommonly glad to be out of the affair at any price.

Seeing some of the infantry engaged on the extreme right, I went there, and met one regiment just coming out of action to recruit, being at that moment commanded by a youth of nineteen, having lost thirteen of its officers since the morning. The number of it was the 52nd, and to the usual inquiring glance that all officers who had not seen me before threw over my most unregimental attire, I replied by offering him a drink of some of the dirtiest water I ever saw, which I had procured from a pond, and which to both of us was better than the best iced champagne.

There was no inquiring then. I was instantly the best fellow he ever saw, and he told me all about what fun it was to be in command, and that he was sure to get something now, and that he meant to have another go in directly, etc. He was the most thoroughly English-German boy I ever saw. We stood under a tree together, and I gave him some cigars and left him. Two hours afterwards I saw his dead body laid out with others in a row, the cigars still stuck between the buttons of his coat. This one little anecdote—when I say it is but a fair sample of other regiments—will show how fearful the loss has been on the Prussian side.

At a subsequent roll call near Tronville it was found that the 24th Regiment had lost 1,000 men and 52 officers, while every officer of the 2nd battalion of the 20th Regiment was killed. It was not till three

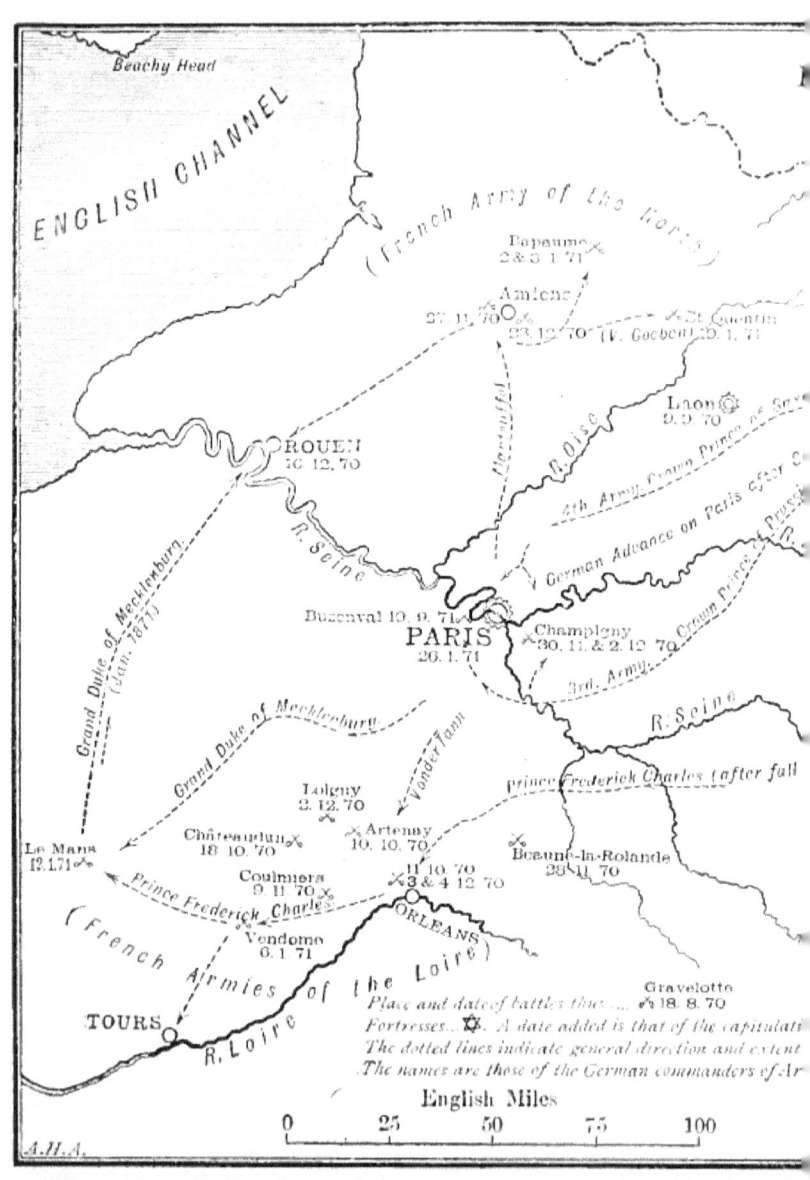

MAP SHOWING SCOPE OF OPERATIONS

NOTE.—Many battlefields are called by some authorities by their German names and by others by Rezonville=Mars-la-Tour or Vionville; Gravelotte=St.

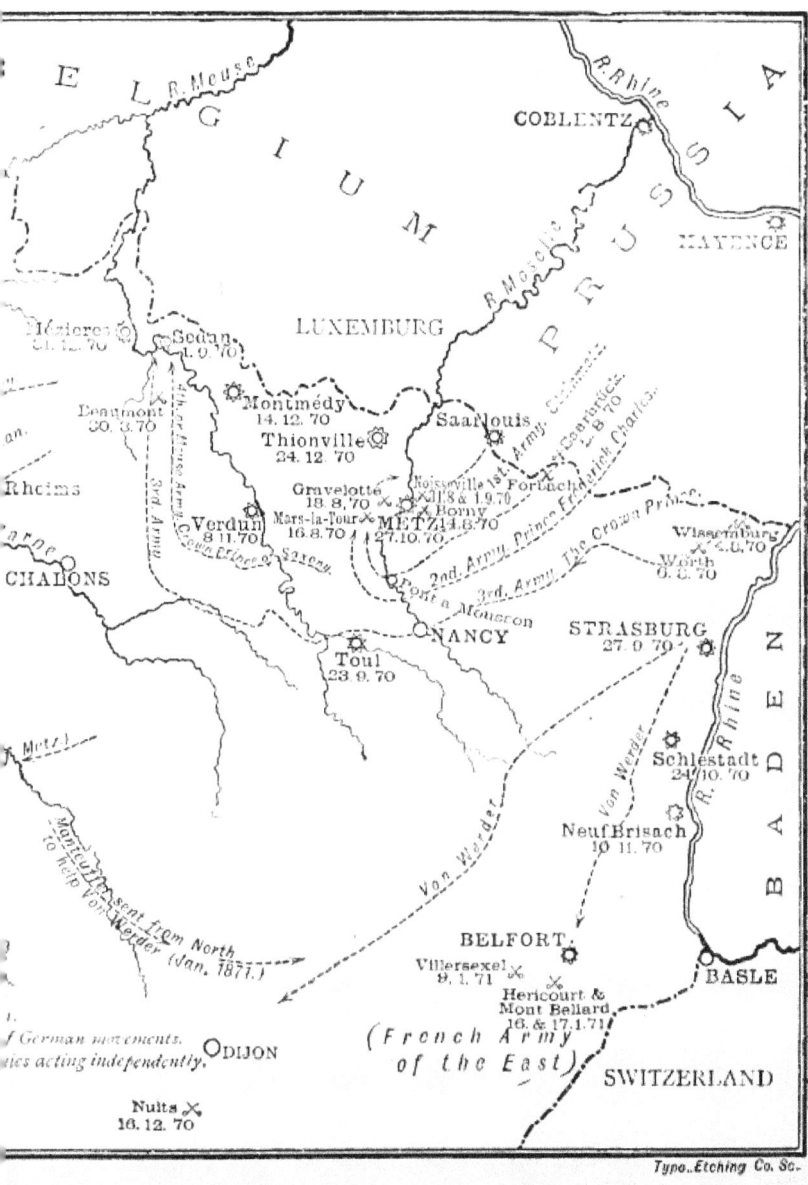

OF THE FRANCO-GERMAN WAR OF 1870-71.

heir French names, thus: Spicheren = Forbach; Wörth = Reichshoffen; Colombey-Nouilly = Borny;
rivat. In all these names the German precedes the French.

in the afternoon that the 3rd Corps, which had been fighting single-handed for five hours against a fivefold force, received any efficient assistance from the 10th Corps, which was now to the Brandenburgers what Blücher's army had been to Wellington at Waterloo. It was only the devotion of the artillery which had meanwhile saved the infantry from complete annihilation. For, after recovering from the shock of Bredow's brigade, the French had again concentrated their attack on the German left, and compelled it to retire, fighting as it went.

But presently reinforcements from the 10th Corps began to come up, and these were followed by the arrival of a man who was a host in himself—Prince Frederick Charles. His headquarters were away at Pont-à-Mousson, about fourteen miles to the south; and on hearing rather late in the day that his own Brandenburgers were up to the hilt in action and so hotly pressed, he mounted his horse and galloped away, without ever once drawing rein, to the field of battle. And now let Mr. Archibald Forbes, the famous war-correspondent, give us one of his telling battle-pictures:—

> It was barely four o'clock when he (the "Red Prince") came galloping up the narrow hill road from Gorze, the powerful bay he rode all foam and sweat, sobbing with the swift exertion up the steep ascent, yet pressed ruthlessly with the spur, staff and escort panting several horse-lengths in rear of the impetuous foremost horseman. On and up he sped, craning forward over the saddle-bow to save his horse, but the attitude suggesting the impression that he burned to project himself faster than the beast could cover the ground. No wolf-skin, but the red tunic of the Zieten Hussars, clad the compact torso; but the straining man's face wore the aspect one associates with that of the *berserkar*.
>
> The bloodshot eyes had in them a sullen lurid gleam of bloodthirst. The fierce sun and the long gallop had flushed the face a deep red, and the veins of the throat stood out. Recalling through the years the memory of that visage with the lowering brow, the fierce eyes, and the strong-set jaw, one can understand how to this day the mothers in the French villages invoke the terrors of 'Le Prince Rouge,' as the Scottish peasants of old used the name of the Black Douglas to awe their children wherewithal into panic-stricken silence.
>
> While as yet his road was through the forest, leaves and twigs

Mitrailleuse (front view).

Mitrailleuse (back view).

cut by bullets showered down upon him. Just as he emerged on the open upland a shell burst almost among his horse's feet. The iron-nerved man gave heed to neither bullet-fire nor bursting shell; no, nor even to the cheers that rose above the roar of battle from the throats of the Brandenburgers through whose masses he was riding, and whose chief he had been for many years. They expected no recognition, for they knew the nature of the man—knew that, after his fashion, he was the soldier's true friend, and also that he was wont to sway the issues of battle. He spurred onward to Flavigny, away yonder in the front line; the bruit of his arrival darted along the fagged ranks; and strangely soon came the recognition that a master-soldier had gripped hold of the command as in a vice.

With the arrival of the "Red Prince" and of reinforcements, the battle now again took the form of a desperate infantry fight. Let me notice only one of its leading incidents, which was graphically described by Moltke. When General von Wedell's Brigade, no more than five battalions strong, advanced to the attack by way of Tronville, he found himself in front of the extensive line of the 4th French Brigade. The two Westphalian regiments advanced steadily under the storm of shell and *mitrailleuse* fire until they suddenly reached the edge of a deep ravine. This, however, they soon crossed; but, after scaling the opposite bank, they were met by a murderous shower of bullets from the French infantry, who were everywhere close upon them.

Almost every one of the generals and officers were killed, the remnant of the broken battalions fell back into the ravine, and 300 men—unable to re-ascend the steep southern slope after the fatigue of a twenty-four-miles march, almost at the double—were taken prisoners. Those who escaped mustered at Tronville around the bullet-riddled colours which Colonel von Cranach—the only officer who still had a horse under him—brought back in his hand. Seventy-two officers and 2,542 men were missing out of 95 officers and 4,546 men—more than a half.

And now there occurred another of those magnificent cavalry charges in which the battle of Vionville-Mars-la-Tour was so sacrificially rich. Raising a shout of triumph over the repulse—almost the annihilation—of Wedell's brigade, the French infantry advanced at the double for the purpose of completing the wreck of the German left, and all seemed lost. But just at this critical moment out rushed the 1st

Dragoon Guards in their sky-blue tunics and dashed straight at the pursuing foe, who poured into the ranks of their assailants a murderous bullet-fire, while shrapnel played upon their flanks. But "*immer vorwärts!*" stormed the devoted dragoons, and plied their sabres on the French *fantassins* with terrible effect.

Again this cavalry regiment had achieved its object—which was to save its own infantry from destruction—but at a frightful cost. Colonel von *Auerswald* was mortally wounded, and it was reserved for the youngest Captain, Prince Hohenlohe, to rally the remnants of the brave regiment and lead it out of action. Only about a third of the troopers afterwards answered to the roll-call. The regiment had left on the field 15 officers, 11 non-commissioned officers, 7 trumpeters, 103 privates, and 250 horses.

The importance of this great sacrifice of life may be gathered from a remark made by the Emperor William two years later, on the occasion of a visit he paid to the barracks in Berlin, he said:

"Gentlemen, but for your gallant attack at Mars-la-Tour, who knows whether we should have been here today?"

This gallant regiment afterwards became the "Queen of England's Own," and a higher military compliment could scarcely have been paid Her Majesty by her German grandson, William II.

Among the ranks of the 1st Dragoon Guards at Mars-la-Tour were the two sons of Prince Bismarck, riding as private troopers; for this happened to be the year in which they were doing their compulsory term of military service. The Chancellor's sons—one in his twenty-first, the other only in his eighteenth year—behaved in action with a courage worthy of their father. The elder, Herbert, had received no fewer than three shots, one through the front of his tunic, another in his watch, and the third in the thigh; while his brother William (Count "Bill" he was always called) had come out of the deadly welter unscathed. Bismarck said once:—

> During the attack at Mars-la-Tour, Count Bill's horse stumbled with him over a dead or wounded Gaul, within fifty feet of the French square. But after a few moments he shook himself together again, jumped up, and not being able to mount, led the brown horse back through a shower of bullets. Then he found a wounded dragoon, whom he set upon his horse, and, covering himself thus from the enemy's fire on one side, he got back to his own people. The horse fell dead after shelter was reached.

But the charge of the 1st Dragoon Guards was scarcely over when it became apparent that the French were preparing for another attack on the invincible left wing of the Germans by hurling upon it a stupendous mass of their cavalry. Three regiments of Le Grand's Division, and both regiments of the Guards Cavalry Brigade, were seen trotting up to the west side of the Grayère ravine. Opposite to them stood the whole of the Prussian cavalry, concentrated to the south of Mars-la-Tour, in the first line being the 13th Uhlans, 4th Cuirassiers, and 19th Dragoons, and behind them the i6th Dragoons and loth Hussars. The 13th Uhlans dashed straight against the foremost French cavalry line; but the regiment had become somewhat disordered, and the French Hussars rode right through it.

Then, however, the 10th Hussars turned up for the second time, and repulsed the enemy's cavalry. The two evenly-balanced masses of horsemen rushed upon each other in an awful cavalry *mêlée*. But, as a mighty cloud of dust concealed the ensuing hand-to-hand encounter of 5,000 men swaying to and fro, it was impossible to follow with minuteness the incidents of the conflict.

Fortune gradually decided in favour of the Prussians, for, man to man, they were heavier than their opponents. General Montaigu was taken prisoner, severely wounded, and General Le Grand fell while leading his Dragoons to the assistance of the Hussars. This, the greatest cavalry combat of the war, had the effect of making the French right wing give up all attempts to act on the offensive. But out of this gigantic combat of horsemen the victorious Prussians had again emerged with great loss; and among those who had fallen was Colonel Finckenstein of the 2nd Dragoon Guards, who had been the midnight bearer of Moltke's momentous message from Gitschin to Königinhof during the Bohemian campaign of 1866.

Darkness was now approaching, and the battle had practically been won by the Germans. The troops were utterly exhausted, most of the ammunition spent, while the horses had been saddled for fifteen hours without anything to eat. Some of the batteries could only be moved at a slow pace, and the nearest Prussian troops on the left bank of the Moselle were a day's march off. Nevertheless, the impetuous Red Prince, desiring to increase the moral impression of the day's endeavours, and, if possible, destroy altogether the internal cohesion of the French, ordered a general advance against their position. But the poor Prussian troops were too utterly fagged out by their incessant exertions during the day to do much more than make a formal response to this cruel and unnecessary command; and, again, they suffered great loss without inflicting a corresponding one on the French.

Fighting did not entirely cease till ten o'clock—that is to say, the bloody battle had lasted for twelve long hours, entailing a loss of about 16,000 officers and men on either side. But the Germans had won the battle. For they had achieved their object—which was to prevent the escape of Bazaine. Yet, in his despatch to the emperor, Bazaine had made bold to assert that:

> The enemy, beaten, retreated on all points, leaving us masters of the battlefield.

Moltke, on the other hand, wrote that

> The troops, worn out by a twelve-hours' struggle, encamped on the victorious but bloody field immediately opposite the French lines.

And Moltke wrote the truth. Bazaine had evidently learned the habit of lying about his reverses from the Great Napoleon, and even from Napoleon the Little.

Yet Mars-la-Tour was only the prologue to the still bloodier and more decisive drama of Gravelotte two days later. The Emperor William II. once said:—

> The Battle of Vionville, is without a parallel in military history, seeing that a single Army Corps, about 20,000 men strong, hung on to and repulsed an enemy more than five times as numerous and well equipped. Such was the glorious deed that was done by the Brandenburgers, and the Hohenzollerns will never forget the debt they owe to their devotion.

Several years later I visited the field of battle just described. Leaving Gorze, with its gilded statue of *la Sainte Vierge* on the brow, of a beetling cliff, I passed up the steep and wooded defile through which the Brandenburgers pressed on the 16th of August, and here the first affecting relics of the bloody strife appeared. In a little, lonely green valley skirted by the road, a few grassy mounds luxuriant with the crimson poppy and the wild fern, each being surmounted by a white wooden cross, told where the *tapfere Krieger* began to drop from the bullets of the *chassepot*. But when the summit is reached, what a touching sight!

The rising plateau on every side is dotted with white crosses,

Charge of the 16th Uhlans

which thicken, thicken, thicken as you advance, and the not far distant horizon edge is bristling with obelisks and stone memorials of more pretentious and lasting form, making the whole region look like one colossal cemetery. An involuntary sadness comes over the traveller, and when approaching every tomb and commemorative tablet he feels instinctively moved by the mute appeal contained in the inscription: "*Sta, viator, heroen calcas!*" The graceful obelisk, with its lengthy death-roll of officers and men, the railing-encircled and ivy-grown mound looking like a well-filled family vault, the silver-edged cross still hung with withered oaken wreaths and immortelles, the slender column snapped in twain to indicate the fate of hopeful youth suddenly cut off, the neatly-trimmed sepulture and the graveyard plot of flowers—conceive all these objects scattered over the summit of a bare plateau facing northwards to the west of Metz, and you will have some idea of the scene.

On an eminence behind Vionville, which formed the centre of the German position, is a pyramidal kind of monument of roughly-hewn stone, surmounted by the Hohenzollern eagle, and surrounded by a railing hung with shieldlike tablets bearing the multitudinous names of those officers of the 5th Division who fell on that fatal day. The reverse and coverless side of the plateau—densely dotted with mounds and monuments testifying to the terrible losses of the brave Brandenburgers—leads you down to the village of Vionville, where tombstones on the public highway point to where the dust of Gaul and German is commingled in the reconciliation of death. "*Mit Gott für König und Vaterland*" is the recorded war-cry on the monument of one Teutonic soldier; while at its side there stands a marble cross, tastefully wreathed with flowers, to the memory of one brave and noble young lieutenant of the Empire who died on the field of honour with these words, preserved in golden letters, on his lips: "*Dites à ma mère,*" he cried, "*que je meurs en soldat et en chrétien. Marchez en avant!*"—"Tell my mother that I died like a soldier and a Christian. Forward!"

French uniforms in 1870.

THE FRANCO-PRUSSIAN WARS
1870-71

The Battle of Gravelotte (St. Privat) August 18, 1870
By A. Hilliard Atteridge

Gravelotte—or, as the French call it, St. Privat—was the decisive battle of the Franco-German War. When night put an end to the fighting around Mars-la-Tour and Rezonville on Tuesday, August 16th, everyone expected that the conflict would be renewed with the first light of the morrow's dawn. But on the Wednesday morning the Germans, who were expecting reinforcements, showed no disposition to immediately resume the attack, and Marshal Bazaine ordered his five *corps d'armée* to withdraw from the positions they had held on the previous evening, and to fall back upon a line of heights that extends in front of the western forts of Metz, from the Moselle to the villages of Amanvilliers and St. Privat. These orders dispirited men and officers alike. They had met and withstood the fierce onset of the day before; when night fell, their line was still unbroken. Could it be that, after all, the terrible battle of the 16th had been one more defeat, seeing that they were thus ordered to abandon their positions to the enemy?

Through the blazing heat of the summer day the long columns plodded back towards Metz. Frossard's Corps, on the left of the line, had the shortest march to make, and was soon in position on the hills behind the deep ravine, through which the Mance Brook flows down to the Moselle. But Canrobert with the 6th Corps, on the extreme right, did not occupy all his positions till evening, for his was the outermost and longest march in this gigantic wheel of a great army 140,000 strong. The roads were encumbered with retiring convoys and long trains of ambulance waggons full of wounded men. Still more of these victims of the strife were left in the farms and villages along the rear of the battlefield.

There was hardly a group of buildings on which the Geneva flag was not flying, roughly improvised, in most cases, by sewing two pieces of red stuff crosswise on a napkin. Gangs of farm labourers were at work burying the dead. In the village church of Doncourt two coffins of rough deal boards lay before the altar. Scrawled in chalk on the lids were the names of "General Legrand" and "General Brayer." Legrand had led the cavalry of the 4th Corps into action the day before, and Brayer had fallen at the head of its first infantry brigade. In the evening a farmer's cart, followed only by a priest and the *maire* of Doncourt, conveyed the coffins to the village cemetery.

As the troops reached the positions assigned to them, the little shelter-tents were pitched, fires were lighted, and cooking began. The baggage-waggons were unloaded, and sent off towards Metz for a further supply of provisions and forage. The ammunition columns of the artillery distributed cartridges. Then came orders that the position was to be entrenched, and working parties were soon busy with pick and spade, under the guidance of engineer officers, along the French left. But on the right, where the work was most needed, little or nothing was done, for Canrobert's Corps reached the ground late, and there was a deficiency of tools, the waggons of his engineer park having, for the most part, got no nearer the frontier than the great camp at Châlons.

In the late hours of the afternoon, strong patrols of the enemy showed themselves along the edges of the woods opposite the French left, and there was some desultory firing, the *mitrailleuse* batteries of Frossard's Corps being particularly active. Their rattling fire broke out whenever a spiked helmet was seen among the trees, but this long-range shooting did very little damage, and the Germans seldom took the trouble to answer it. So, the long summer day went by; and when night fell, the French lay down beside their thousand bivouac fires, fully assured that next day would witness a great battle.

Bazaine slept in the village of Plappeville, with the regiments of the Imperial Guard camped close by in the hollow, between the two fort-crowned heights of Plappeville and St. Quentin. Curiously enough, the marshal told his staff that he did not anticipate a battle. He would give his men a day's rest, and then resume his march to the north-westward and rejoin MacMahon.

And what were the Germans doing all this time? After the war, there grew up a kind of legend about the way in which the victors had conducted their operations. According to this story they were always doing something, and it was always the right thing to do. They

THE ROADS WERE ENCUMBERED WITH RELIEVING CONVOYS AND LONG TRAINS OF AMBULANCE WAGGONS

had a plan of campaign which worked out with the precision of an approved chess-opening, and made victory a certainty. Their cavalry was always in touch with the enemy. The *Uhlans* were everywhere, watching every move of the French, and when their reports reached headquarters, they were made the basis of orders that directed overwhelming masses with the certainty of fate against the weak points of the French positions.

There is something of this legendary view of the war to be traced even in the German official account of the campaign; but since the staff history was published, a whole literature of the war has come from the printing-presses of both France and Germany, and the evidence thus made available has done much to discredit the traditional view of what happened on many important occasions. It is now tolerably clear that on the 17th the Germans were acting in a way that was hardly worthy of such past-masters in the art of war. On the right the outposts of the First Army, under the command of General von Steinmetz, were in sight of the French left on the hills beyond the Mance Brook, and were, indeed, occasionally exchanging fire with them; but no attempt had been made to keep in touch with the retiring corps on the French right, though there was a strong force of cavalry available for this purpose.

On the extreme left of the Germans, the Crown Prince (now the King) of Saxony, one of the best leaders in the invading army, pushed forward some of his cavalry to Pasondrupt, on the Metz-Verdun road, and ascertained that there were no French troops in that direction. But nothing was done to make sure that the greater part of Bazaine's army was not in retreat across the Orne river, by the Metz-Briey route. Nor were the hills held by the corps of the French right and centre reconnoitred, so that next day very serious loss of time and of life resulted from a mistake as to where the French right really lay. The orders for the movement which resulted in the battle of Gravelotte were, indeed, drawn up before 2 a.m. on the 17th, on the basis of insufficient information. It was only through the superiority in numbers of the Germans, and the general soundness of their position compared with that of the French, that these orders worked out so well next day.

When night fell the two armies, therefore, were in bivouac in the same order in which they fought on the morrow; but, instead of facing each other, the two lines formed a right angle, the French left and the German right being in touch near the Moselle, while the other extremities of the lines were about nine miles apart. Next day the German armies were to be flung against the French position by a great wheel to the eastward, across the same ground that had been traversed by the French on the morning of the 17th. The annexed sketch map shows, more clearly than any description, the position of the two armies on the night before the great battle, and the movements of the morning of the 18th.

The night was clear, and starlit overhead. It was warm, and the men hardly needed their bivouac fires. In the French lines, there were two alarms during the hours of darkness. The first was about 2 a.m., when the cry "To arms!" started somewhere in the middle of the outpost lines, and ran like lightning all through the bivouacs. The men sprang up, and seized their rifles; many of the batteries hooked in their teams, ready to gallop up their guns to the front. But in a few minutes the word was passed that it was nothing. There was another alarm a little later, and after this in many of the bivouacs the men sat chatting and smoking round the fires.

At four o'clock the sky was already whitening with the dawn, and then bugle and trumpet began to sound the reveille along the plateau from Rozerieulles to St. Privat; and after the morning roll-call the men got their breakfasts, while the sun rose brightly in the clear sky.

The Germans were already in movement. Some of the corps marched off at four o'clock, others had not to start till six; but some of the divisions had been marching all night. The Pomeranians of the 2nd corps had left their bivouac near Pont-à-Mousson soon after midnight, and had been tramping northward by starlight ever since, the guns and cavalry on the high road, the infantry moving by tracks among the vineyards on the slopes above it. Towards morning they had cheered the old King of Prussia as he passed their columns on the road in his carriage, driving from Pont-à-Mousson, where he had had a short sleep, to Flavigny, where he was in the saddle with Moltke and the headquarters' staff by six o'clock.

Prince Frederick Charles, who commanded the Second Army, forming the German left, had slept at Mars-la-Tour. At half-past five he was in the saddle, directing the march of his corps to the northward. The Saxons were the first to move off at six o'clock, but such is the space occupied by an army corps, that it was not till nine that the last of their battalions was clear of Mars-la-Tour and the Guards began their march. The corps under Steinmetz on the right had not so far to go. Their business for the present was to close up and watch the French, and to issue from the woods to attack them as soon as the

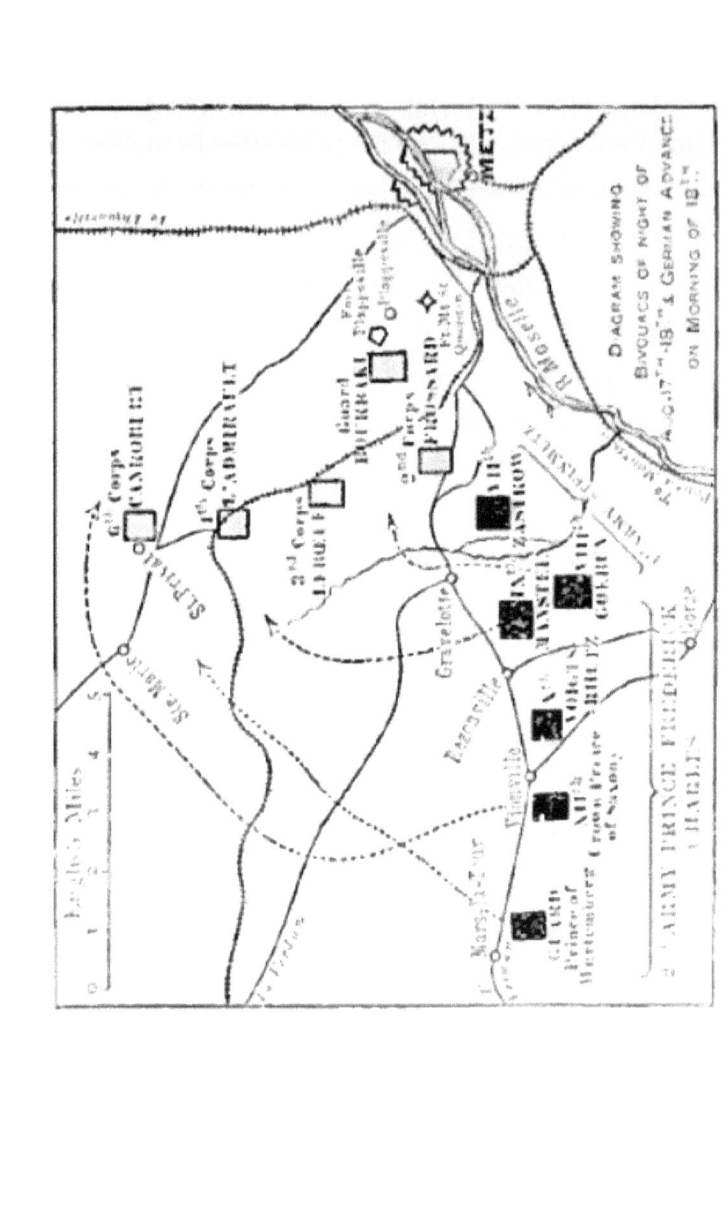

sound of cannon from the northward told that Frederick Charles was in touch with the enemy.

So, the great wheel, first to the northward and then to the eastward, went on through the summer morning, 220,000 Germans, with 800 guns, pushing on to the line of heights that runs from Habonville by Gravelotte to the ravines above Gorze, facing the corresponding line held by Bazaine. It was the first great battle in which troops from every part of Germany were to fight side by side. Here flew the black and white flag of Prussia; there the black, white, and red colours of the North German Confederation, or the white and green banner of Saxony; and the white and red pennons of Hessian contingents; and the flags of Mecklenburg, Brunswick, and Oldenburg; and the historic colours of the Hanseatic League.

At ten the cavalry in front of the German left reported that the enemy had not retired to the northward. French tents were standing along the hills about Amanvilliers, and there was an advanced detachment holding the village of Ste. Marie aux Chênes. At first it was supposed that the French line of battle extended no further than Amanvilliers village. Later it was ascertained that there were also troops in St. Privat; but where precisely the French right lay was not clearly known until the attack had made some progress. Reports sent to the royal headquarters at Flavigny brought back orders for the German left to march eastwards against the French positions. But even before these orders reached him Prince Frederick Charles was directing his columns toward Amanvilliers and St. Privat, the Saxons and the Guards moving on his extreme left, expecting to find nothing but weak detachments in their immediate front, and to turn the French right without much fighting.

Marshal Bazaine spent the morning with his chief of the staff, General Jarras, in a house at Plappeville, busy with preparing a list of promotions to replace the officers killed and wounded in the battles of the 14th and 16th. At half-past nine an officer of Marshal Leboeuf's staff arrived with a report that masses of the enemy were moving in his front, and asking for orders. The commander-in-chief of the French army sent word to Leboeuf that in the position he held he ought to be quite safe if he was attacked, and that meanwhile he had better push on the work at the shelter-trenches and other fieldworks planned and begun the day before.

When the staff officer went away Bazaine told Jarras that he doubted if the enemy would venture on a serious attack, for the ground held by the Imperial Army was so strong as to leave few chances of success to such an enterprise. To messages from other corps commanders he sent much the same reply he had given to Leboeuf. So, the morning was spent in mere routine duties at the French headquarters. A better soldier than Bazaine would have been early in the saddle, seeing for himself what was the state of affairs along his line of defence. But he had apparently deluded himself into the idea that all that was necessary had been done when he had placed his five corps in position along the plateau of Amanvilliers. Even when, about noon, the sound of cannon came echoing along the hills from the westward he remained at his desk, and it was not till two o'clock that he mounted and rode up the hill of St. Quentin, taking only two off his officers with him, and again telling Jarras that he was sure the affair would not be serious.

But by two o'clock the battle had been some time in progress over miles of country. The first shots were fired a few minutes after noon by the 9th German Corps—Schleswig-Holsteiners and Hessians—commanded by Von Manstein. As his vanguard reached the farm of Champenois just before twelve o'clock, a French camp could be seen on the opposite slope of the valley. He thought it was going to be another surprise—a Wissemburg on a grand scale—so he gave the word, and promptly a couple of batteries galloped up, unlimbered, and sent a shower of shells bursting among the French tents.

Manstein was acting against orders in thus precipitating the attack, for Moltke had intended that the French should be assailed simultaneously on the left and right, as soon as Prince Frederick Charles had begun to seriously develop his flank movement north of Amanvilliers, but not till then. But now, as on more than one previous occasion, the eagerness of the subordinate commanders hurried on the battle. Manstein could not resist the temptation of suddenly opening fire on the camp in front of him. But the French were not surprised. The infantry rushed to their shelter-trenches. The artillery promptly replied to the German guns from the higher ground beyond.

Moltke, sitting on his horse beside the king, on the hill near Flavigny, heard the roar of Manstein's guns. He knew the Guard and the Saxons could not yet be in a position to cooperate in the attack, and he did what he could to prevent Steinmetz from flinging the troops on the right prematurely against the French left. He hurriedly wrote and sent him an order telling him that the action which he could hear beginning near Verneville was an isolated affair, and there was no need yet of showing his troops. If he must act, let it be only by using his artillery as a prelude to the attack which would come later. But Steinmetz, on the heights beyond Gravelotte, had heard Manstein's guns before Moltke's galloper reached him, and had not only brought his batteries into action, but had begun to push on his infantry through the woods in his front. So it was that about noon the great battle began, as it were, by an accident.

A few words as to the character of the battlefield:—The high ground to the west of Metz is made up of three nearly parallel ranges of hills, running north and south, those nearest the city being the highest. The valleys between them are from 1½ to 2 miles wide from crest to crest, and the slopes are gentlest towards the northern end of the heights, where also the valleys are more shallow, all the forms of the ground being bolder in the southern part of the region. In the hollows, there are extensive woods—those near Gravelotte village, the Bois de Vaux and the Bois de Genivaux, being at the time of the battle so full of thick undergrowth that they could only be traversed by following the paths and a few narrow glades. The hills are sufficiently elevated above the valleys to enable one in most places to see across from ridge to ridge over the trees. The central line of heights was that held by the French. The Germans advanced to the attack across the western ridge.

On their right, at Gravelotte village, the Verdun-Metz road drops into the valley, passing through a defile with steep rocks on either side, traversing a narrow belt of wood by a clearing, and ascending the opposite slope, having on one side a mass of quarries that made a ready shelter for the defence, and on the other the farm-house and stables of St. Hubert, which the French had occupied, as well as the quarries and the belts of wood below. But all these were only the advanced posts of their left.

About 250 yards eastward of St. Hubert their shelter-trenches ran along the upper slope of the hill; and in places, where it was steepest, they were arranged in double and triple tiers. A wall at the bend of the road was lined with rifles. The farms of Moscou and Point du Jour had been prepared for defence, and just above them at the crest of the hill there were three groups of cannon and *mitrailleuses*. These were pointed at the opposite ridge beyond Gravelotte, while the rifles of the infantry could sweep all the slopes down to the edge of the woods. Frossard with the 2nd Corps held this splendid position. An officer of Engineers, he had carefully entrenched all his front, and made the most of the natural advantages of the ground. To his right Marshal

Leboeuf with the 3rd Corps, chiefly made up of the garrison of Paris, prolonged the line along the ridge by the farm of Leipzig and La Folie to Montigny la Grange. Here, too, the spade had been busy providing shelter for the defence.

Behind the left centre, the Imperial Guard and the reserve artillery were stationed near Plappeville. General Ladmirault with the 4th Corps came next to Leboeuf, the strong point of his position being the large walled village of Amanvilliers, which he had carefully prepared for defence. Then on the right Marshal Canrobert with the 6th Corps occupied St. Privat, with a strong detachment in Roncourt to guard his flank, and an advanced post in the village of Ste. Marie aux Chênes. Here on the right, where such work was most needed, very little had been done to entrench the position, chiefly because there was a deficiency of tools.

But even without such help it was strong, for St. Privat was partly hidden from view and fire by the crest of the long slope which descends to the westward and north-westward, a gentle slope of open fields, which the *chassepot* bullets could sweep with that grazing fire which is always far more deadly than the plunging fire from a bolder slope. For two thousand yards there was practically no cover for the attack. It was a huge natural glacis destined to be the scene of terrible slaughter before the day was won.

Begun on the centre at noon, the cannonade spread rapidly to the

GENERAL STEINMETZ

southward. Steinmetz had opened with his guns against the French left, and Frossard's artillery was replying. The shells were screaming high above the trees in the Mance valley, as they flew from crest to crest. Battery after battery came galloping up on the German side, and in twenty minutes Von Goeben, who commanded the 7th Corps (the first of Steinmetz's to come into action), had more than a hundred guns in line on the slope above Gravelotte, while his infantry were pushing into the thick belt of woods in the valley below and exchanging rifle fire with the French advanced posts. It was soon evident that the Germans were going to have the best of this artillery duel.

To begin with, they had more guns than the French. Then the German guns were breech-loading cannon, while the French were rifled muzzle-loaders of the same type that they had used eleven years before in Italy; and the result was that the German gunners fired faster, were less exposed as they worked their guns, and shot better. Finally, the Germans had better ammunition. Their shells, fitted with percussion fuses, almost invariably burst on contact with the hot hard ground of the ridge at which they fired; whilst the French time fuses acted irregularly, sometimes burst the shells too soon, and, oftenest of all, failed to explode them at all, so that the projectiles were practically solid shot. Frossard's gunners made very fair practice, but they were handicapped from the very outset. Near some of Von Goeben's batteries, as the day went on, the ground was scored with long furrows cut by the grazing but unburst shells from the French batteries. But on the opposite side of the valley, in and around the farms at which the Germans chiefly directed their fire, as soon as they had got the upper hand of the French artillery, the results were fearful.

St. Hubert was early in the day a mass of ruins, and a little later Moscou and Point du Jour were set on fire by bursting shells. To quote a German account of the appearance of the two farms after the fight. Major Hoenig tells us how:—

> At these points hardly any French were found killed or wounded by infantry bullets; almost all had been destroyed by the fire of the guns. In the large heaps of ruins the defenders, especially in Moscou, lay all around, fearfully torn and mutilated by the German shell; limbs and bodies were blown from thirty to fifty paces apart, and the stones and sand were here and there covered with pools of blood. In Moscou and Point du Jour some French were found burnt in their defensive positions, and

a large number of the wounded showed marks of the flames, which had destroyed both uniforms and limbs. All around there lay rifles and swords, knapsacks and cartridges, the remains of limbers which had been blown up, broken gun-carriages and wheels, and a large number of hideously torn and mangled horses. The ground was changed by the German artillery fire into a desert covered with many corpses. The interiors of Point du Jour and Moscou were not passable after the battle until they had been cleared.

Such was the storm of fire which the French had to face once their own artillery was partly silenced. And along the left of their position they faced it successfully. Driven from the blazing farms, they held the entrenched slopes none the less doggedly. Up to a certain point the Germans made progress, that point being within close range of the French main position. Thus, at one o'clock—when, after an unaccountable delay, Moltke's *aide-de-camp* reached Steinmetz and told him not to precipitate his attack—the infantry were already in the woods in the hollow. The French had no intention of making a prolonged resistance here, and in the next hour they let go the woods and drew back their advanced troops to the slope beyond, though not till they had made the Germans pay dearly for their success.

St. Hubert then became the object of attack. Two German corps, the 7th and 8th (Von Goeben and Zastrow), had now their artillery in position. St. Hubert was crumbling under the shower of shells. The batteries further back on the crest of the French slope were all but silent. Forced to change their position continually, sometimes after firing only a single gun, they hardly counted for anything in the struggle. It had become a fight of French rifles against German rifles and cannon.

The quarries and gravel-pits south of St. Hubert were occupied after a sharp fight. Regiment after regiment, each company working independently under its captain, pressed up to St. Hubert, till at last a thick German firing-line was lying down two hundred yards from its ruined walls, blazing away at the French garrison, the German artillery now devoting its energies to prevent their being reinforced or supported from the main position. At three o'clock the 60th Infantry pushed up from the woods, and, thus reinforced, the firing line surged forward with the bayonet, and the remnant of the French garrison were made prisoners or driven out by the east gate of the farmyard.

A THICK GERMAN FIRING LINE WAS BLAZING AWAY
AT THE FRENCH GARRISON

The capture of St. Hubert had cost the lives of so many of the senior officers that the troops who had stormed it, belonging as they did to three regiments, found themselves under the command of a major of the both, the sole survivor of the regimental or battalion commanders.

In and around the buildings the victors found some shelter, and opened fire on the French position about Moscou and Point du Jour. But it was only the superiority of their own artillery which, by crushing the French fire, enabled them to retain possession of St. Hubert for a single hour. They got no further; for hours, the ruined farm was the high-water mark of the German advance, and Frossard's main line was not only intact but victorious.

Meanwhile, how had the first three hours of the battle gone on the rest of the field? In the centre Manstein's Corps had made little or no progress. When he opened fire upon the French near Amanvilliers, the ground in front had been so badly reconnoitred, and his view was so limited by the woods to the northward, that he thought he was engaged with the extreme right of the enemy. He therefore boldly pushed forward the left of his own line of guns, with the result that it was promptly taken in flank, and enfiladed by the batteries of the French 6th Corps between Amanvilliers and St. Privat.

Thus, the German gunners had to face a heavy fire, while another storm of shells raked their line from the left. Outnumbered and badly posted, it was no wonder that for some time Manstein's artillery had decidedly the worst of the fight. Some of the batteries were silenced. The teams were brought up to withdraw them, but the horses were shot down in struggling heaps in front of the limbers. And now swarms of French skirmishers pressed forward. At one point, they had for a while several guns in their possession, though they were unable to carry them off. The German infantry came to the rescue. Three times the French rushed forward, and three times they were driven back; and then the artillery of the Prussian Guard began to come into action in support of Manstein, and made the conflict more equal.

The Prussian Guard, led by the Prince of Würtemberg, had been marching northward and eastward to the left rear of Manstein's Schleswigers. When the "cannon thunder" began, its artillery hurried up to the front. But it was soon discovered that, instead of being in a position to turn the enemy's right, the Guards had French troops in their front at St. Privat, and an advanced detachment on their own flank at Ste. Marie aux Chênes.

This village, a mass of stone houses, with gardens surrounded by walls and hedges, and with very little cover for the attack within a thousand yards of its outer fences, was held by a French regiment, the 94th of the line, two and a half battalions strong, and commanded by the veteran Colonel Geslin. The Germans waited to attack it until the heads of the Saxon columns, moving still further to the westward, began to appear beyond the village. Meanwhile, it was shelled by the batteries of the Guard. When at last, the Saxons were ready to cooperate, seven of their battalions moved against the village from the west, while four battalions of the Guard attacked from the south.

Advancing by successive rushes, lying down to fire, and then pushing on again, the attack reached a point two hundred yards from the village. Then, after a long burst of rifle fire, Saxons and Guardsmen dashed in with the bayonet. The Frenchmen made a hard fight, especially at the head of the village street, where Von Eckert, the colonel of the leading Guard battalion, was killed. But to have protracted the defence would have been to risk being cut off, and Geslin withdrew the bulk of his force to the main French position, his defence and retreat ill the face of such superior forces being alike honourable. This was at half-past three, the capture of Ste. Marie, on the German left, coming just after that of St. Hubert, on their right, both being alike advanced posts outside the French main position.

And now the crisis of the fight was approaching. The artillery began to concentrate its fire on St. Privat, and while the Guards waited for the order to attack it in front, the Saxons were sweeping round to the northward by Roncourt, in order to outflank it, and, perhaps, even take it in rear. As the heads of the Saxon columns gained the Orne valley, the Crown Prince sent some of his squadrons away towards the Moselle to cut the railway and telegraph lines between Metz and Thionville. They did their work effectually. There certainly should have been French cavalry watching the valley, but Bazaine's troopers were standing idly by their horses here and there at various points behind his long line.

For nearly an hour and a half the storm of bursting shells descended upon St. Privat, and swept the crest of the heights around and beyond it. The French artillery was gradually silenced, some of the batteries because they were already running short of ammunition. On the other side more than two hundred guns, drawn up in a line a mile and a half long, were hurling destruction and death upon the devoted village. House after house collapsed. Of the *mairie*, in the centre of the village, only a few fragments of the walls were standing. Towards five o'clock the lull in the French rifle fire, the silence of Canrobert's batteries, the sight of a column moving southwards near St. Privat, all suggested to Würtemberg that the 6th Corps was ready to let go its hold of the village under any serious pressure. So, the word was given for the leading divisions of the Guard, 15,000 strong, the picked soldiers of all Prussia, the men who had broken the Austrian centre at Sadowa, to advance to the attack.

On they went, drums beating, battle-flags waving in the sultry air, their generals and field officers mounted, at the head of brigades and regiments. General von Rape's division marched on the left of the St. Privat road, General von Budritzki's on the right to the south of it, each in its massive column of half-battalions; and as they moved out, they looked not as if they were upon a fire-swept battlefield, but as if they were drawn up for some grand parade under the eyes of the king, on the dusty Tempelhof Platz at Berlin. Before them, with gentle unbroken slope, a mile and a half of open ground rose up towards the hill-top where St. Privat just showed its first houses and its church tower above the crest.

The poplar avenue of the high road linked it with Ste. Marie. There had been of late only a dropping fire from the village, but now from the houses and the hill-top came the sharp volleys of the *chassepot*, and a rain of lead began to patter on the sunburnt slope. But as yet the range was too long for the fire to do much damage. Then the leading companies broke into lines of skirmishers, replying to the French volleys, while the columns pressed on behind them, continually reinforcing them. But as the range lessened, the chassepot *fire* from the crest rose into a wild storm, the levelled rifles pouring out their bullets as fast as deft hands could work levers and triggers. The Guardsmen were falling fast. In a few minutes, all the mounted officers were down.

Of the *Jäger* battalion which led the left attack seventeen officers had fallen, and a young ensign found himself in command of the handful of riflemen that were still marching onwards. "Forward! Forward!" rang out the voices of the leaders, as with waving swords they moved in front of their men, and dropped one by one. Now there were only 600 yards to the crest, but here the Guards were going down like grass before a scythe. They could advance no further, but they would not go back. They lay down, and replied to the fire of the defenders. Many of them never rose again.

Along that terrible hillside there stretched before long a broad belt of dead, wounded, and dying, piled up in places three and four deep.

THE CHASSEPOT FIRE FROM THE CREST
ROSE INTO A WILD STORM

Of the 15,000 who advanced to the attack, 4,500 were struck down. It was an heroic failure, and it taught the lesson that against the modern rifle even the best infantry could no longer advance in the massive columns that had decided the fate of many a European battlefield.

To the right of the Guards, Manstein had begun to push forward an attack against Amanvilliers, but when he saw the failure before St. Privat he checked his own advancing battalions. It was clear that nothing more could be done against the French on this part of the field until the turning movement of the Saxons had begun to tell upon them. Meanwhile the fire of nearly three hundred guns, ranged in a vast semi-circle, was concentrated upon St. Privat.

On the German right, where the First Army under Steinmetz faced the French left under Frossard and Leboeuf, fortune had been equally adverse to the invaders. The 7th and 8th Corps had, it is true, silenced the French artillery, and captured the farm of St. Hubert and the quarries of Rozerieulles to the south of it, but the French main position was as solid as ever; and though the farms of Moscou and Point du Jour were bursting into flames under the German shell fire, the men who held the crest of the hill between and on either side of them were not of the kind that can hi driven from their position by a mere bombardment, however terrible.

But Steinmetz, seeing the farms blazing, and noticing that the French artillery was absolutely silent and their rifle fire seemed dying away, came to the conclusion that they were about to retreat. He wrote an order to his cavalry commander telling him that he was to push through the Gravelotte defile, wheel left at St. Hubert, and charge the enemy, "who was inclined to give way." The charge was to be continued "right up to the glacis of Metz." Several batteries were to cross the valley with the cavalry, and to open fire from near St. Hubert at close range, and the infantry was to advance over the ground swept by the victorious squadrons.

So nearly a third of the guns limbered up, and began to trot down the narrow road that led across the valley. With them went a regiment of *Uhlans* (the 4th), and a great mass of heavy *cuirassier* cavalry, and at the same time the infantry already engaged with the French began to push forward from St. Hubert. But Steinmetz had made a bad mistake—a mistake that cost him his command. The enemy was not in the least inclined to give way.

On the contrary, the temporary silence of so many of the German guns gave them the chance they wanted to bring back their own batteries into action. As the head of the column of German artillery, lancers, and cuirassiers began to come up the slope out of the defile, a hurricane of shells and bullets swept down from the opposite crest. Between the blazing farms, and right and left of them, the white smoke of cannon, *mitrailleuse*, and *chassepot* rose in a dense bank, torn here and there by the long flashes of the guns. A crowd of wounded and unwounded fugitives from St. Hubert struggled to pass the advancing column. The teams of a couple of artillery tumbrils in the first battery took fright, and madly plunged down the defile.

Bursting shells and showering bullets began to strike down men and horses, and the narrow way was blocked by a struggling mass of horses, men, waggons, and guns. Out of the confusion four batteries and the lancer regiment pushed up to St. Hubert; but in one battery the first gun stopped short with all its horses killed, the other five were no sooner in position than their teams broke away in a mad gallop down the crowded road. Then the guns opened against the French, only to lose rapidly the greater part of the brave officers and men who served them; while the *Uhlans*, seeing that a charge would have been mere madness, halted at the edge of the wood as an escort to the artillery, and there lost men and horses, without being able to attempt anything against the French line.

Rearwards the *Cuirassiers* and the other batteries moved back to Gravelotte, but they were followed by a confused crowd of broken infantry, for Frossard had charged with the bayonet, recaptured the quarries, and for the moment broken the front line of the German attack. The woods in the hollow were full of wounded and unwounded men who had given up the fight. Others, many of them unhelmeted and without their weapons, straggled back to Gravelotte, where efforts were made to rally them.

Thus, at St. Hubert four German batteries were being destroyed, while about Gravelotte the rest of the guns were working to regain their superiority over the French artillery, and along the valley a number of isolated attacks on the French front were breaking uselessly like waves upon a reef. So far it did not look like victory for Germany; but then only half the infantry and not all even of the artillery had been brought into action.

On right and left two huge masses were approaching the scene of action. Northwards the Saxons were closing in upon Roncourt, and behind the German right the French saw, about six o'clock, what looked like a great sea of moving helmets flashing in the western sun.

German Hussar

It was the 2nd Corps, the Pomeranians, under Franzecky, hurrying up in three columns to the rescue of the First Army. Canrobert, on the French right, was terribly short of ammunition. His men had fired so fast in the repulse of the Guard that their pouches were empty. They were looking for cartridges in the pouches of the dead and wounded, and they got a small supply and a few shells for the guns from the 4th Corps.

Bazaine had done little all day but watch the fight on the left from near St. Quentin. In response to a pressing' request from Leboeuf and Frossard, who had seen, from the high ground near Point du Jour, the advance of the Pomeranians, he sent the Light Infantry of the Imperial Guard to their help, and a little later moved some of the other regiments and part of his reserve artillery towards the right. If he had had the insight and energy to throw the Imperial Guard and the artillery somewhat earlier, either against the German left or across, the Mance valley against their right, Gravelotte might easily have been a great French victory. But he frittered away his reserves or kept them idle till it was too late.

What a vigorous counter attack towards Gravelotte village might have done was shown by the wild scene of confusion that followed the charge of a single French brigade down the elope south of St. Hubert and towards the woods in the valley. Everything gave way before them. The only battery still in action near St. Hubert was saved chiefly because the wave of the French advance rolled past it on its flank. But everything on the slope was swept away.

The German artillery from the opposite side of the valley checked the French rush with its well-placed shells, but out of the woods there came a mad, panic-stricken rush of German infantry, several regiments mixed together. The mob poured directly towards its own artillery, silencing its fire for the moment, heedless of the threats of officers, who menaced them with sword and pistol.

Even behind the guns they could not be rallied, and the old king and his staff were nearly swept away by the crowd. The French, checked by the shell-fire, withdrew up the slope, but a few minutes later there was another panic as a stampede of frightened horses cleared the Gravelotte road and thundered through the village. Well might Moltke and the king welcome Franzecky's hardy Pomeranians as the cheering column of dust-stained men marched with a springing step down the slope of Gravelotte to restore the fight in the brief interval of summer twilight that remained.

An Incident of the Battle of Gravelotte.

But far away to the northward the tide of battle had turned, though it would be hours yet before the tidings of defeat and victory would reach King William at Gravelotte or Bazaine at Plappeville, such is the vast scale of a great modern battle. Between six and seven the Saxons, after a sharp fight, had driven the French out of Roncourt, and closed in upon St. Privat from the north and north-eastward. This was the signal for the Guards, reinforced by a fresh brigade, to renew their advance against the west side of the village, now a mass of ruins, with many of the houses burning fiercely. But against this new advance there was nothing like the storm of fire that had repelled the first assault.

For a few minutes the *chassepots* poured out their deadly hail; then there was only a dropping fire, and the Saxons and Guardsmen were able to close with Canrobert's lines. But there was still a fierce struggle. In the burning streets and the ruined church of St. Privat, bayonet, revolver, and sabre were busy, and the Frenchmen only gave way as they were forced back by superior numbers. A rumour had spread that the Imperial Guard was close at hand, and they held on doggedly in the hope that once more the Guard would bring victory with the onward rush of its eagles. As the Prussians approached the village cemetery, there was not a shot fired from its wall, and they thought it was abandoned; but they found there the 9th Chasseurs, who held it with the bayonet long after the rest of the place had been captured. It was in the gathering darkness that the 6th Corps fell back along the heights towards Metz, some of Bourbaki's regiments of the Imperial Guard helping to cover their retreat.

The capture of St. Privat made Amanvilliers untenable. Manstein, supported by the 3rd Corps, advanced upon the village as soon as the attack of the Guards had pushed into St. Privat. Amanvilliers was by this time in flames. But L'Admirault held his ground until his colleague's retreat made further resistance impossible. Even then he checked the German pursuit with more than one bold counter-attack, the last of these, a bayonet charge by the light of the burning village, being made by the 41st of the line led by Colonel Saussier, now the chief commander of the armies of the French Republic.

But away to the southwards, where the king and Moltke watched the battle near Gravelotte, the French were still holding their own. Brigade after brigade of Franzecky's corps plunged down into the valley, where what was left of the 7th and 8th Corps were struggling with the soldiers of Leboeuf and Frossard, now reinforced by the Guard.

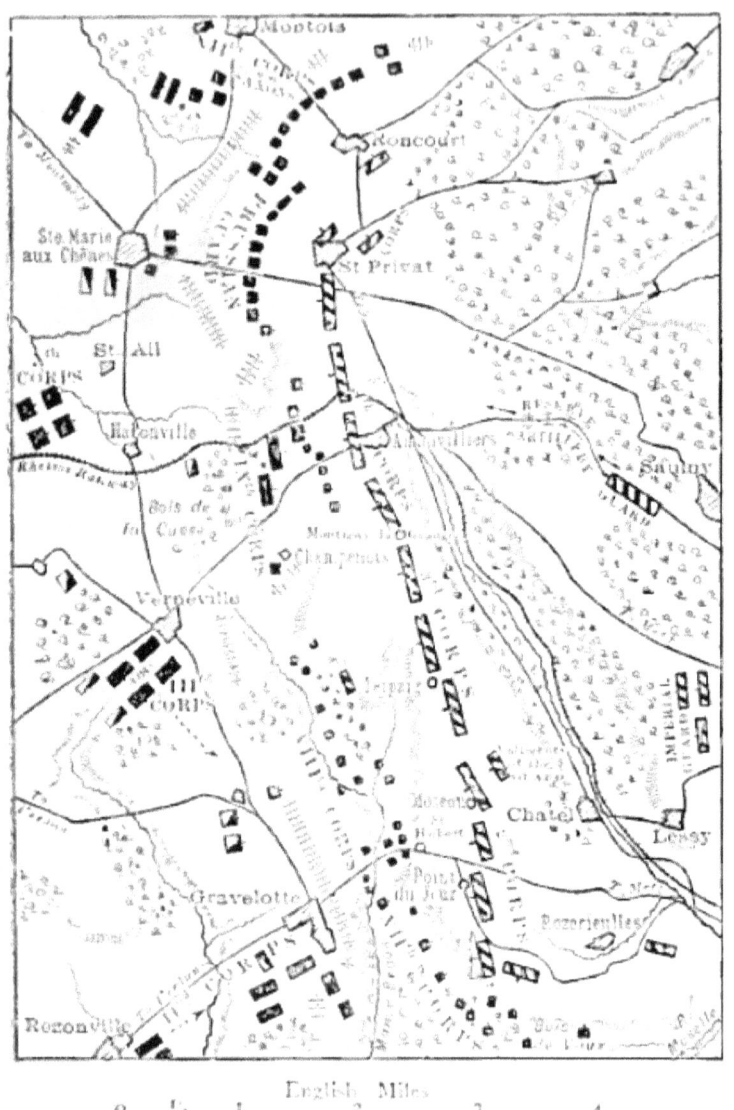

Battle of GRAVELOTTE (ST. PRIVAT) Aug. 18. 1870.
Position about 7 p.m.

Here the French fought with the sense of hard-earned victory. As for the Germans, unaware of the success won far to the north by Prince Frederick Charles, and lately witness of the disgraceful panic round Gravelotte, no wonder the royal headquarters staff watched the fight with anxiety.

Mr. Archibald Forbes, who was on this part of the field, has told how he saw the old king resting with his back against a wall, his seat being a ladder with one end resting on a dead horse, while Bismarck, close by, hid his anxiety by reading, or seeming to read, some letters by the light of some houses set on fire by the French shells. Out of the valley below rose the din of the fight. Suddenly Von Moltke rode up the slope with the tidings that all was well—"it was a victory."

One wonders what was the precise event on which the great strategist based his comforting piece of news. Perhaps it was the recapture of the quarries near St. Hubert, for no other success was won on the right at this hour. Long after—in fact, till next day—on the German side the valley was held only by detached bodies of formed troops, mostly of the 2nd Corps, who were expecting every moment to have to meet a renewed French advance. Behind them, between them, all around them, were crowds of disorganised men, who broke away more than once in local panics. It was not till far into the night that something like order was restored in this part of the field, and officers and men began to realise that they were not beaten, but victorious.

But on the left the German triumph was clear and unmistakable. Although the French artillery kept up a fire from beyond and above Amanvilliers till long after ten o'clock, the plateau here was held by three German corps, and all the French right was in full retreat. How little there was of either rout or panic among the French is shown by the fact that they did not leave a gun or a standard as trophies to the victors. But for all that they were defeated at the point where defeat was most fatal. It might almost be said that there were two battles that day—St. Privat, won by Frederick Charles; and Gravelotte, lost—or all but lost—by Steinmetz.

But even so the success of St. Privat outweighed the failure at Gravelotte. Bazaine was cut off from Verdun and Châlons and flung back upon Metz. Yet as night deepened over the field he did not realise the extent of the catastrophe that had befallen his army. He rode back to Plappeville, while the sky was reddening with the light of blazing villages and farmsteads, and streaked to the northwards with the flaming curves of the shells flying over Amanvilliers. At his head-

Under Fire

quarters, he told his staff he was satisfied with the way in which the army had held its own. But then came tidings from Canrobert and L'Admirault that they were driven back from their positions on the plateau. Still the marshal affected to treat the great battle as a matter of no importance. "In that case," he said, "we shall merely occupy tomorrow the positions nearer Metz, which I would have taken up even if there had been no battle"—a curious self-contradiction, for only the previous day he had talked of continuing his march to the northwards.

Towards midnight the Germans were aware everywhere of their success, though its full extent was not grasped till next day, when the retreat of the French to the ground covered by the forts of Metz left the victors in possession of the battlefield, strewn with thirty thousand killed and wounded, the victims of the great battle, so great that in all our warlike century only two other days—those of Leipzig and Sadowa—saw such vast armies set in battle array. Of those who fell two-thirds belonged to the invading army, so dearly had the victory been bought.

THE FRANCO-PRUSSIAN WARS
1870-71

The Battle of Sedan
September 1, 1870
By Charles Lowe

War between France and Germany had been declared on 19th July, 1870; and as early as August 2nd—so swiftly had been accomplished the work of mobilising the hosts of the Fatherland as the "Watch on the Rhine"—King William of Prussia, now in his seventieth year, took command of the united German armies at Mayence.

These armies were three in number—the First, on the right, consisting of 60,000 men, commanded by General Steinmetz; the Second, in the centre, 104,000 strong, under the "Red Prince" (Frederick Charles); and the Third, on the left, 130,000, led by the Crown Prince of Prussia. An additional 100,000 men, still at the disposal of any of these three hosts, brought up the German field-army to a figure of 484,000.

Altogether, Germany now had under arms no fewer than 1,183,389 men, with 250,373 horses! Many of these, however, had to remain behind in the Fatherland itself to man the fortresses and maintain communication with the front; while others belonged to the category of supplementary troops, or reserves, held ready to supply the gaps made in the fighting field-army of nearly half a million men, as above.

The corresponding field array of the French was considerably inferior in point of numbers (336,500), equipment, organisation, and discipline—in all respects, in fact, save that of the chassepot rifle, which was decidedly superior to the German needle-gun. The French, too, had a large number of *mitrailleuses*, or machine-guns, which ground out the bullets at what they deemed would be a terribly murderous rate. But these instruments of wholesale massacre did not, in the end, come up to the French expectation of them; while, on the other hand, the Prussian field-artillery proved itself to be far superior in all respects to that of the French.

Finally, the Germans had a plan; the French had none. Profound forethought was stamped on everything the Germans did; but, on the other hand, it was stamped on scarcely one single act of their enemies. The Germans had at their head a man of design, while the corresponding director of the French was only a "Man of Destiny."

The first serious battle was fought on the 4th August at Wissemburg, when the crown prince fell upon the French and smote them hip and thigh, following up this victory, on the 6th, at Worth, when he again assaulted and tumbled back the overweening hosts of MacMahon in hideous ruin, partly on Strasburg, partly on Chalons. On this same day, Steinmetz, on the right, carried the Spicheren Heights with terrific carnage, and all but annihilated Frossard's Corps.

It was now the turn of the "Red Prince," in the centre, to strike in; and this he did on the 16th, with glorious success, at Mars-la-Tour, when, against fivefold odds, he hung on to Marshal Bazaine's army and thwarted it in its attempt to escape from Metz. Two days later, the 18th, on very nearly the same ground, there was fought the bloodiest battle of all the war, that of Gravelotte-St. Privat—which resulted in the hurling back of Bazaine into Metz, there to be cooped up and beleaguered by Prince Frederick Charles and forced to capitulate within a couple of months.

Moltke's immediate object was now to dispose of MacMahon, who had retired on Chalons—thence either to fall back on Paris, or march by a circuitous route to the relief of Bazaine. Which course he meant to adopt the German leaders did not as yet know, though it was of life-and-death importance that they should find out with the least possible delay. Meanwhile the Crown Prince of Prussia with the Third Army continued his pursuit of MacMahon, as if towards Chalons; and with him co-operated the Crown Prince of Saxony at the head of a Fourth Army (of the Meuse), which had now been created out of such of the "Red Prince's" forces (First and Second Armies) as were not required for the investment of Metz.

For several days, the pursuing Germans continued their rapid march to the west, but on the 25th, word reached Moltke, the real directing head of the campaign, that MacMahon in hot haste had evacuated the camp at Chalons, and marched to the north-west on Rheims, with the apparent intention of doubling back on Metz. Meanwhile, until his intention should become unmistakably plain, the German leaders did no more than give a right half-front direction to the enormous host of about 200,000 men which, on an irregular frontage of nearly fifty miles, was sweeping forward to the west, Pariswards.

For three more days, this altered movement was continued, and then "Right-half-wheel!" again resounded all along the enormous line, there being now executed by the German armies one of the grandest feats of strategical combination that had ever been performed. The German cavalry had already done wonders of scouting, but it was believed that Moltke's knowledge of the altered movements of Mac-Mahon was now mainly derived from Paris telegrams to a London newspaper, which were promptly re-communicated, by way of Berlin, to the German headquarters—a proof of how the revelations of the war-correspondent—whom Lord Wolseley once denounced as the "curse of modern armies"—may sometimes affect the whole course of a campaign.

Not long was it now before the heads of the German columns were within striking distance of MacMahon, who was hastening eastward to cross the Meuse in the direction of Metz; but his movement became ever more flurried in proportion to the swiftness wherewith the Germans deployed their armies on a frontage parallel to his flank line of march. Alternately obeying his own military instincts and the political orders from Paris, MacMahon dodged and doubled in the basin of the Meuse like a breathless and bewildered hare.

On the 30th August, an action at Beaumont proved to the French the utter hopelessness of their attempting to pursue their Metzward march. As the Battle of Mars-la-Tour had compelled Bazaine to relinquish his plan of reaching Verdun and to fight for his life with his back to Metz, so the victory of Beaumont proved to MacMahon that his only resource left was to abandon the attempt to reach the virgin fortress on the Moselle, and concentrate his demoralised and rabble army around the frontier stronghold of Sedan.

As Sedan, had been the birthplace of one of the greatest of French marshals, Turenne, who had unrighteously seized Strasburg and the left bank of the Rhine for France, and been the scourge of Germany, it was peculiarly fitting that it should now become the scene of the battle which was to restore Alsace-Lorraine to the Fatherland, and destroy the Continental supremacy of the Gauls.

Standing on the right bank of the Meuse, in a projecting angle between Luxemburg and Belgian territory, the fortressed old town of Sedan is surrounded by meadows, gardens, cultivated fields, ravines, and wet-ditches; while the citadel, or castle, rises on a cliff-like emi-

The Crown Prince of Saxony.

General de Wimpffen.

nence to the south-west of the place. Away in the distance towards the Belgian frontier stretch the Ardennes—that verdant forest of Arden in which Touchstone jested and Orlando loved, but which was now to become the scene of a great tragedy—of one of the most crushing disasters that ever befell a mighty nation.

In retiring on Sedan, MacMahon had not intended to offer battle there, but simply to give his troops a short rest, of which they stood so much in need, and provide them with food and ammunition. These troops were worn out with their efforts by day and night and by continuous rain; while their apparently aimless marching to and fro had undermined their confidence in their leaders, and a series of defeats had shaken their own self-trust. Thousands of fugitives, crying for bread, crowded round the waggons as they made their way to the little fortress which had thus so suddenly become the goal of a vast army.

On the 31st of August, after making all his strategic preparations, and taking a general survey of the situation, Moltke quietly remarked with a chuckle:

"The trap is now closed, and the mouse is in it."

That night headquarters were at Vendresse, a townlet about fourteen miles to the south of Sedan; and early on the morning of the 1st of September, King William and his brilliant suite of generals, princes, and foreign officers were up and away to the hillslope of Fresnois, which commands a view of the town and valley of Sedan as a box on the grand tiers of an opera does that of the stage. Bismarck, Moltke, and Roon—the king's mighty men of wisdom and of valour—were also in his Majesty's suite.

"Why," remarked a Prussian soldier on seeing this brilliant assemblage take up its position on the brow of the hill and produce its field-glasses, "why, all this is just the same as at our autumn manoeuvres!"

The morning had broken in a thick fog, under cover of which the Germans had marched up to their various positions, some of the columns having moved off at midnight; and by the time King William had taken his stand on the Fresnois height, a little to the east of where his son, the crown prince, had similarly posted himself in order to direct the movements of the Third Army, the hot September sun had raised the curtain of the mist and disclosed the progress which had already been made by the stupendous battle drama.

This had been opened by the Bavarians, under Von der Tann, who, crossing the Meuse on pontoons, advanced to attack the village of

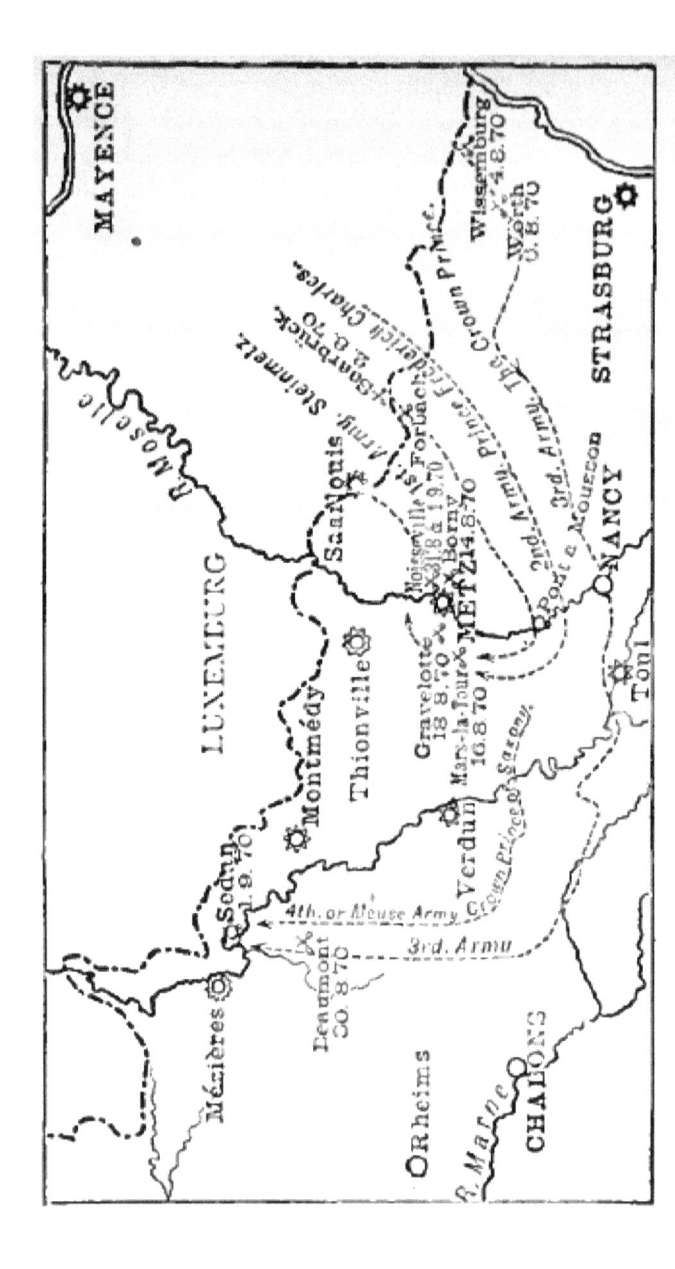

STRATEGIC MOVEMENTS PRIOR TO SEDAN.

Bazeilles, a suburb of Sedan outside the fortifications on the southeast. The Bavarians had already shelled this suburb on the previous evening so severely that pillars of flame and smoke shot up into the air during the night. In no other battle of the war was such fighting ferocity shown as in this hand-to-hand struggle for Bazeilles. For the Bavarians were met with such a stubborn resistance on the part of the French marine infantry posted there, that they were twice compelled to abandon their hold on that place by vehement counter-assaults.

The inhabitants of the village, too—women as well as men—joined in its defence by firing out of the houses and cellars on the Bavarians as they pressed onward, and by perpetrating most revolting barbarities on the wounded Germans. left behind when their comrades had repeatedly to retreat. The Bavarians, on their part, were so dreadfully embittered and enraged by these things that they gave no quarter, acting with relentless rigour towards all the inhabitants found with arms in their hands or caught in the act of inflicting cruelties on the wounded.

The struggle for the village became one of mutual annihilation. House by house and street by street had to be stormed and taken by the Bavarians, and the only way of ejecting the enemy from some of these massively built and strongly garrisoned buildings was by employing pioneers to breach the walls in the rear or from the side streets and throw in lighted torches. Notwithstanding all the desperate bravery of the Bavarians, the battle fluctuated for nearly six hours in the streets of Bazeilles, fresh troops, or freshly rallied ones, being constantly thrown by both sides into the seething fight.

It was not till about 10 a.m. that the Bavarians had acquired hill possession of the village itself—now reduced to mere heaps of smoking ruins; but as the combat died away in the streets it was continued with equal desperation in the adjacent gardens on the north, where the French made a fresh stand, defending their ground with the most admirable valour.

Bazeilles was certainly the scene of some of the most shocking atrocities which had been perpetrated by European soldiers since the siege and sack of Badajoz by the victorious troops of Wellington, and the storming of Lucknow by the infuriated Highlanders of Sir Colin Campbell. But it must be remembered that in all three cases the blood of the assailants had been roused to almost tiger-heat by barbarous provocation from the other side.

Simultaneously with the sanguinary struggle for Bazeilles, the

German uniforms, 1870

battle had also been developing at other points. Advancing on the right of the Bavarians the Crown Prince of Saxony—afterwards King Albert—pushed forward towards Givonne with intent to complete the environment of the French on this side. In order to facilitate their marching, the Saxon soldiers had been ordered to lay aside their knapsacks, and by great efforts they succeeded in reaching their appointed section of the ring of investment early in the day, taking the enemy completely by surprise, and hurling them back in confusion both at La Moncelle and Daigny. At the latter place the French, soon after 7 a.m., made two offensive sallies with their renowned *Zouaves* and dreaded Turcos belonging to the 1st Corps, but were beaten back by a crushing artillery and needle-gun fire.

For some time, the scales of battle hung uncertain on this portion of the field, but reinforcements coming up to the Saxons, the latter made an impetuous push across the valley, capturing three guns and three *mitrailleuses* from the French after half an hour's street-fighting in the village (Daigny), which was now finally wrested from the enemy. Soon after this the Saxon right was rendered secure by the advance of the Prussian Guards, under Prince August of Würtemberg, who had made a wide detour to reach their objective, Givonne.

A considerable body of French cavalry and numerous trains were seen by the Guards on the opposite side of the valley. These offered the corps artillery of the Guards an immediate target for its fire; and scarcely had the first shells fallen among the French columns when the entire mass scattered in all directions in the greatest confusion, leaving everywhere traces of a complete panic. The cavalry of the Guard was sent by a detour to the right, to bar the road to Belgium, and also establish touch with the crown prince's (Third) army, which had been pushed round on the German left.

At Givonne the Guards, at a great loss, stormed and captured seven guns and three *mitrailleuses*, whose gunners were all killed or made prisoners. Beaten out of Daigny and Givonne, the French hereabouts fled in a disorderly crowd into the woods, or fell back upon the centre, which they incommoded and discouraged by their precipitate appearance on a part of the field where they were not wanted. Shortly after, the junction between the Prussian Guards and the crown prince was accomplished, and the ring was now complete. Successes equal to those at Daigny and Givonne were obtained by the Germans in other directions, and the French centre began to recede, though the contest was still prolonged with desperate tenacity, the French fiercely disputing every hill-slope and point of vantage, and inflicting as well as sustaining tremendous losses.

Meanwhile the French right had been hotly engaged. A railway bridge which crosses the Meuse near Le Dancourt had been broken down by MacMahon, but in the early morning the crown prince had thrown some of his troops across the river on pontoons, and was thus enabled to plant his batteries on the crest of a hill which overlooks Floing and the surrounding country. The French, suddenly attacked in the rear, were more than astonished at the position in which they now found themselves; but fronting up towards their assailants with all their available strength, they maintained a prolonged resistance. Their musketry fire was poured in with such deadliness and determination that it was heard even above the deeper notes of the *mitrailleuse*, now playing with terrible effect on the Germans. General Sheridan said he had never heard so well-sustained and long-continued a small-arm fire.

By noon, however, the Prussian battery on the slope above the broken bridge over the Meuse, above La Vilette, had silenced two French batteries near Floing, and now the enemy were compelled to retire from the position. About half-past twelve large numbers of retreating French were seen on the hill between Floing and Sedan, their ranks shelled by a Prussian battery in front of St. Menges. The Germans now advanced and seized Floing in the valley, holding it against all attempts to dislodge them; but it still remained for them to scale the heights beyond, from the entrenched slopes and vineyards of which they were exposed to a murderous fire. Here the French had all the advantages of position, and the Germans could make but little headway in spite of their repeated efforts, so that at this point the battle came to something like a standstill for nearly an hour and a half, the time being consumed in assaults and counter-assaults.

At last, on receiving reinforcements, which brought up their strength in this portion of the field to seventeen battalions, the Germans once more advanced to the attack, and the French saw that something desperate must be done if their position was to be saved. Hitherto the French cavalry had done little or nothing, but now was their chance. Emerging from the Bois de la Garenne at the head of the 4th Reserve Cavalry Division, consisting of four Scots-Grey-looking regiments of *Chasseurs d'Afrique* and two regiments of Lancers, General Marguerite prepared to charge down upon the Germans. But he himself was severely wounded before his imposing mass of picturesque horsemen had fairly got in motion, and then the command

devolved on General Gallifet, one of the bravest and most brilliant cavalry officers in all France—in all Europe.

Placing himself at the head of his magnificent array of horsemen, Gallifet now launched them against the seventeen battalions of the Germans. Thundering down the slope, the shining squadrons broke through the line of skirmishers, scattering them like chaff. But then, in the further pursuit of their stormful career, they were received by the deployed battalions in front and flank with such a murderous fire of musketry, supplemented by hurricanes of grapeshot from the batteries, as made them reel and roll to the ground—man and horse—in struggling, convulsive heaps. Nowhere throughout the war was the terrible pageantry of battle so picturesquely displayed as now on these sacrificial slopes of Sedan, when the finest and fairest chivalry of France was broken and shivered by bullet and bayonet as a furious wave is shattered into spray by an opposing rock.

Moltke wrote:—

These attacks, (supported by Bonnemain's division of four *Cuirassier* regiments), were repeated, by the French again and again, and the murderous turmoil lasted for half an hour, with steadily diminishing success for the French. The infantry volleys fired at short range strewed the whole field with dead and wounded. Many fell into the quarries or over the steep precipices, a few may have escaped by swimming the Meuse, and scarcely more than half of these brave troops were left to return to the protection of the fortress.

The scene was well described by an eyewitness, Mr. Archibald Forbes:—

At a gallop through the ragged intervals in the confused masses of the infantry came dashing the *Chasseurs d'Afrique*. The squadrons halted, fronted, and then wheeled into line, at a pace and with a regularity which would have done them credit in the Champ de Mars, and did them double credit executed as was the evolution under a warm fire. That fire, as one could tell by the dying away of the smoke-jets, ceased all of a sudden, as if the trumpets which rang out the 'Charge!' for the *Chasseurs* had sounded also the 'Cease firing!' for the German artillery and infantry. Not a needle-gun gave fire as the splendid horsemen crashed down the gentle slope with the velocity of an avalanche.

I have seen not a few cavalry charges, but I never saw a finer one, whether from a spectator's or an adjutant's point of view, than this one of the *Chasseurs d'Afrique*. It was destined to a sudden arrestment, and that without the ceremony of the trumpets sounding the 'Halt.' The horsemen and the footmen might have seen the colour of each other's moustaches (to use Havelock's favourite phrase), when along the line of the latter there flashed out a sudden, simultaneous streak of fire. Like thunder-claps sounding over the din of a hurricane, rose the measured crash of the battery guns, and the cloud of white smoke drifted away towards the *Chasseurs*, enveloping them for the moment from one's sight.

When it blew away, there was visible a line of bright uniforms and grey horses struggling prostrate among the potato drills, or lying still in death. Only a handful of all the gallant show of five minutes before were galloping backward up the slope, leaving tokens at intervals of their progress as they retreated. So thorough a destruction by what may be called a single volley probably the oldest soldier now alive never witnessed.

The French had played their last card. they had endeavoured to give the tide of battle a favourable turn by sacrificing their cavalry, but in vain. The Germans now stormed and captured the heights of Floing and Cazal, and from this time the battle became little more than a mere *battue*. The French were thoroughly disheartened, and rapidly becoming an undisciplined rabble. Hundreds and thousands of them allowed themselves to be taken prisoners; ammunition-waggons were exploding in their midst, while the German artillery were ever contracting their murderous fire, and walls of bayonets closed every issue. The fugitive troopers, rushing about in search of cover, increased the frightful confusion which began to prevail throughout the circumscribed space in which the French army had been cooped up.

Still, from the German point of view, a decisive blow was imperative, so that the results of the mighty battle might be secured without a doubt. With this in view, the Prussian Guards and the Saxons from the Givonne quarter were launched against the Bois de la Garenne, which had become the last refuge of the battered and broken French; and these were soon driven back from every point, with the loss of many guns and prisoners—back on the fortress of Sedan in wild turmoil and disorganised flight.

It is to the inside of this fortress that the scene must now change, in order that we may pick up and follow what may be called the personal thread of the great battle-drama, of which we have but given the leading episodes. For it is only at this point that the battle-drama began to enter its most interesting, because most surprising phase.

Marshal MacMahon, the French commander-in-chief, had been in the saddle as early as 5 a.m. When riding along the high ground above La Moncelle he was severely wounded in the thigh by the fragment of a shell, and then he nominated Ducrot his successor in command. By 8 o'clock the latter was exercising this command, in virtue of which he had ordered a retreat westward to Mezières; but presently he was superseded by General de Wimpffen, who had but just arrived from Algeria, and who hastened to countermand the retreat on Mezières in favour of an attempt to break out in the opposite direction towards Carignan. This chaos of commanders and confusion of plans proved fatal to the distracted French, who now began to see that there was no hope for them.

When riding out in the direction of the hardest fighting, Napoleon had met the wounded marshal being brought in on a stretcher. The unfortunate emperor mooned about the field for hours under fire, but he had no influence whatever on the conduct of the battle. He had already almost ceased to be emperor in the eyes of his generals, and even of his soldiers. De Wimpffen sent a letter begging his imperial master "to place himself in the midst of his troops, who could be relied on to force a passage through the German lines;" but to this exhortation His Majesty vouchsafed no reply.

Eventually he returned into the town and, already showing the white feather, gave orders for the hoisting of the white flag. Up flew this white flag as a request to the Germans to suspend their infernal fire; but this signal of distress had not long fluttered aloft when it was indignantly cut down by General Faure, chief-of-staff to the wounded MacMahon, acting on his own responsibility alone. For some time, longer, the useless slaughter went on, and then Napoleon, who had meanwhile taken refuge in the *sous-préfecture*, made another attempt to sue for mercy.

"Why does this useless struggle go on?" he said to Lebrun, who entered the presence of His Majesty shortly before 3 p.m. "An hour ago, and more, I bade the white flag be displayed in order to sue for an armistice."

Lebrun explained that, in addition to the flying of the white flag,

THUNDERING DOWN THE SLOPE THE SQUADRONS BROKE THROUGH THE LINE OF SKIRMISHERS

there were other formalities to be observed in such a case—the signing of a letter by the commander-in-chief, and the sending of it by an officer accompanied by a trumpeter and a flag of truce.

These things being seen to, Lebrun now repaired to where Wimpffen was rallying some troops for an assault on the Germans in Balan, near Bazeilles; and on seeing Lebrun approach with all his paraphernalia for a parley, the angry commander-in-chief shouted: "No capitulation! Drop that rag! I mean to fight on!" and forthwith he started for Balan, carrying Lebrun with him into the fray.

Meanwhile Ducrot, who had been fighting hard about the Bois de la Garenne, in the desperate attempt to retard the contraction of the German circle of fire and steel, resolved about this time to pass through Sedan and join in Wimpffen's proposed attempt to cut a way out towards Carignan. What he saw in the interior of the town may be described almost in his own words.

The streets, the open places, the gates, were blocked up by waggons, guns, and the impedimenta and debris of a routed army. Bands of soldiers without arms, without packs, were rushing about, throwing themselves into the churches or breaking into private houses. Many unfortunate men were trampled underfoot. The few soldiers who still preserved a remnant of energy seemed to be expending it in accusations and curses. "We have been betrayed," they cried; "we have been sold by traitors and cowards."

Nothing could be done with such men, and Ducrot, desisting from his intention to join De Wimpffen, hastened to seek out the emperor.

The air was all on fire; shells fell on roofs, and struck masses of masonry, which crashed down on the pavements.

"I cannot understand," said the emperor, "why the enemy continues his fire. I have ordered the white flag to be hoisted. I hope to obtain an interview with the King of Prussia, and may succeed in getting advantageous terms for the army."

While the emperor and Ducrot were thus conversing, the German cannonade increased in deadly violence. Fires burst out; women, children, and wounded were destroyed, and the air was filled with shrieks, curses, and groans. The *sous-préfecture* itself was struck; shells were exploding every minute in the garden and courtyard.

"It is absolutely necessary to stop this firing," at last exclaimed the emperor, in a state of pallid perturbation. "Here, write this: 'The flag of truce having been displayed, negotiations are about to be opened with the enemy. The firing must cease all along the line.' Now sign it!"

"Oh, no, sire," replied Ducrot; "I cannot sign. By what right could I do so? General Wimpffen is in chief command."

"Yes," rejoined the emperor; "but I know not where General Wimpffen is to be found. Someone must sign!"

"Let his chief-of-staff do so," suggested Ducrot; "or General Douay."

"Yes," said the emperor; "let the chief-of-staff sign the order."

But what became of this order is not exactly known. All that is known is, that the brave Wimpffen scorned even to open the emperor's letter, calling upon His Majesty instead to come and help in cutting a way out; that the emperor did not respond to this appeal; that Wimpffen, failing in his gallant attempt on Balan for want of proper support, then retired on Sedan, and indignantly sent in his resignation to the emperor; that then, in the presence of his Majesty, there was a scene of violent altercation between Wimpffen and Ducrot, in the course of which it was believed that blows were actually exchanged; and that finally Napoleon brought Wimpffen to understand that, having commanded during the battle, it was his duty not to desert his post in circumstances so critical.

Let the scene now again shift to the hill-top of Fresnois, where King William and his suite were viewing, as from the dress-circle of a theatre, the course of the awful battle-drama in the town and valley below. The first white flag run up by order of Napoleon had not been noticed by the Germans, and thinking thus that the French meant to fight it out to the bitter end, the king, between 4 and 5 p.m., ordered the whole available artillery to concentrate a crushing fire on Sedan, crowded as it was with fugitives and troops, so as to bring the enemy to their senses as soon as possible, no matter by what amount of carnage, while at the same time, under cover of this cannonade, a Bavarian force prepared to storm the Torcy Gate.

The batteries opened fire with fearful effect, and in a short time Sedan seemed to be in flames. This was the cannonade which had burst out daring the emperor's conversation with Ducrot, making His Majesty once more give orders for the hoisting of the white flag; and no sooner was it at length seen flying from the citadel than the German fire at once ceased, when the king despatched Colonel Bronsart von Schellendorff, of his staff, to ride down into Sedan under a flag of truce and summon the garrison to surrender.

Penetrating into the town, and asking for the commander-in-chief, this officer, to his utter astonishment, was led into the presence of Napoleon!

For the Germans, had not yet the faintest idea that the emperor was in Sedan. Just as Colonel Bronsart was starting off. General Sheridan, of the United States Army, who was attached to the royal headquarters, remarked to Bismarck that Napoleon himself would likely be one of the prizes. "Oh, no," replied the Iron Chancellor, "the old fox is too cunning to be caught in such a trap; he has doubtless slipped off to Paris."

What, then, was the surprise of all when Colonel Bronsart galloped back to the hill-slope of Fresnois with the astounding news that the emperor himself was in the fortress, and would himself at once communicate direct with the king!

This Colonel Bronsart was a man of French extraction, being descended (like so many in Prussia) from one of those Huguenot families who had been driven into exile by the cruel despotism of Louis XIV. And now—strange Nemesis of history—to the lineal representative of a victim of this tyranny was given the satisfaction of demanding, on behalf of his royal Prussian master, the sword of the historical successor in French despotism to Louis XIV.

The effect on the field of battle, as the fact of a surrender became obvious to the troops, was most extraordinary. The opening of one of the gates of Sedan to permit the exit of the officer bearing the flag of truce gave the first impression of an approaching capitulation. This gradually gained strength until it acquired all the force of actual knowledge, and ringing cheers ran along the whole German line of battle. Shakoes, helmets, bayonets, and sabres were raised high in the air, and the vast army swayed to and fro in the excitement of an unequalled triumph.

Even the dying shared in the general enthusiasm. One huge Prussian, who had been lying with his hand to his side in mortal agony, suddenly rose to his feet as he comprehended the meaning of the cries, uttered a loud "Hurrah!" waved his hands on high, and then, as the blood rushed from his wound, fell dead across a Frenchman.

On Bronsart returning to the king with his momentous message, murmured cries of "*Der Kaiser ist da!*" ran through the brilliant gathering, and then there was a moment of dumfounded silence.

"This is, indeed, a great success," then said the king to his retinue. "And I thank thee (turning to the crown prince) that thou hast helped to achieve it."

With that the king gave his hand to his son, who kissed it; then to Moltke, who kissed it also. Lastly, he gave his hand to the chancellor,

SEDAN

and talked with him for some time alone.

Presently several other horsemen—some escorting-troopers—were seen ascending the hill. The chief of them was General Reille, the bearer of Napoleon's flag of truce.

Dismounting about ten paces from the king, Reille, who wore no sword and carried a cane in his hand, approached his Majesty with most humble reverence, and presented him with a sealed letter.

All stepped back from the king, who, after saying, "But I demand, as the first condition, that the army lay down their arms," broke the seal and read—

> *Monsieur*, my Brother,—Not having been able to die in the midst of my troops, it only remains for me to place my sword in the hands of your Majesty. I am your Majesty's good brother,
>
> Napoleon.
>
> Sedan, 1st September.

Certainly, it seemed that the emperor might have tried very much harder than he had done to die in the midst of his troops, but his own heart was his best judge in this respect.'

On reading this imperial letter, the king, as well he might, was deeply moved. His first impulse, as was his pious wont, was to offer thanks to God; and then, turning to the silent and gazing group behind him, he told them the contents of the imperial captive's letter.

The crown prince with Moltke and others talked a little with General Reille, whilst the king conferred with his chancellor, who then commissioned Count Hatzfeldt to draft an answer to the emperor's missive.

In a few minutes it was ready, and His Majesty wrote it out sitting on a rush-bottomed chair, while another was held up to him by way of desk:—

> *Monsieur*, my Brother,—Whilst regretting the circumstances in which we meet, I accept your Majesty's sword, and beg you to appoint one of your officers, provided with full powers, to treat for the capitulation of the army which has fought so bravely under your command. On my part I have nominated General von Moltke for this purpose. I am your Majesty's good brother,
>
> William.
>
> Before Sedan, 1st September, 1870.

While the king was writing this answer, Bismarck held a conversa-

MEETING OF WILLIAM AND NAPOLEON.

tion with General Reille, who represented to the chancellor that hard conditions ought not to be imposed on an army which had fought so well.

"I shrugged my shoulders," said Bismarck.

Reille rejoined that, before accepting such conditions, they would blow themselves up sky-high with the fortress.

"Do it, if you like; *faites sauter*," replied Bismarck; and the king's reply was now handed to the envoy of the captured emperor.

The twilight was beginning to deepen when General Reille rode back to Sedan, but his way was lighted by the lurid gleam of the conflagrations in and around the fortress which crimsoned the evening sky. And swift as the upshooting flames of shell-struck magazine, flew all around the circling German lines the great and glorious tidings that the emperor with his army were prisoners of war!

In marching and in fighting, the troops had performed prodigies of exertion and of valour, but their fatigues were for the time forgotten in the fierce intoxication of victory; and when the stars began to twinkle overhead, and the hilltops around Sedan to glow with flickering watch-fires, up then arose from more than a hundred thousand grateful German throats, loud and clear through the ethereal summer night, the deeply pious strains of "Now thank we all our God;" and then the curtain of darkness fell on one of the most tragic and momentous spectacles ever witnessed by this age of dramatic change and wonders.

Mr. Archibald Forbes—the prince, if not the father, of war-correspondents—wrote:

> Before going to sleep, I took a walk round the half-obliterated ramparts which surround the once fortified town of Donchery. The scene was very fine. The whole horizon was lurid with the reflection of fire. All along the valley of the Meuse, on either side, were the bivouacs of the German host. Two hundred thousand men lay here around their king. On the horizon glowed the flames of the burning villages, the flicker occasionally reflecting itself on a link of the placid Meuse. Over all the quiet moon waded through a sky cumbered with wind-clouds.
>
> What were the Germans doing on this their night of triumph? Celebrating their victory by wassail and riot? No. There arose from every camp one unanimous chorus of song, but not the song of ribaldry. Verily they are a great race these Germans—a masterful, fighting, praying people; surely in many respects not

unlike the men whom Cromwell led. The chant that filled the night air was Luther's hymn, the glorious—

'*Nun danket alle Gott*,'

the 'Old Hundredth' of Germany. To hear this great martial orchestra singing this noble hymn under such circumstances was alone worth a journey to Sedan, with all its vicissitudes and difficulties.

Of the 200,000 men whom the Germans had marched up towards Sedan, only about 120,000 had taken actual part in the battle; and of these their glorious victory had entailed a loss of 460 officers and 8,500 men in killed and wounded. The French, on the other hand, had to lament the terrible loss of 17,000 killed and wounded, and 24,000 prisoners taken on the field (including 3,000 who had fled over into Belgium and been disarmed). On the part of the Germans, the Bavarians and the men of Posen had been the heaviest sufferers.

On the night of the battle King William returned to Vendresse, "being greeted," as he himself wrote, "on the road by the loud hurrahs of the advancing troops, who were singing the national hymn," and extemporising illuminations in honour of their stupendous victory; while Bismarck, with Moltke, Blumenthal, and several other staff-officers, remained behind at the village of Donchery—a mile or two from Sedan—to treat for the capitulation of the French army.

For this purpose, an armistice had been concluded till four o'clock next morning. The chief French negotiators were Generals de Wimpffen and Castelnau—the former for the army, the latter for the emperor.

Both pleaded very hard for a mitigation of Moltke's brief but comprehensive condition—unconditional surrender of Sedan and all within it. But the German strategist was as hard and unbending as adamant; and when De Wimpffen, with the burning shame of a patriot and the grief of a brave soldier convulsing his heart, talked of resuming the conflict rather than submit to such humiliating terms, Moltke merely pointed to the 500 guns that were now encircling Sedan on its ring of heights, and at the same time invited Wimpffen to send one of his officers to make a thorough inspection of the German position, so as to convince himself of the utter hopelessness of renewed resistance.

The negotiations lasted for several hours, and it was past midnight when the broken-hearted De Wimpffen and his colleagues returned to Sedan, having meanwhile achieved no other result than the prolongation of the armistice from 4 to 9 a.m. on the 2nd September, at which hour to the minute, said Moltke, the fortress would become the target of half a thousand guns unless his terms were accepted.

On returning to Sedan about 1 a.m., De Wimpffen at once went to the emperor to make a report on the sad state of affairs, and beg His Majesty to exert his personal influence to obtain more favourable terms for the army. For this purpose, Napoleon readily undertook to go to the German headquarters at 5 a.m.

Soon after he had driven out of the fortress, Wimpffen called a council of war, consisting of all the commanding generals, and put the question whether further resistance was possible. It was answered in the despairing negative by all the thirty-two generals present, save only two, Pellé and Carré de Bellemare; while even these two in the end acquiesced in the absolute necessity of accepting Moltke's terms on its being shown them that another attempt to break through the investing lines would only lead to useless slaughter. For in the course of the night the Germans had further tightened their iron grip on the fortress, and thickened the girdle of their guns. No; there was clearly nothing left for the poor, demoralised French but to yield to the inevitable, and their only chance lay in the hope that the emperor himself would be able to procure some mollification of their terrible fate.

But the hope proved a vain one. Driving forth with several high officers from the fortress about 5 a.m., the emperor, who was wearing white kid gloves and smoking his everlasting cigarette, sent on General Reille to Donchery in search of Bismarck; and the latter, "unwashed and unbreakfasted," was soon galloping towards Sedan to learn the wishes of his fallen Majesty.

He had not ridden far when he encountered the emperor, sitting in an open carriage, apparently a hired one, in which were also three officers of high rank, and as many on horseback. Bismarck had his revolver in his belt, and on the emperor catching sight of this he gave a start; but the chancellor, saluting and dismounting, approached the Emperor with as much courtesy as if he had been at the Tuileries, and begged to know His Majesty's commands.

Napoleon replied that he wanted to see the king, but Bismarck explained that this was impossible, His Majesty being quartered fourteen miles away. Had not the king, then, appointed any place for him, the emperor, to go to?

Bismarck knew not, but meanwhile his own quarters were at His Majesty's disposal. The emperor accepted the offer, and began to drive slowly towards Donchery, but, hesitating on account of the possible crowd, stopped at a solitary cottage, that of a poor weaver, a few hundred paces from the Meuse bridge, and asked if he could remain there. Bismarck said:—

I requested my cousin to inspect the house, and he reported that, though free from wounded, it was mean and dirty. '*N'importe*,' said Napoleon, and with him I ascended a rickety, narrow staircase. In a small, one-windowed room, with a deal table and two rush-bottomed chairs, we sat alone for about an hour—a great contrast to our last meeting in the Tuileries in 1867. (the year of the Paris Exhibition). Our conversation was a difficult thing, wanting, as I did, to avoid touching on topics which could not but painfully affect the man whom God's mighty hand had cast down.

Whenever Napoleon led this conversation, as he was for ever doing, to the terribly hard terms of the capitulation, Bismarck met him with the assurance that this was a purely military question, and quite beyond his province. Moltke was the man to speak to about such things.

In the meantime, efforts, had been made to find better accommodation for the emperor, and this was at last discovered in the Chateau Bellevue, a little further up the Meuse. Leaving Napoleon in the weaver's cottage, Bismarck hurried back to his quarters on the market-place at Donchery to array himself in his full uniform, and then, as he said, "I conducted His Majesty to Bellevue, with a squadron of *Cuirassiers* as escort." At the conference, which now began, the emperor wished to have the king present, from whom he expected softness and magnanimity; but His Majesty was told that his wish in this respect could not possibly be gratified until after the capitulation had been signed.

Oh! if he could but see and plead with the king—was the anguished emperor's constant thought; but the king took very good care, or his counsellors for him, that he should not expose himself to any personal appeal for pity until the German Army had safely garnered all its splendid harvest of victory.

Meanwhile De Wimpffen had come out of Sedan with the despairing decision of the council of war, and the determination to accept Moltke's inexorable terms. But even Moltke, the least sentimental and emotional of men, could not help feeling a genuine throb of pity for the very hard fate of De Wimpffen—a man of German origin, as his name implied—on whom it thus fell to sign away the existence of an army, of which he had not been four-and-twenty hours in supreme command. Napoleon, the crowned cutthroat of the *coup d'état*, the sawdust "Man of Destiny," the intriguer, the selfish adventurer, the author of the meddling policy which had involved his country in this unparalleled calamity—this "Napoleon the Little" had richly deserved his fate. But as for De Wimpffen—no wonder that *his* misfortune even touched the adamantine heart of his German co-signatory to the capitulation.

After his interview with Napoleon, Bismarck rode to Chéhery (on the road to Vendresse), in the hope of meeting the king and informing him how things stood. On the way he was met by Moltke, who had the text of the capitulation as approved by His Majesty; and on their return to Bellevue it was signed without opposition.

By this unparalleled capitulation 83,000 men were surrendered as prisoners of war in addition to the fortress of Sedan with its 138 pieces of artillery, 420 field-guns, including 70 *mitrailleuses*, 6,000 horses fit for service, 66,000 stand of arms, 1,000 baggage and other waggons, an enormous quantity of military stores, and three standards. Among the prisoners yielded up were the emperor and one of his field-marshals (MacMahon), 40 generals, and 2,825 various other officers, all of whom, by the special mercy of King William, were offered release on parole, though only 500 of them took advantage of this condition, the others being sent to Germany. By the catastrophe of Sedan, the French had lost—in killed, wounded, and prisoners—no fewer than 124,000 men at one fell swoop!

With the capitulation sealed and signed, Bismarck and Moltke now hastened back to the king, whom they found on the heights above Donchery about noon. His Majesty ordered the important document to be read aloud to his numerous and brilliant suite, which included several German princes.

Now that an appeal *ad misericordiam* had been put out of the emperor's power, the king, accompanied by the crown prince, rode down to the *château* of Bellevue to meet the fallen monarch. His Majesty wrote to Queen Augusta:

> At one o'clock, I and Fritz set out, accompanied by an escort of cavalry belonging to the staff. I dismounted at the *château*, and the emperor came out to meet me. The visit lasted for a quar-

KING WILLIAM STARTED ON A RIDE THROUGH ALL THE POSITIONS OCCUPIED BY THE GERMAN ARMIES.

ter of an hour. We were both deeply moved. I cannot describe what I felt at the interview, having seen Napoleon only three years ago, at the height of his power.

And now, while the crushed and broken-hearted emperor was left to spend his last day on the soil of France prior to his departure for the place of his detention at Wilhelmshöhe, near Cassel (once, strange to say, the residence of his uncle, King Jerome of Westphalia), King William, accompanied by Moltke, Roon, Bismarck, and the rest of his paladins, started on a ride through all the positions occupied by the German Armies round Sedan. For five long hours, over hill and dale, from battery to battalion, and from corps to corps, through all the various tribes of the Fatherland in arms, rode the brilliant cavalcade, greeted with triumphant music and frantic cheering wherever it went.

The king wrote:—

I cannot describe the reception given me by the troops, nor my meeting with the Guards, who have been decimated. I was deeply affected by so many proofs of love and devotion.

No wonder the Germans very nearly went mad with joy. For no victory, had ever been like this crowning masterpiece of Moltke's genius—so colossal, so complete, so momentous in its political results—which converted the French Empire into a Republic and the Germanic Confederation into an Empire.

THE FRANCO-PRUSSIAN WARS
1870-71

The Battle of Saarbrück August 2, 1870
By Archibald Forbes

The pleasant little frontier town of Saarbrück was a very interesting place at the beginning of the Franco-German war. Within the distance of a mile from the low heights covering Saarbrück towards the west, ran the frontier line dividing France from Germany. The place was being held "on the bounce," for its garrison consisted merely of one battalion of the Hohenzollern infantry regiment and two squadrons of the 7th Rhineland Uhlans. All along this frontier line down in the broad smooth valley between the Saarbrück heights and the loftier and more abrupt Spicheren heights inside of the French border, the hostile piquets and videttes confronted each other.

As one stood in front of the little "Bellevue" public-house on the Reppertsberg, one saw in the plain below among the trees a Prussian piquet of *Uhlans* and infantry; and on the little knolls further in advance the videttes circling singly, their lance-pennons fluttering in the wind. Several hundred yards further away, by the side of the Forbach road, was the frontier custom-house which the French now used as a piquet house. Outside of it the red-breeched linesmen were to be seen sitting or lounging about in considerable numbers. In their front was the chain of their videttes. All along the frontier line, to the right and left of this point, there ran this arrangement of outposts confronting each other. On the Spicheren upland a French force was gradually gathering until, by the end of July, the whole of Frossard's army corps was massed on the Spicheren, within gunshot distance of the low heights covering Saarbrück.

In those pleasant early days, while as yet there were no graves on the Spicheren Berg and no shattered men lying in the Saarbrück hospitals or littering the platform of the Saarbrück railway station on the blood-stained stretchers, the opposing piquets and videttes formed quite the diversion of the Saarbrück people. After the day's work was over, the labouring folk used regularly to stroll up to the "Bellevue" to watch, as they drank their beer, the dropping fire, fain to see a German marksman proving his skill by hitting a Frenchman. Both sides were very cautious and few casualties occurred. As yet the Saarbrück hospital contained but two wounded Germans, both linesmen of the Hohenzollern regiment. The French were reputed to be in force in Forbach as well as on the Spicheren Berg—as many, it was said, as 15,000 men. Saarbrück, however, was in no trepidation and kept a good face with its little garrison of some 1,200 men all told.

It was on one of the earliest of those early days that the midday *table d'hôte* in the Rheinischer Hof was broken up abruptly by the report that French cannon were being moved forward to the edge of the Spicheren Berg. Immediately the drummers paraded the town, beating to arms. A company of the Hohenzollerns occupied each of the two bridges and a third marched up the hill and took up a position among the trees skirting the exercise-field. A detachment of the *Uhlans* rode up on to the heights, while the rest stood to their horses in the Central Platz. From the "Bellevue" the French cannon were easily discernible through the field-glass, as they were being drawn forward into position by infantrymen.

Almost immediately came a puff of white smoke from the mouth of one of the guns, and a shell struck on the road close by the little beer-house, bursting as it fell. There was a stampede on the part of the civilians from their beer-mugs in the "Bellevue," and they hurried into cover behind the crest of the height. They were only just in time. Another shell, ricocheting off the road, struck the front of the beer-house, went through the wall as if it had been paper, and burst inside, blowing out the windows and part of the roof. Four more shots were fired, and then the French withdrew their cannon. Their practice, no doubt experimental, was very good—of the six shells fired, three struck the "Bellevue." Two rooms of it had been blown into one, the bar knocked into little pieces, the furniture wrecked, and a great gap in the floor made by a shell on its way to the cellar to cause a smash-royal among the bottles.

The outposts blazed away at each other until dusk. One of the last shots killed a soldier on patrol—he was the first man killed in the war. The poor fellow was hit full on the forehead, and he must have died instantaneously. His comrades carried in the corpse on a stretcher improvised of their rifles. The drops of blood pit-patted on the road as they carried him past, the moonbeams falling on the pale dead face. Quite a lad he was, with the down hardly grown on his face—likely enough a mother might have been thinking of and praying for her lad, little knowing that he was lying stark and cold, waiting for a grave.

The slow days passed in a strange bewildering calm, unbroken save by the trivial skirmishes occurring in the course of the constant reconnaissances and patrolling parties.

Frossard lay passive on the Spicheren save for the "potato-reconnaissances" his hungry soldiers occasionally made, sending out a screen of skirmishers to the front while the working parties dug potatoes with great industry.

Brave old Major von Pestel of the Lancers, who commanded the handful of men holding Saarbrück, had received an order from Moltke to evacuate a place which was regarded as untenable; but von Pestel pleaded successfully to be left where he was, on the undertaking that he would not compromise his little command, but would fall back as soon as serious danger threatened.

Meanwhile he was never out of the saddle. Every afternoon he would come cantering over the Bellevue height with his cheery greeting and his shout, "Come along, English sir! I go to draw de shoots of de enemy!" The French marksmen expended a considerable quantity of ammunition on the worthy major; but the range was long and they never succeeded in hitting him, although certainly he gave them plenty of chances.

But in spite of Major von Pestel's cordiality, it was rather a tedious time. Men asked each other if it were possible that the French on the Spicheren were not aware of the weakness of the land on the other side of the frontier. The Prussian infantrymen and *Uhlans*, it was true, were manipulated dexterously and assiduously to make a battalion seem a brigade and a couple of squadrons a powerful cavalry force; yet it was felt that the place was being held only by dint of sheer impudence—for there were no supports as yet nigh at hand—and that the bubble must burst summarily if Frossard should abandon his unaccountable inactivity. Why the soldiers in red breeches lay so long basking lazily in the sun on the Spicheren slopes the men of Saarbrück could not comprehend; but the day must surely be near now, they said one to the other, when the red-breeches would gird up their loins and roll their columns on over the Reppertsberg, the exercise-ground, and

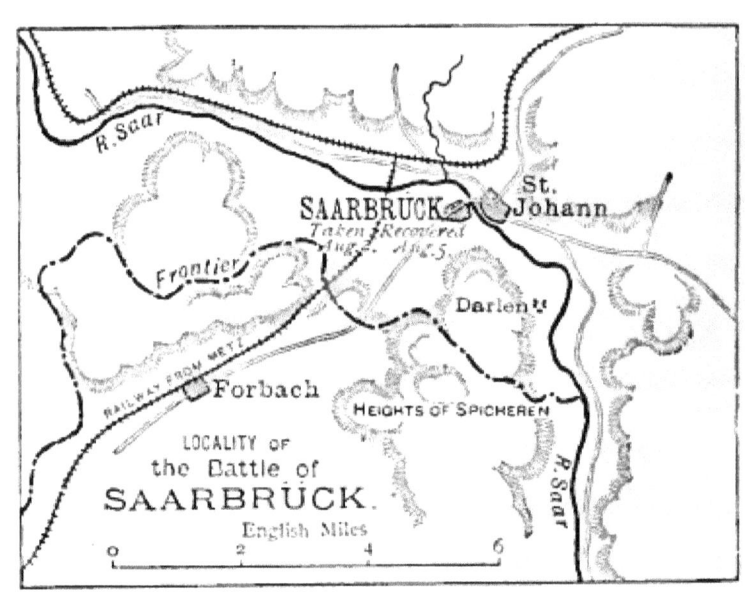

the Winterberg, and across the Saar into the Köllerthaler Wald or the Pfalz.

In their path—surely they must have known it—there stood but an open town, a couple of bridges partially barricaded with barrels, a single battalion of infantry and two reasonably strong squadrons of *Uhlans*. The 1st of August, while the French on the Spicheren Berg were still supine, brought to near Saarbrück what all hoped was the earnest at last of a host, not alone of resistance, but also of invasion. On the afternoon of that day, the 1st and 3rd battalions of the Hohenzollern regiment, with a battery of artillery, reached the vicinity and bivouacked on the edge of the forest at Raschpfuhl, some two miles north-west of the town. General Gneisenau also arrived and assumed the command.

On the morning of the 2nd, when the Hohenzollerns were basking in their sunshiny bivouac, the French emperor, with his son, was travelling by train from Metz to Forbach. The German videttes down the valley heard the gusts of cheering with which Frossard's soldiers welcomed the Head of the State and his heir. Ignorant of the cause, some attributed the cheering to the announcement of a French success somewhere; others ascribed it to an extra issue of wine. How were the honest *Uhlans* to discern that the imperial parent had come to the frontier to make a military promenade wherewithal to throw dust in the eyes of his Parisians, and that "Lulu," as they impertinently styled the heir of the dynasty, accompanied his father that he might receive his "baptism of fire"?

The night had passed in quiet along the frontier, and in the morning, it seemed as if the 2nd of August was to be as monotonous as had been the 1st. General Gneisenau and old von Pestel, now a lieutenant-colonel, had made a reconnaissance from the "Bellevue" and had come back to a leisurely breakfast. The soldiers in the barrack-yards and in the several posts on the environs of the town, slept and smoked and gossiped, their arms stacked as usual; the officers sat under the trees drinking their Rhine wine, and the whole place seemed oppressed by the drowsiness of a fervently hot day.

But the torpor was soon to give place to alert activity. At ten a.m. Saarbrück awoke at the announcement sent in from the outposts that the enemy was at last advancing. The two companies in front of Saarbrück moved at once into the line of defence. The company from St. Johann hurried by at the double to occupy the "Red House." Major von Horn hastened to strengthen the post on the Winterberg,

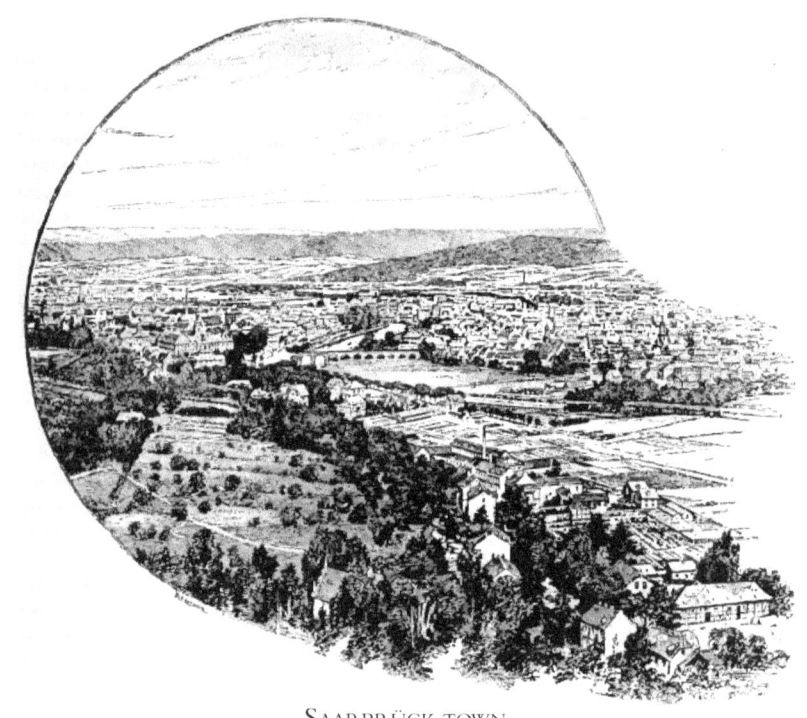

SAARBRÜCK TOWN

which was most imminently threatened. Captain Gründer occupied the Löwenberg, and moved with Leydecker's company and the rest of his own out to St. Arnual, where his rifle fire and the fire of two guns sent to him from Raschpfuhi gave a warm reception to the enemy debouching from the Stiftswald. As some English spectators hurried up to the "Bellevue" height, there rattled past them at a sharp trot a couple of guns which the general had ordered to be put in position on the Exercise Platz. The battery chief waved his hand cheerily as he galloped to the front.

From the "Bellevue" one looked upon an imposing spectacle. Three roads, crossing the plain from the wooded heights on the French side of the frontier, converge on Saarbrück. One of these is the great post-road from Forbach. Another, starting from the village of Spicheren, winds tortuously down the right flank of the precipitous "Rothe Berg"—the "Red Crag"—crosses the hollow and enters Saarbrück between the Reppertsberg and the Nussberg. The third, further to the east, is a mere green track of considerable breadth, which falls abruptly down into the valley by the poplar-clad slope from the plateau towards St. Arnual.

Down all these three roads were flowing from the upland dense and glittering streams of French troops, the stream on the great road flowing swiftest and fastest. The sunrays flashed on the bright bayonets, and threw up from the green or grey background the red and blue of the uniforms. The troops came on in the true careless, irregular French style, with scarcely a pretence of formation, but with a speed that was remarkable. The moment that the head of a column reached the valley, it broke into spray. As file after file reached a certain point, it became dissipated; the nimble linesmen extended further and further to right and left, till by the time that the heads of all three columns were in the valley, an unbroken but loose chain of skirmishers was drawn across the plain several hundred yards in advance.

Then began the steady deployments of company after company, battalion after battalion, regiment after regiment; and almost before one had realised the situation, a long dense line had been ruled along the valley behind the more ragged line of the skirmishers. Squadrons of cavalry streamed down, and forming line at a gallop, rapidly overtook the infantry. Passing through the intervals, they reformed and pushed on to occupy and cover the flanks of the advance.

While all this was going on in the valley, the streams from behind the wood and the hill seemed to flow from a source that never would

LULU'S DEBUT.

run dry. It was hardly a break that was caused in it by the two batteries that came down and wheeled off the road on to the verge of the plateau, the gunners unlimbering and standing ready by the venomous pieces that presently gave fire from their wicked black, mouths. Higher up on the crest were visible other batteries, apparently of larger guns. The peculiarity of the movements described was their perfect quietness and uninterruption. The French *tirailleurs* had already begun to breast the gentle slope leading up to the positions held by the Germans, when the chassepots began to give tongue; and then the silence gave place to a steady rattle of musketry fire, through the smoke of which the main advance moved steadily and swiftly forward.

Bataille's division formed the first line; of it Bastoul's brigade on the right of the main road moved against the Reppertsberg, the Winterberg, and St. Arnual; Pouget's brigade on the left of the road moved towards the exercise-ground. In the second line were the brigades of Michelet and Valazé; the remainder of Frossard's corps, the strength of which reached 35,000 men, followed in reserve. An army corps was marching against a couple of battalions.

Despite the disproportion, the Prussian defence was obstinate. It was only after a brisk combat that the weak detachment were driven from St. Arnual, the Winterberg, and the Reppertsberg. On the latter height, a Prussian half-company met the French skirmishers with the bayonet, and then held them for a time at bay by a fire from behind the hedges.

The final withdrawal was conducted slowly, in excellent order. Baron von Rosen held his company to the last on the exercise-ground. His steadfast soldiers, lying down between the trees, waited until Pouget's skirmishers were within 300 yards, and then poured in a fire so heavy that the French assailants were compelled to halt and lie down for a time.

It was just as Rosen had received a peremptory order to retire that the few spectators who waited to accompany that movement witnessed the descent from the Spicheren height of a great *cortége* of mounted officers. The glittering procession rode forward at a slow trot, crossed the intervening level, and then ascended the slope of the Folster height, around which was massed the regiments of Valazé's brigade.

The *cortége* halted on the low crest of the Folster height; and through the telescope one saw the group open out and leave isolated two personages on horseback, one of whom was clearly discerned to be Napoleon III. The boyish figure on the smaller horse, whose gestures were so animated, was presumed to be the young Prince Imperial; and the cheers which rose above the din of the musketry-fire were taken to indicate the congratulations of the soldiers at the prince's receiving his "baptism of fire"—which, indeed, it has been supposed, was the object of the otherwise pointless demonstration. Not on the Folster Höhe, but nearer to Saarbrück, under the trees of the exercise-ground, is now a stone with a somewhat brusque inscription, which being translated reads:—

> Lulu's Début, 2nd August, 1870. Erected by H. H. Baumann, Veteran of 1814-1815.

It was just as Rosen was withdrawing his company from the immediate front of Pouget's advance that a curious and characteristic incident occurred. Among the few civilians who remained on the exercise-ground to the bitter end was a gallant British officer, Wigram Battye of the famous "Guides," who died fighting in Afghanistan in the campaign of 1878. A soldier was shot down close to him, whereupon Battye, who had been rebelling against the retirement, snatched up the dead man's needle-gun and pouch-belt, ran out into the open, dropped on one knee, and opened fire on Pouget's brigade. Pouget's brigade replied with alacrity, and presently Battye was bowled over with a *chassepot* bullet in the ribs. A German professor and a brother Briton ran out and brought him in, conveyed him later to a village in the rear, plastered successive layers of brown paper over the damaged ribs, and started him off in a waggon to the Kreuznach hospital.

The French did not press upon the orderly Prussian retirement, and, indeed, both of the bridges across the Saar remained in the possession of the Prussians. The firing had almost died out when, soon after noon, the French began to bombard the lower bridge and the railway station from three batteries which they had brought up on to the heights overhanging Saarbrück. One of these was a *mitrailleuse*, the storm of bullets from which swept the bridge so that nothing could live on it, and an unfortunate *burgher*, who did not believe in the *mitrailleuse*, had to alter his views on this subject when the lower part of his person was riddled by the bullets it poured forth.

The Prussian artillery about Malstatt tried with four guns to make head against the French batteries, but had to give up the attempt and retire. The final detachment of Prussians remained under the shelter of Hagen's Hotel while the French were shelling the railway station, but ultimately ran the gauntlet and found refuge in the Köllerthal. The casualties of the day were trivial. The Prussians had eight men killed, four officers and seventy-one men wounded. The French loss amounted to six officers and eighty men.

During their short stay in and about Saarbrück the French behaved with great moderation. General Frossard, on the evening of the attack, sent for the Mayor of Saarbrück, and told him that his orders were very strict against marauding, and that if any cases occurred the townspeople were to take the numbers on the caps of the evil-doers, when the fellows would be severely punished. But there was little occasion for complaint: the French soldiers paid their way honestly. They did, to be sure, drink a brewery dry, but the brewer refrained from reporting them. A corporal attempted to kiss pretty Fraulein Sophie— the *dame du comptoir* of the Rhinescher Hof; but a captain caught him in the act, ran him off the premises, and himself kissed the winsome lass. On the morning of the 6th the Prussian troops were back again in Saarbrück: the French had gone back to the Spicheren position on the previous night.

THE FRANCO-PRUSSIAN WARS
1870-71

The Battle of Champigny November 29–December 2, 1870
By A. Hilliard Atteridge

It was in the second month of the siege of Paris. The pigeon post had brought in news of the gathering of armies on the Loire and in the North destined to come to the rescue of the beleaguered capital; but, so far, there were many hopes but few signs of the promised succour. The iron ring of the German siege-works cut off the city so effectually from the rest of France that it was only at long intervals that some daring adventurer succeeded in passing the enemy's outposts and bringing to the besieged tidings of what was passing just outside the German lines of investment.

On Sunday morning, November 13th, at the outposts near Creteil to the south-east of Paris, a sentry challenged a man who had crept up to his post half-seen in the grey light of the dawn. The man answered the challenge in French, and declared that he was a farmer of Valenton who had, at the risk of his life, passed the German sentries in the dark in order to bring important news into the city. He refused to give his information to anyone but the governor, General Trochu, or one of his staff-officers. He was at last brought to the headquarters at the Louvre, and there Trochu gave him an interview. The farmer said that for the last three days the Germans had seemed anxious and uneasy. He had heard them talking among themselves of something serious that had occurred at Orleans: the force holding the villages to the south of Paris had been reduced, and the troops thus withdrawn had marched away to the southwards. Trochu discussed the news with General Ducrot, his most trusted colleague during the siege. They agreed that it was most probable that the new French Army of the Loire was advancing and pressing the Prussians seriously, and that it had perhaps even won a victory near Orleans.

Next day all uncertainty was at an end. A pigeon arrived from Tours bringing a despatch from Gambetta, and soon all Paris was reading it, for it was posted on the walls with a proclamation from the governor. This was the good news:—

Gambetta to Trochu.
Tours. November 11th, 1870.
The Army of the Loire, under the orders of General Aurelle de Paladines, took Orleans yesterday, after two days' fighting. Our losses in killed and wounded do not exceed 2,000. Those of the enemy are heavier. We have made more than a thousand prisoners, and the pursuit is adding to the number. We have taken two Prussian guns, twenty waggon-loads of ammunition, and a great quantity of carts laden with provisions and stores. The chief fighting was round Coulmiers on the 9th. The *élan* of the troops is remarkable, notwithstanding the wretched weather.

Paris was wild with joy. At last it had been proved that the Prussians were not invincible! The new armies that had arisen at the call of the Republic had done what the legions of the Empire had failed to accomplish. They were pressing on to the rescue of the capital; surely the time w-as come when the army of Paris should burst through the German besieging lines, and join hands with the victorious soldiers of the south and west. The very name of Orleans seemed of good augury. Was it not at Orleans that Jeanne d'Arc had won her first triumph over another invader? Might one not hope that again the tide of war had turned in favour of France at the same historic spot?

The newspapers all called for a grand sortie against the German lines. Everyone felt that the decisive moment was coming—that the fate of Paris and of France would be decided within the next few weeks, or even days. On the 18th there arrived a despatch from Gambetta calling on Trochu to co-operate with the relieving armies by acting vigorously against the Germans before Paris, and so preventing them from detaching any more troops to the help of their armies in the provinces. The generals in Paris were already preparing to act. They had been arranging for a sortie across the Seine from the west of the city, with a view to breaking through the investing lines to the north-west. But now, with a victorious army pressing on the Germans to the southwards, they decided on changing the direction of the blow; and though to the last moment the change of plans was kept secret, and attempts were made to lead the Germans to still expect an

GENERAL CLÉMENT-THOMAS

GENERAL TROCHU

GENERAL VINOY

attack on the side of Mount Valérien, General Ducrot was directed by Trochu to concentrate all the best troops in Paris for a sortie to the southwards, across the Marne, just above the point where it joins the Seine.

The ground in this direction was eminently favourable for such an enterprise. The German line of investment ran across the Marne near Noisy-le-Grand, followed the river bank near Brie, and then ran across a swell of rising ground to Champigny, the river between these two villages curving away sharply towards Paris, the peninsula thus formed being about a mile and a quarter across. The fort of Nogent, on the French side of the Marne north of the curve, commanded the ground within it, and crossed its fire with the guns of the redoubt of St. Maur south of the curve. At the western end of the space thus enclosed the French held Joinville.

If they crossed the river here under cover of the guns at Nogent and St. Maur, they might hope to turn the Prussian outposts out of Brie and Champigny, hold the neck of the peninsula while reinforcements crossed in their rear, and then break through the German lines in their front, their retreat across the river being fairly secure in the event of a disaster. The Marne, before joining the Seine, makes a second and still sharper curve round the height of St. Maur, and a canal cuts across the loop, passing under the hill by a short tunnel. This passage, known as the Canal of St. Maur, played an important pail in the plans for the sortie.

The ground about the loops of the Marne, which was destined to be the scene of one of the fiercest and most prolonged struggles of the siege of Paris, was not so built over as it is at the present time; but it was a suburban rather than a country district, with numerous roads, detached houses, walled parks and gardens, and plantations, so that there was abundance of cover. The large walled parks of Villiers and Coeuilly had been put in a state of defence by the Germans, the walls being loop-holed and the gates barricaded. The park walls stood a little back from the edge of the plateau on which the villages of the same name are built. This line of high ground formed the main position of the Germans, their outposts being nearer the river in Brie-sur-Marne and Champigny.

Nearly a fortnight was spent by the French in preparing for their great effort. There were to be several false attacks, to mislead the Germans and prevent them from moving troops to reinforce the position actually assailed—a position held by portions of the Wurtemberg and the 12th Saxon Corps. These false attacks were to be made by the troops under "General Vinoy's direction, but all the best regiments in Paris were formed into a field-army under Ducrot. In all, there were three armies organised in Paris during November. The "First Army" consisted of the National Guard, under General Clément-Thomas, afterwards one of the first victims of the Commune. Clément-Thomas was rather a politician than a soldier. He had no record of service, and the hundreds of thousands under his command were rightly described as mostly mere "men with muskets."

They had, generally, very little fight in them. They drilled in Paris; they drew their pay and rations; they mounted guard at the ramparts (which no one attacked); and the Government did not venture to put them in line of battle until the closing days of the siege, when they were marched out to be shown what a battle really was, and for the most part they behaved very badly.

The "Second Army," under Ducrot, was composed of very different materials. The infantry were made up of the 35th and 42nd of the line, who had been withdrawn from Rome at the outset of the war, and the line regiments that had formed Vinoy's corps, which he had saved from the catastrophe of Sedan by his splendid retreat from Mezières. These were nearly all the troops of the line that were now left to France—all the rest had been made prisoners at Metz, Sedan, Strasburg, and elsewhere. To bring their numbers up to war strength and repair their losses men had been drafted into them from the depots, and to these had been added reservists who had been late in joining their proper regiments. A *Zouave* regiment thus formed was largely made up of recruits; it was brigaded with the 136th of the line.

The rest of the infantry consisted of thirty-three battalions of mobiles, drafted in from the provinces—the fine battalions of the West, the men of Brittany and La Vendée, Normans from the neighbourhood of Rouen, sturdy countryfolk from Orleans, the men of the central plateau from the Côte d'Or, and fiery, dark-eyed volunteers of the South from Languedoc. The upper valleys of the Seine and Marne sent their contingents, but of the Parisian battalions not one was to take part in the main operation for the rescue of the capital.

The "Second Army" was divided into three corps the first under General Blanchard, the second under General Renault (a distinguished soldier of Africa), and the third under General d'Exéa. A cavalry division, under General de Champeron, was partly made up of old soldiers, partly of new levies. Altogether Ducrot had about 120,000 men

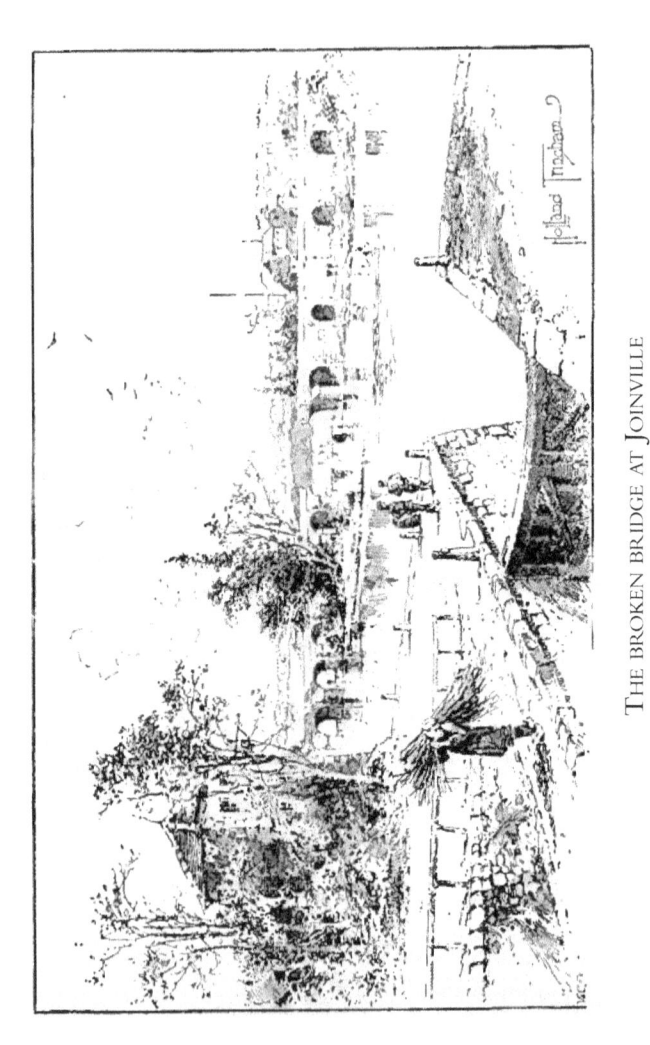

The broken bridge at Joinville

under his command, the pick of the army of Paris.

The "Third Army," under General Vinoy, was composed of very various elements. One brigade was formed chiefly of *gendarmerie* and the depot troops of the old Imperial Guard; a second was made up of custom-house officers and men of the State forest service, with the depot troops of two line regiments. Two line regiments and two brigades of sailors and marines supplied further excellent material; and the other battalions were formed of mobiles from the provinces and regiments of volunteers picked from the Paris National Guard. This army was organised as a single corps of six divisions.

In the first days of the siege, when the defenders of Paris were in a very excited frame of mind, and full of the idea that the best way to resist the Prussians was to recklessly destroy their own property in the neighbourhood of the capital, the fine bridge which crossed the Marne at Joinville had been blown up, its central arch being destroyed and the debris forming a kind of rough dam across the stream. This bridge would have been invaluable for the sortie, but as it was broken temporary means of crossing had to be substituted; and as over 100,000 men had to pass the river, several such bridges would be necessary. The material for these was collected on the Seine within the walls of Paris, and it was decided that on the very eve of battle it should be towed through the tunnel of the canal of St. Maur into the Marne.

Thus, up to the very last moment the preparations for the sortie would be concealed from the enemy. In order to add to the already powerful array of heavy artillery that swept the banks of the Marne, the plateau of Avron was to be seized on the eve of the sortie, and heavy naval artillery placed in battery there by the sailors, so as to be ready to open fire at dawn. Ducrot concentrated his army near the scene of action in the last week of November. His first and second corps (Blanchard and Renault) bivouacked near Joinville and in the park and wood of Vincennes. The third corps (d'Exéa) concentrated to the south of Nogent.

To the north of it gathered the troops destined for the *coup-de-main* against Mont Avron. Southwards, westwards, and northwards, at various points, Vinoy placed in position the detachments that were to make the false attacks. It was a whole series of battles that were thus being prepared, and Ducrot's army was accompanied by an immense train of waggons destined to convey its ammunition and other supplies in the event of its breaking through. The regular ambulances of the army were ordered to follow well to the rear, and reserve themselves for the further stages of the march towards the Loire; while the wounded of the sortie were succoured by the ambulances of the various Parisian volunteer Red Cross societies, and by floating ambulances established on river steamers, which could convey the wounded rapidly and smoothly by water to the central hospitals of Paris.

Proclamations from Trochu and Ducrot were posted on the walls, announcing that a great effort was to be made. Ducrot's, issued at the last moment, ended with the somewhat melodramatic phrase:

> I will return either dead or victorious.

The gates were closed, and no one was allowed to pass the ramparts, the object of this precaution being to prevent possible spies from conveying information to the Prussians. All Paris soon knew where the blow would fall, for the march of Ducrot's troops to Vincennes and Nogent took some days, and was accompanied by so much noisy display that everyone's attention was attracted to the great concentration that was in progress. Finally, on the eve of the sortie, the forts all round the circle of the fortifications poured a storm of shells against the German lines. This wild firing did very little harm, and while hardly effecting anything in the way of preparing the ground for the morrow's fight, it certainly served to keep the besiegers on the *qui vive*.

Yet, with all this, Ducrot persuaded himself that he was keeping the secret of his enterprise. He wrote out his orders at first with blanks for the names and dates, only filling in these on the day before the battle, the 29th of November being selected for the great sortie. These orders, were far too complicated. While the German commanders in France in 1870 contented themselves with broadly indicating to their subordinates what they wanted done, and left to the commanders of corps, divisions, and brigades great latitude in arranging the details of attack. or defence, the French commanders seem to have had a mania for drawing up detailed programmes of their battles, in which every movement was carefully defined as to hour, place, and numbers to be employed, with the result that it any part of the programme failed to come off, all the subsequent movements which depended, on such or such an occurrence being noted by a corps commander were likely to be left unexecuted.

Ducrot's main idea was that Avron having been seized during the night, and several pontoon bridges thrown across the Marne at and above Joinville, in the early morning while the Prussians were distracted by the false attacks, and the immediate field of battle was swept by the guns of St. Maur on the right, and Nogent and Avron on the left, Renault and Blanchard were to cross the Marne and attack Brie and Champigny first, and then the heights beyond d'Exéa watching their progress from the right bank above the bend, and, when certain points were reached by the French attack, crossing on the flank and rear of the German lines. Or supporting the French left by immediately reinforcing it.

On the evening of the 28th everything was supposed to be ready. Ducrot came down to Joinville to watch the throwing across of the bridges, and Trochu was close at hand at Nogent. All round Paris the forts were blazing with the flashes of their heavy guns, and the long rocketlike trails of their shells lit up the sky. North of Nogent, through the cold and rainy evening, 6,000 mobiles were tramping across the valley and up the slopes of Avron, scouts feeling the way in front, and behind long teams of carthorses tugging at the heavy guns which the sailors were to place in position.

Through the dark tunnel of St. Maur came the first of the little tug-boats with the pontoons and framework of one of the bridges trailing behind it. Engineers were at work on the Joinville bridge. They had thrown some more stones down on the rubbish heap under the central arch, and on the mound thus formed had fixed wooden trestles and constructed a foot-bridge. The steamer, with its train of pontoons, made for the arch nearer the bank on the Joinville side of the stream. Under the arch the river was rushing down with a loud ripple that suggested that the stream was in flood. The steamer tried to pass through the arch, but the current first held her and then swept her down below the bridge.

Behind her other boats arrived. The river was black with the great mass of pontoons and boats. Lights flickered here and there, but not many, for it would be dangerous to arouse the attention of the Germans, away in those villages on the kit bank. The attempt to pass the bridge was renewed. It failed again. Then despairing efforts were put forth, but apparently with little method or intelligence. After a while it was realised that so much time had been lost that, even if the materials could be got through, the eight bridges could not be completed before daybreak. In the small hours of the morning the engineers announced to Ducrot that the river was in flood. The attempt must be put off for another day. The bridge material was hidden away, partly behind the island at Joinville, partly in the tunnel and the canal. A hurried council of war was held. Would it not be better to stop the false attacks? There was some hesitation. Then it was resolved to allow the generals to act, and to add one more to a night of mischances it was not till next morning that the commanders of the various detachments told off for these minor sorties were informed that the main effort had been deferred for twenty-four hours.

And now comes the strangest part of the story. It has been proved since then that there was no flood in the Marne that night. The rush of water under the Joinville bridge had been augmented by the ill directed efforts of the engineers, who had added to the mass of debris that blocked the middle of the stream. Men who knew their business would have rather tried to clear away the obstruction under the broken arch before they brought up their heavy convoy of bridge material. The mistake was fatal to the success of the whole operation.

At Avron all had gone well, and in the early morning the naval guns, worked by Admiral Saisset's blue-jackets, opened on the German posts across the Marne. Out to the south-west of Paris, across the loops of the river, Vinoy and Admiral Pothuau stormed the advanced Prussian, posts at Choisy and at the big cattle station on the railway near the village. Elsewhere there were minor sorties. The roar of guns from Avron at first confirmed Vinoy in his belief that all was going well with Ducrot. At the barriers of Paris anxious crowds waited for the news of a great victory. Tidings came that Mont Avron had been occupied, that success had crowned Vinoy's arms at Choisy. The first wounded were brought in along the river by the steamers. But there was no news of the crossing of the Marne. At last came the chilling announcement that the one serious operation of the day had been put off. Something was wrong with the bridges. So Vinoy and his colleagues abandoned the ground they had won, sad at the thought of useless sacrifices made, and blood shed freely, because "someone had blundered."

With the early twilight of the November evening work was resumed at Joinville, and the bridge material was got past the broken bridge, chiefly through the channel behind the island. In the small hours of the 30th the bridges were ready, and before dawn the strong columns began slowly to cross. The temperature had fallen suddenly, and it was bitterly cold, but with the frost there had come fog, which favoured the march of the besieged, and would have concealed their movements still better if the cannonade from the forts had not been resumed. It was hoped the noise would prevent the Germans from hearing the approach of their foes. Perhaps it did. Perhaps they thought that the weak sorties of the previous day indicated the collapse of the great French effort to break their lines.

In any case, it seems to be fairly clear that while they had been on the *qui vive* all through the 29th, they felt a little more secure on the morning of the 30th. The Saxons were to relieve the Wurtembergers at the outposts across the peninsula of the Marne that morning, the latter handing over the care of Brie and Champigny to the former about 6.30, while it was still quite dark. This was again lucky for the French, for the Saxons did not know their way about in the villages. The 107th Infantry held Champigny, and their patrols were searching the roads towards the bend of the river, when about half-past seven, just as it was beginning to get brighter, one of them rushed breathless into the village, calling out that at least four French battalions were coming on after him.

The alarm was sounded through the village, but the French were into the western end of its main street, and, driving the Saxons before them, they gradually cleared the place, and by eight o'clock held the whole of it. The German garrison consisted only of three companies, or about 500 men, and it was no discredit to them that they had to give way before the French column, but it looks as if they might have kept a better watch to their front, and discovered somewhat earlier that a whole army was pouring across the bridges. If the sortie had come the day before there would have been only a brigade of Wurtembergers in position to meet it. Now, besides the Saxons in the first line, the Wurtembergers whom they had relieved were close at hand, and gallopers were sent off to bring them back.

To the left of Champigny another column, linesmen and mobiles of the western departments, advanced through the village of La Plante into the little valley of the Lande, passed the smoking limekilns outside Champigny, and pushed on to the barricaded embankment of the Mulhouse railway, the Germans falling back before it, a thin firing line, that was reinforced as it withdrew. On the higher ground, behind the Germans, a battery came into action, and one of its first shells, bursting on the railway line, wounded General Renault, shattering his leg.

Renault was a soldier of the old school. Though a corps commander, he insisted on being in front of one of his divisions, and he had told his men that their best plan was not to fire, but to press on with the bayonet. He died four days after the battle.

Boissonet, who commanded his artillery, was killed by another shell soon after the fall of his chief. But though the German fire was becoming heavier, and there were serious losses in the dense marching columns that crowded the peninsula, the first rush had been successful. The railway had been crossed, and the French *tirailleurs* were dashing up the hollow of the Lande valley, towards the plateau of Villiers. More to the left Brie, on the river bank, had been stormed, the Germans giving way before superior numbers, and effecting their retreat with difficulty.

And now the French began to press forward against the heights of Villiers and Coeuilly, and the resistance became, more serious. More than once they gained the edge of the plateau only to be driven back by the storm of bullets from the loop-holed park walls. Artillery brought up to close quarters might have cleared away these obstacles, but only a battery of *mitrailleuses* was available, and its stream of balls produced no effect on bricks and mortar. The brave captain who brought it into action was killed beside one of his pieces. Up to noon no impression whatever had been made on the second German line.

Meanwhile, across the river to the south-west, another French column had marched out of Creteil and attacked the Germans in Mesley, only to be driven back with the loss, among others, of its commander. General Ladreyt de la Chavrière, who was shot down while cheering on his men within fifty yards of the Prussian line. To the north of Paris another attack was made from St. Denis, and obtained temporary possession of Epinay. These and other minor attacks prevented the German staff at Versailles from rapidly reinforcing the position which Ducrot was assailing. They did not feel certain till the middle of the day as to which was the main attack.

It was only after one o'clock that D'Exéa brought his corps into action, crossing the river by the bridges north of Brie and pressing the German right. An earlier attack might have had serious results for the besiegers. As it was, the effect of his advance was to renew the fierce onslaught upon Villiery. The 107th and 136th of the line, the Mobiles of the Seine and Marne, the Bretons of Morbihan, and the 4th Zouaves threw their lives away recklessly in the attempt to gain a footing on the plateau. Three times the firing line of the *Zouaves* pressed close up to the north-west corner of the park of Villiers, and three times they fell back, leaving at last nearly all their officers and half the rank and file strewing the ground, killed and wounded.

At four the sun set red in the cloudy western sky, and the darkness came on rapidly, the French drawing off to the villages they had

THE FIRST RUSH HAD BEEN SUCCESSFUL

won, and bivouacking for the night on the frozen ground, without blankets or even overcoats to cover them; for by order of Ducrot all these *impedimenta* had been left with the train on the other side of the river to lighten the load of the men—a blunder for which they had to pay dearly.

Over 100,000 French had been in action, and about 26,000 Germans had successfully held the fortified heights against them. But still the French had won ground which the Germans held in the morning, and in so far they might claim a success. About 2,000 Germans and 3,000 French had fallen in the fight.

There is an old saying about "*lying like a bulletin*," and the bulletin despatched that night from the royal headquarters at Versailles was anything but truthful. This was what King William sent by wire to Queen Augusta:—

> Royal Headquarters, Versailles,
> November 30th, 1870.
>
> Today important sorties were made on the east of Paris against the Wurtembergers and Saxons at Bonneuil-sur-Marne, Champigny, and Villiers, which were captured by the French and afterwards recaptured by our own troops with the aid of our 7th Brigade. Before nightfall less important sorties were made simultaneously towards the north-east at St. Denis against the Guards and 4th Army Corps. I was unable to leave Versailles, as I desired to remain in the centre.
>
> William.

Not a word to show that on this Monday evening the German headquarters were seriously anxious about the situation, seeing that, so far from the villages on the Marne being recaptured, they were held by the French, who were busy fortifying the ground they had won. True, the besieged had not broken out. The attacks on the plateau of Villiers and Coeuilly had been repulsed, but it was also true that the French had not been driven from the ground they had won in their first onset. The fact is that up till now the German staff had sent out true information as to the progress of the war because it had gone in their favour; but the truth about the fighting on the Marne was suppressed for three days, and a false version of the story was officially put in circulation. It may be that the old king was himself deceived by the staff. Of Podbielski—the adjutant-general who was responsible for the official *communiqués*—General Beauchamp Walker, the English *attaché* at the royal headquarters, wrote a few days later:—

> Podbielski told an official lie which is a disgrace to our profession.

The news of the first day's battle was sent out of Paris by a balloon on the night between November 30th and December 1st. It fell at Palais, in Morbihan, the following morning, and the tidings of what was represented as a complete victory were telegraphed to Tours and thence all over France. The despatch was so brief that it led to a most serious misunderstanding. It announced that Ducrot had successfully crossed the Marne and defeated the Germans, and that the French had taken Brie, Champigny, and Epinay.

The mention of Epinay was particularly unfortunate. Gambetta supposed that the place mentioned was not Epinay-sur-Seine, but Epinay-sur-Orge, a good day's journey towards the Loire. He announced that the Army of Paris was in full march for Orléans, and against the advice of his generals he insisted on the Army of the Loire, which had just received a serious check at Beaune-la-Rolande, advancing at all hazards against the army of Prince Frederick Charles. The result was widespread disaster. Two words added to the name in the despatch would have prevented the possibility of mistake.

To return to the battlefield, hundreds of the wounded died of the bitter cold in the early hours of the 1st of December. The soldiers of Ducrot's army, huddled together waiting for the dawn, were chilled through and through, so that sleep was barely possible, and numbers of those who lay on the ground awoke frost-bitten or so seriously ill that they had to be carried to the ambulances. There was little ammunition left in the men's pouches, and before daylight of Thursday, December 1st, Ducrot and Trochu had decided that it would not be possible to renew the attack on the German lines till Friday.

So the Thursday was spent by the French in renewing their supplies of ammunition, rapidly fortifying Brie and Champigny, entrenching the ground between the two villages, carrying off the wounded, and burying the dead. A truce was arranged for these latter purposes in the afternoon. Nor were the Germans less busy. They had expected to be attacked at dawn. When the early hours passed without an advance on the part of the French, they employed this despite in strengthening their hold on the Villiers plateau. General Fransecky took command of the lines facing the loops of the Marne, and reinforced the Saxons and Wurtembergers with some 16,000 Prussians and several batteries.

At four o'clock the truce for the burial of the dead came to an end. It was dark very soon after, and on both sides the soldiers lay down with a tolerable certainty that the dawn would see another great battle.

The first snow of the winter fell during the second night's bivouac. The French had had very little rest, and had suffered terribly from exposure. A day of battle, another of hard work, and two nights passed in frost and snow without even an overcoat, would have been trying even to veterans, and the greater number of Ducrot's soldiers, even in the so-called line regiments, were new levies. The French throughout the war were very careless about their outposts. No wonder that on that snowy Friday morning the soldiers were half-asleep and some of them cowering under cover. Just before dawn there came a rush of German infantry and rifles into Champigny and Brie, and through the plantations in the Lande valley where the French centre lay.

Brie was taken by this sudden onset, and at Champigny the French were swept out of the greater part of the village, and, what was worse, the Mobiles of the Côte d'Or and of the Ille-et-Vilaine broke and fled, a panic-stricken crowd, towards the ridges. Ducrot, who had turned out of his quarters between Champigny and Joinville at the first alarm, met the fugitives as he rode with his staff at headlong speed towards the scene of action. Speaking words of encouragement to some, threatening others with sword or revolver, he and his officers rallied the mobiles and brought them back towards Champigny.

There the French had recovered from the first surprise, and were rapidly driving the Germans out of the place. It was a hard fight, in which again, and again the bayonets crossed in the lanes among the houses. At Brie, also, the village was attacked and retaken by the French, and in the centre, they held their own gallantly against the German onset. From the heights—the scene of the battle of two days before—a hundred German guns opened on the French positions. The heavy artillery of the forts and outworks of Paris and the few batteries of Ducrot's army replied. But in the broken ground, and among the numerous enclosures along the front of the two armies, the battle was mainly an infantry fight.

Three times during the eight hours that the battle lasted the villages were taken and retaken, remaining at the close of the day still in the hands of the French. In Champigny the fighting was close and desperate—from house to house, from barricade to barricade. Late in the afternoon the Comte d'Hérisson, one of Trochu's *aides-de-camp*, rode out from Paris along the frozen roads, bringing a message from the headquarters at the Louvre to the governor, who was with Ducrot on the battlefield. He looked for him first in Champigny. In his journal, he noted that though he had seen many campaigns he had never heard or seen such a fire as that which raged round the village. Infantry were exchanging volleys at close quarters, and the German shells were falling on every side. One of them burst in a cottage as he passed by, and the window with its shutters attached was blown out and flew over the head of his horse. He inquired of a mounted officer if he had seen the general, and though their horses were pulled up side by side, and the riders leant over and shouted into each other's ears, it was with difficulty they could make themselves heard.

Outside Champigny, near the cross road to Brie, he found Trochu and his staff. The general seemed to him to be seeking for death on the field, for he rode slowly across a stretch of open ground where the enemy's shells were bursting on all sides, the hard ground making their explosions all the more dangerous. The *aide-de-camp* gave him the message from Paris. A pigeon had come in from Tours, and it brought a letter from Gambetta, informing him that the Army of the Loire was in full march for the forest of Fontainebleau, and bidding him meet them there with the Army of Paris. For a moment Trochu's face brightened as he heard the news, but he had already realised that Ducrot could not break through the circle of iron in which Paris was enclosed.

The most that the Army of Paris could do that day was to hold the narrow tract of ground it had won on the left bank of the Marne. Even if the Army of the Loire was so near at hand, all he could hope would be that next day its pressure on the German rear would enable him to resume the offensive with some better hope of success. But, alas! the pigeon despatch was the outcome only of Gambetta's sanguine spirit. He spoke of his projects as if they were accomplished facts. True, on November 30th he had ordered the advance of all the corps of the Loire army towards Fontainebleau; true, that yesterday the movement had begun; but this Friday, December 2nd, they were still slowly marching to the north-west of Orléans, engaged with the advance troops of Prince Frederick Charles. It was the first day of the disastrous Battle of Loigny.

Ducrot had also acted as if he meant to keep the promise of his proclamation, and find death if not victory on the field of Champigny. He had more than once rallied his young troops and led them in person against the enemy. In one of the numerous melees he had dashed

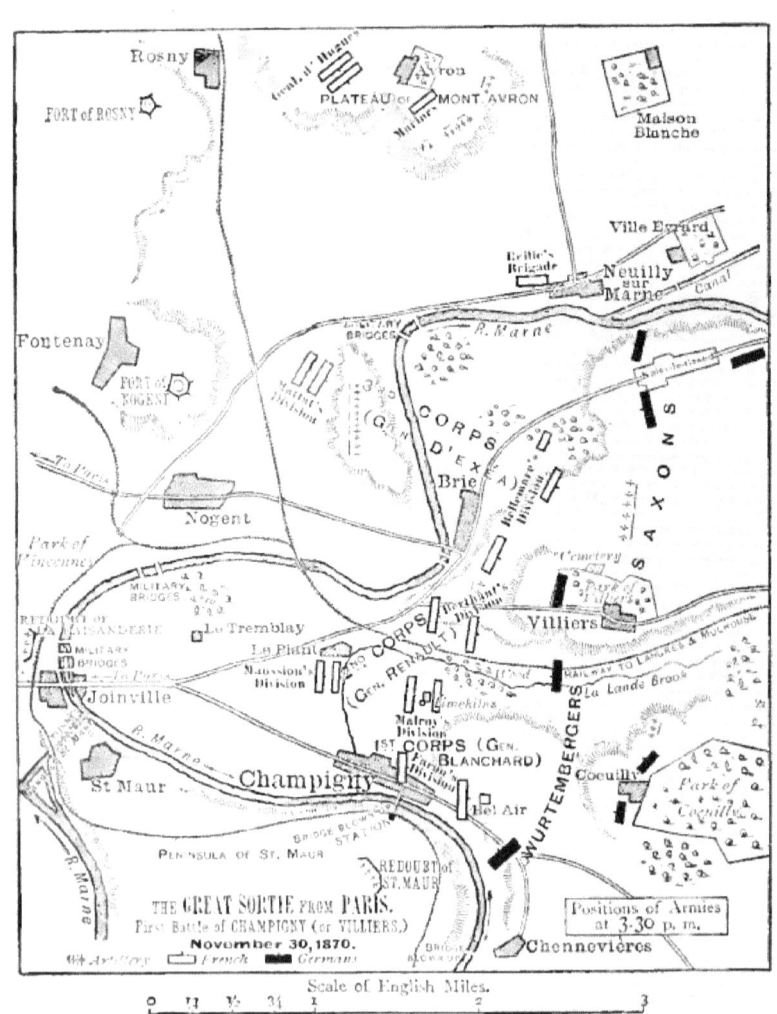

in among the enemy's bayonets, and fought sword in hand until he was disarmed by his blade breaking off short in the body of a German infantry soldier. It was a sword that had been presented to him by some of his soldier friends before the war. But in spite of this dashing bravery, it must be said that it was hardly the work for a general commanding three army corps. His place was not among the bayonets, but at some central point whence he could direct and combine the operations of his corps and divisions.

Towards four o'clock the fire began to slacken. The Germans, inferior in numbers to the French, and attacking them in partly entrenched positions, had failed to break through their line. The second battle of Champigny had ended like the first, leaving the French in possession of the villages on the Marne, but making their chance of breaking out more hopeless than ever. Thus, though the French had held their own when attacked, and though they claimed the day as a victory, the main advantage was with the Germans, had failed.

And it was a costly failure. The Germans had lost in the two days of battle 259 officers and 5,913 men, the French more than double the number—539 officers and 11,546 men. In all, more than 18,000 men had fallen in the fight for the villages on the Marne. The third night of the bivouac on the battlefield was for the French the most wretched of all. The frost was keener than ever, and something like a thousand men were invalided by the cold of that terrible night, many of them dying before the end of the year. In the early morning of Saturday, December 3rd, Trochu and Ducrot visited the bivouacs, and were horrified at the look of weariness and misery on the faces of officers and soldiers. They had sent their picked regiments into battle. They knew they had no troops of the same quality with which to relieve them.

They knew, too, that the Germans in their front had been further reinforced with men and guns. To hold on to Brie and Champigny any longer would have been to risk a fearful disaster. Orders were given to retreat. At various points along the front there was desultory skirmishing with the Prussian outposts, and the artillery was for a while in action on both sides. Meanwhile, division after division fell back across the bridges of Joinville. The Germans did nothing to disturb this retreat. It was only on Sunday morning, December 4th, that they reoccupied Brie and Champigny. A French post held Le Plant to the north-west of the latter village till the morning of the 5th.

Thus, ended the most hopeful effort that the French had made to break through the German besieging lines. The mistake about the

OUTSIDE CHAMPIGNY HE FOUND TROCHU AND HIS STAFF

bridges at the outset did much to increase the difficulties of what was never an easy enterprise. The unfortunate part of the situation was that the French commanders, with such an enormous number of armed men at their disposal in Paris, were able to make only a comparatively small part of them into reliable soldiers. If Trochu had been able to seriously menace other portions of the German lines on the day of Champigny, he could have prevented Von Moltke from reinforcing the Saxons and Wurtembergers along the Marne; and if he had possessed solid reserves of fresh troops he could have replaced the regiments that suffered most in the first day's fight with troops that would have been in condition to renew the battle on the morrow.

As it was, the soldiers of Ducrot's three corps failed, but failed with honour. Whilst they were fighting in front of Paris their comrades of the Loire army were fighting as bravely but with as little result at Loigny. The day that saw the retreat of Ducrot's army across the Marne saw also the defeat of Chanzy on the field of Loigny, and the two events sealed the fate of Paris and of France.

The Franco-Prussian Wars
1870-71

The Battle of Villersexel
January 9-10, 1871
By A. Hilliard Atteridge

The New Year's Day of 1871 was a dark one for France. Two whole armies were captives in Germany. The Prussian flag flew over Metz and Strasburg. Paris was besieged—held fast in a ring of iron through which it had proved impossible, so far, to break a way. The armies of the provinces, Faidherbe's in the north and Chanzy's on the Loire, for all their gallant efforts had suffered repeated defeats. Faidherbe had lost Amiens; Chanzy had been forced to abandon Orléans. And yet amid all this darkness there was just one gleam of hope; and, while most of the defenders of France fought only with the courage of despair, there were among her chiefs some who thought that even at the eleventh hour the tide of conquest might be turned back. Fired with this hope, they played a bold game, and nearly won. For a brief moment in the midst of defeat they had the joy of victory.

After the surrender of Strasburg, the 14th German corps, under the command of General von Werder, which had captured the place, was ordered to complete the conquest of Alsace—on the one hand keeping in check the corps of *franc-tireurs* and volunteers, which, if they were allowed to make any progress in the Vosges, might endanger the communications of the main army with Germany; and, on the other, reducing one by one the minor fortresses of the east of France.

A division of Baden troops, provided with a siege-train, was brought across the Rhine; and Werder, having secured Strasburg by the end of September, pushed forward by Epinal towards Dijon, while, protected by this movement, the Badeners had by the end of October reduced the little fortresses of Neuf-Brisach on the Rhine and Schlestadt on the Ill. During November Werder held Dijon, fighting a number of minor actions with the new French levies under Garibaldi and Cremer; whilst the Badeners, reinforced from his army, began the siege of Belfort, the one place in Alsace over which the tricolour still flew.

Between the southern end of the main range of the Vosges and the first outlying ridges of the Jura there is a gap some miles wide, where the mountains sink down into low hills. Through the central valley of these hills the canal that joins the Rhine and Rhone makes its way. The gap is known to French geographers as the *trouée de Belfort*, taking its name from the fortress on its northern side, which closes it against an invader coming from the direction of the Rhine. Belfort has been a place of strength ever since it was acquired by France under Louis XIV. and fortified by Vauban. Perched on a spur of the Vosges, with its citadel surrounded by a triple girdle of works, it was practically impregnable in the days of the old short-range artillery. If attacked with modern guns, it could be brought under fire from several of the adjacent hilltops.

Under the Second Empire some of these were crowned with outlying forts, but the system of defence was still very incomplete when the war of 1870 began. Colonel Denfert-Rochereau, a man of great resource and determination and a skilful engineer, was put in command of the place after the 4th of September by Gambetta, and he at once proceeded to fortify with earthwork redoubts a circle of positions round the town; working with such a will that, while on September 4th the circuit of the outworks was five miles, on November 3rd, when the Germans closed in upon the northern works, they had to occupy a line of investment nearly twelve miles long.

With a garrison of 17,000 men, chiefly mobiles, national guards, and volunteers, Denfert-Rochereau doggedly defended every inch of ground; and it was not till November 25th that the Germans were able to complete even the investment of the place. Till the end of the year they were still battering at his outworks, and the citadel and the town were untouched.

After the second Battle of Orléans, on December 4th, the left of the Loire army under Chanzy had retired towards Vendôme along the right bank of the river, pursued by the Germans under Prince Frederick Charles. The right, composed of the 15th, 18th, and 20th *corps d'arm*ée, had retreated by the left bank, then to the southward and eastward by Gien to the neighbourhood of Bourges, where General Bourbaki rallied and reorganised it. Ill-fed, incompletely equipped and badly uniformed, the troops had suffered terribly in the retreat to Bourges, but a few days' rest did wonders for them, and by the middle of December the army was again ready to take the field. Gambetta himself had come to Bourges to encourage the troops and co-operate with Bourbaki; and on the 19th the army began to move northward towards Paris, its object being to threaten the communications of Prince Frederick Charles with Versailles and so force him to slacken his pursuit of Chanzy.

On this same day M. de Serres, a young engineer, who had often acted as Gambetta's adviser, arrived at Bourges with a new plan which the government at Bordeaux had already approved—a plan for sending Bourbaki's army to the east of France, where it was to raise the siege of Belfort, and, uniting with Garibaldi and Cremer's troops and the corps which was being formed by General de Bressolles at Lyons, it was to strike northwards at the German communications or make a raid across the Rhine into southern Germany.

It was hoped that Bourbaki's forces could be rapidly conveyed by railway to the east; that Werder could be overwhelmed before he even realised that he had any serious force in his front; and that Belfort and Langres and the south of France could be made the basis for a new campaign, the first effect of which would be to force the Germans to stop their advance on the Loire and think more of guarding the communications by which they were supplied from Germany than of hunting down Chanzy or reducing Paris.

At first sight the plan looked a wild one, but it was sound, and it very nearly succeeded. It is difficult for most people to realise what are the conditions under which an army of some 800,000 men maintains itself in a hostile country in the depth of winter, carrying on at the same time the siege of a great capital like Paris. It is true that some supplies could be obtained in France itself by purchase and requisition, but by December the resources of the districts occupied were nearly exhausted. The army before Paris, the armies that faced Faidherbe in the north and Chanzy in the west, had to be supplied in great part with the ordinary necessaries of life from Germany itself.

Ammunition for the Paris siege-guns, renewed supplies for the armies in the field, all this came by the lines of railway that stretched across eastern France through Champagne and Lorraine, guarded partly by detachments on the lines themselves and in the towns through which they passed, but chiefly protected by Werder's army preventing any stroke from the southward and Manteuffel holding back the levies of the north.

Werder had at most 43,000 men at his disposal. He had had some difficulty in holding on at Dijon and at the same time maintaining before Belfort a sufficient force to press the siege. If 80,000 or 100,000 men, even of inferior quality to his own, could be suddenly thrown against him, he must go, and then the main German Army would have to take swift and effectual means to stay the French advance in the east. Otherwise it would be cut off from Germany and starved. But the crisis in the east would coincide with renewed sorties from Paris, a renewed advance on the Loire and in the north; and it might well be that, under such pressure, the siege of Paris would be raised if only for the brief period necessary to refill its magazine, bring out a large number of the civil inhabitants, reinforce the provincial armies with some of Trochu's best troops, and so change the whole face of the situation.

As in the earlier project for raising the siege of Metz by the march of MacMahon's army to Montmédy, everything depended on rapid movement. Otherwise this bold stroke for the deliverance of Belfort and of France would end in another disaster like that of the previous enterprise. But in the first few hours there was certainly no loss of time. When de Serres submitted his plan to Gambetta, the dictator hesitated to approve it. The movement northwards towards Paris had begun that morning; he based great hopes on it, and this stroke at the German communications seemed too daring. He told de Serres he would leave the decision to Bourbaki himself, and the engineer hurried off to Baugy, north of Bourges, where he found Bourbaki had established his headquarters in one of the houses of the village.

By candlelight in the little room the engineer and the general bent over the map of the east of France, and discussed the plan. The conference was a brief one. Bourbaki thought the bold game could be successfully played, and gave de Serres a note in which he informed Gambetta that, as soon as he received an authorisation cancelling previous orders, he would put his army in movement for the east of France. The order came back by telegraph, and next morning the troops were being moved to the points where they were to entrain, and the southern railways were collecting engines and rolling stock about Bourges.

Gambetta expected great things of Bourbaki. He was one of the most popular soldiers of the Second Empire. He had a record of service extending over thirty-four years. He had fought in Africa, the Crimea, and Italy—everywhere with distinction. Englishmen should remember his name as that of the brigadier who brought up the two first French battalions to the help of our hard-pressed soldiers on

General Von Werder.

General Bourbaki

Léon Gambetta

the terrible morning of Inkerman. At the outbreak of the war with Germany he was in command of the Imperial Guard. He had been brought out of Metz before the end of the siege on a mysterious mission to Chislehurst, and, when he was refused permission to re-enter the fortress, he at once offered his sword to Gambetta, not that he was a Republican, but because all dynastic and partly feelings disappeared in the general interest of the defence of France against the invader.

But unfortunately, Bourbaki during this his last campaign seems to have been a different man from the fiery soldier of Algeria and the Crimea. On the battlefield, when he heard the cannon again, he showed something of his old vigour; but on the march and at the council-board he hesitated, changed his plans, and seemed to labour under a depressing feeling that as an old general of the Empire he could not rely upon those who now followed him to stand by him after a single check. he wrote to a friend

> If it rains or snows too much, they will say it is my fault, and that I have betrayed them.

Though everything depended on speed, the railway transport of the troops to the eastern departments was terribly slow. All was confusion. Trains were blocked for hours on the line, while the men, huddled together in the carriages, shivered with cold, for the ground was deep with snow and all the streams were frozen. Only a single line was available for the greater part of the way from Bourges to Chalons-sur-Saône. The 24th corps from Lyons reached the same point by another line. It had originally been intended to move only two corps—the 18th (General Billot) and the 20th (General Clinchant) from Bourges, leaving the 15th to hold in check the Prussian corps of observation under Zastrow, which had moved southwards from Versailles. But Bourbaki, though the resources of transport were already taxed to the utmost, insisted on the 15th being also placed at his disposal, and after some hesitation the government granted his request.

At last, in the first week of January, the four corps were concentrated between Besançon and Chalons-sur-Saône—a movement which ought to have been completed before New Year's Day.

Werder had already found out that a considerable force was being accumulated in his front, and on December 26th he abandoned his advanced position at Dijon. One of the German regiments marched out of the town carrying its gaily-decorated Christmas tree on a cart, and as they passed along the street the soldiers threw some of the

The Germans took the defenders of the barricade in reverse

bonbons to the children. In order to be ready to oppose any attempt to relieve Belfort, Werder concentrated his forces between Vesoul and Villersexel in the valley of the Ognon. On January 4th, he received orders to push reconnaissances to the southward, and the result was some skirmishing between the German scouting parties and Bourbaki's advanced troops.

Three days later the German headquarters staff at Versailles telegraphed to Werder orders and information which showed that Moltke considered that a very serious danger was threatening the Germans in Eastern France. Werder was informed that he would be largely reinforced from the north, and that Manteuffel would presently take over the eastern command. Meanwhile he was at any cost to keep Belfort blockaded; use the most severe measures of repression in case the population of the occupied departments attempted an insurrection; fall back before Bourbaki if he could not hold his ground, but even so take care not to lose touch of him. At the same time, he was directed to be ready to block the southern passes of the Vosges, and to prepare to destroy the Basle and Mulhouse railway-, so as to make a French *coup-de-main* on the upper Rhine more difficult. A hundred thousand Frenchmen were gathering round Besançon, and Werder was outnumbered nearly three to one.

Bourbaki had been hesitating as to whether he should march direct on Vesoul in order to strike at the field-army under Werder, or move immediately to the relief of Belfort. On this same 7th of January he decided on the latter course. On the 8th he concentrated three of his corps about Montbozon in the Ognon valley—Billot on the left, Clinchant in the centre. Bressolles on the right. Two battalions and a squadron of cavalry were pushed forward to the little town of Villersexel, where there was a bridge across the river and an important junction of roads. The main body of the French was about eight miles south-west of the town. Eight miles north-west of the same point Werder had concentrated his army about Noroy-le-Bourg, intending next day to fall on the flank of the French, trusting to the superior quality of his troops to more than compensate for inferior numbers.

Early on the morning of the 9th the two armies were thus converging on Villersexel, which was held by the French advanced guard. The first division of Billot's corps (nine battalions and fourteen guns) was moving up the right bank of the Ognon, and had reached the village of Esprels at nine in the morning, when the cavalry scouts brought in news that the Germans were about a mile in front near the village of Marast. This was Von der Goltz's infantry division, forming Werder's right. Within half an hour the two divisions were in contact, and all day long the fight continued among the snowy woods between Marast and Esprels. The French, mostly young troops, stood their ground well, and resisted every effort of the Germans to break through or turn them.

Once only, towards one o'clock, there was a temporary panic in the Bois des Brosses, which was held by chasseurs and *franc-tireurs*. The 34th Pomeranian infantry fought their way into the wood, and had captured half of it when they were driven out by a counter attack made by fresh troops, a brigade of linesmen and mobiles which was gallantly led to the charge by its brigadier. General Robert. On this part of the field the fighting ended with the short winter day, soon after four o'clock.

But in Villersexel itself and on the other side of the river the fight was a much more serious affair. In 1870 the town numbered about 1,500 inhabitants. It is built on the slope of a hill on the left bank of the Ognon. The main street runs from the Place Neuve (at the point where the Belfort road enters the town) to the stone bridge which crosses the river. Close to the bridge several side streets run into the main street. On the west side of the town stood the splendid *château* of Grammont—a three-storeyed building, with two wings, ending in high-roofed pavilions. Beyond the *château* extended a wooded park, and at the western end of the park a large island divided the Ognon, and both branches were crossed by foot-bridges, that nearest the park being a small suspension bridge.

On the evening of the 8th the town had been occupied by two battalions of the 20th corps (Clinchant), one being a battalion of Corsican mobiles and the other a battalion of mobiles of the Vosges. General Ségard commanded this advanced guard. He barricaded the stone bridge, loop-holed the houses along the river, and put a company of the Corsicans into the *château*; but by a strange oversight he took no precautions to guard the foot-bridge at the end of the park.

At nine on the morning of the 9th the sound of cannon was heard away to the left on the north bank of the river. It was the beginning of Von der Goltz's attack on Billot's first division. This put the little garrison of Villersexel on the alert, and soon they saw the head of a column issuing from the wood of Le Grand Fougeret, opposite the town. They opened fire from the houses and the barricade, and the Germans threw forward a line of skirmishers, while two batteries took up a position on the high ground beyond the wood, and began to throw shells into the streets and the park. Higher up the German engineers had bridged the river near Aillevans, and a division was crossing there, with orders to move down to the eastward of the town and stop the advance of the main body of the 20th corps, which was coming up in that direction.

The Germans repeatedly advanced towards the long bridge as if they meant to rush it, but each time they fell back under the heavy fire from the houses. Along the banks of the river the rival firing lines exchanged volleys at close range. Twelve o'clock came, and the Germans had made no progress. But about this time a lieutenant, with half a company of the 25th Fusilier regiment working along the river bank, reached the hamlet of La Forge, and, to his surprise and delight, found an unguarded foot-bridge leading across to the big island in the Ognon. Cautiously reconnoitring the island, he came on the suspension bridge, giving free access to the park. He could hardly believe his good luck. Sending back word to his captain of what he had discovered, he hastened to secure a footing among the trees of the park.

The rest of the company, and after it the greater part of the battalion, stole across the bridge into the trees, and then the word was given to advance. The *château* was taken with a rush. Surprised by an attack from a quarter which they thought quite secure, some of tile Corsicans were bayoneted, about a hundred were taken prisoners, the rest fled into the town. Pressing down through the streets, the Germans took the defenders of the barricade in reverse, and the bridge was captured. By one o'clock the Germans held the town. To the eastward, the heads of their columns had reached Villers-la-Ville and the woods towards Magny.

Between one and two o'clock there was a lull in the fight on the south side of the Ognon. Then Bourbaki and Clinchant, the commander of the 20th corps, rode up by Magny and directed a general attack upon the positions held by the Germans. Two divisions moved against their left, while a third pushed forward to attempt the recapture of Villersexel. Further down the river, at Pont-sur-Ognon, a division of the 18th corps crossed to the south side of the stream to support its comrades of the 20th in their attack on Villersexel. It was commanded by Admiral Penhoat, a brave Breton sailor, who that day showed himself a good general. Between three and four o'clock Villers-la-Ville was captured.

It was a strong position: the village, with a wood close beside it,

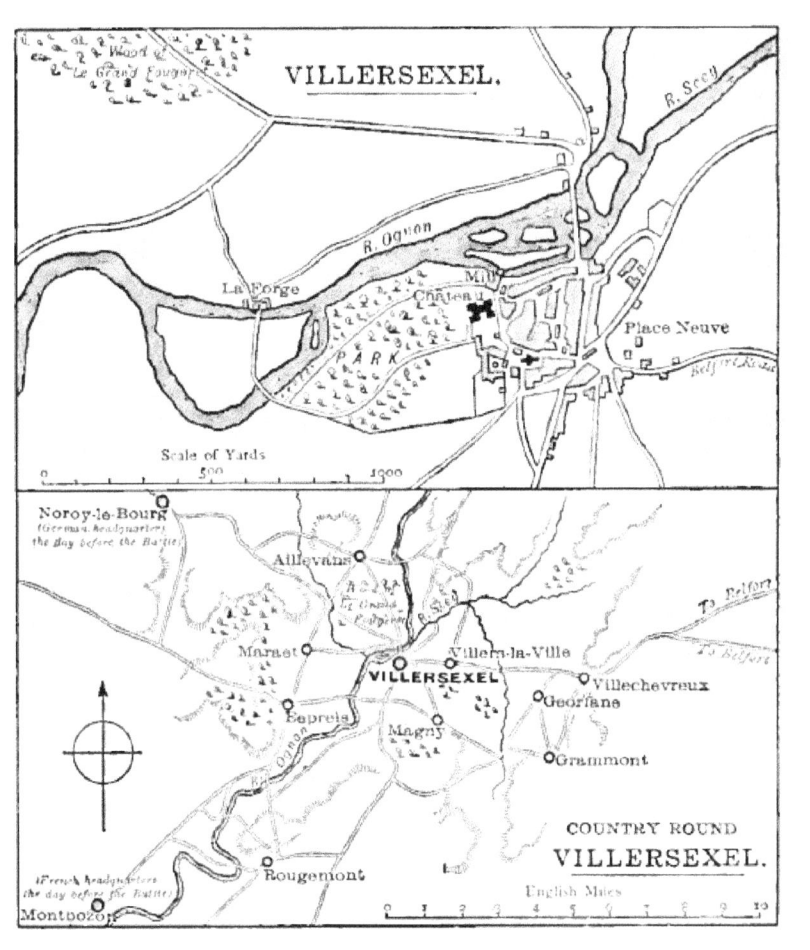

stands at the crest of a long, gentle slope—a natural glacis, like that which made the attack of St. Privat so terrible for the Prussian Guard on August 18th. Now, covered as it was with deep snow, this long slope gave the garrison of the village a splendid field of fire. Nevertheless, Logerot's brigade of two battalions of the mobiles of the Jura moved steadily to the attack, a battalion deployed on each side of the road, the general on horseback between them, quietly signalling, now to one, now to the other, with his kept, escaping the balls that whistled round him as it by a miracle. But, bravely as it was made, this front attack would probably have failed if it had not been combined with a turning movement against the left of the village by Polignac's brigade. Under this double attack the Germans gave way.

But they had a further reason for not making a prolonged or desperate defence of this part of the position. Werder was now aware that he had in his front on the south side of the river the three divisions of Clinchant's corps and one of Billot's. True, all these troops were not actually engaged, but they could come into action very soon. Further east, the 24th corps, under de Bressolles, was marching by the villages of Grammont, Georfans, and Villechevreux—a movement which outflanked the whole German position.

Bressolles, with a woeful lack of initiative, was marching quietly to the points assigned to him in the general order for the advance of the army on the 9th. He could hear the cannon thundering away to his left, but only four companies of one of his battalions marched towards the fight and took some part in it. Had de Bressolles pushed boldly in behind Werder's left, the battle might have been, not a defeat, but a disaster for the Germans. Werder, used as he was to the German habit of each corps commander moving at once to the help of a comrade who was actually engaged in a battle, evidently expected some such movement on his left; and, seeing that the French were making a good fight of it, and that there were nowhere signs of that collapse of the new levies on which he had counted, he sent an order between three and four o'clock to withdraw all the troops to the north bank of the river, except those actually holding Villersexel. His guns retired partly by the stone bridge in the town, but mostly by the temporary bridges at Aillevans.

Then the French attack came rolling on to the boundary walls of the park and the outlying houses of the town. A little after four the sun had set, and the attack on Villersexel began amid the gathering twilight of the winter evening. But the sky was clear, the stars began to

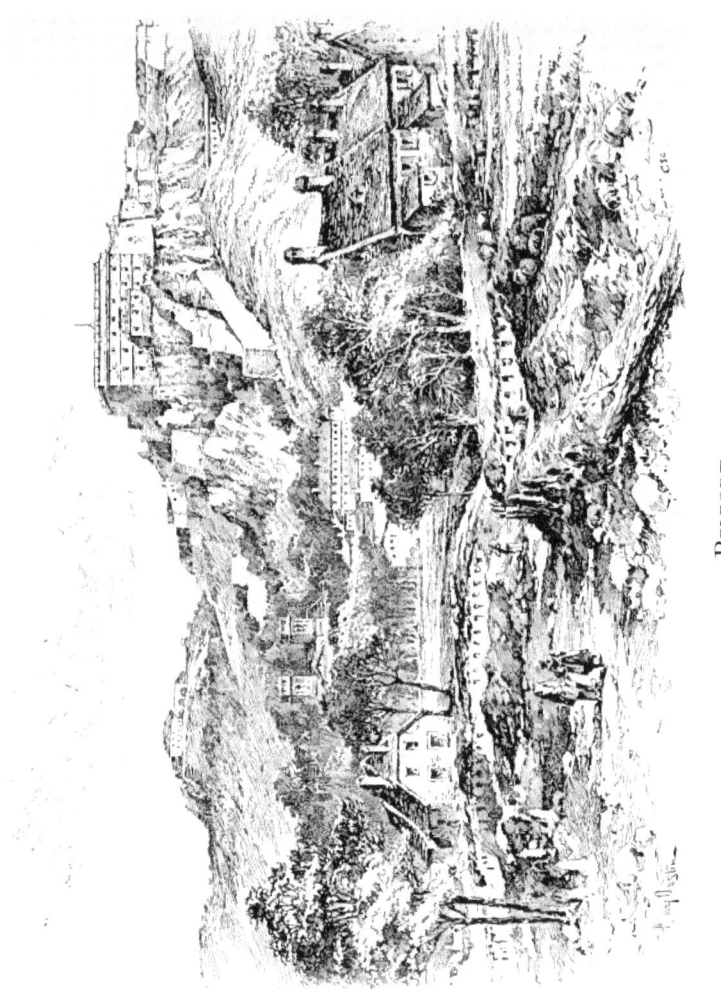

Belfort

come out, and the moon, near the full, shining on the snow gave light enough to continue the struggle. Bourbaki, flushed with something of the old eagerness which had made him famous in Africa and in Italy, was well up to the front. When the mobiles of the Pyrenees and the Vosges began to fall back under the heavy fire that met them as they advanced against the park, Bourbaki pushed through them, and, sword in hand, placed himself at their head. "À *moi, l'infanterie!*" he called out. "Stand by me. Have French soldiers forgotten how to charge?" And they rallied and dashed forward with the shout of "*Vive la France! Vive la République!*" One of Clinchant's divisions was attacking the town. Admiral Penhoat's battalions won on their way with the bayonet into the park and attacked the *château*. The Germans set it on fire as they gave way. But the victors arrived in time to extinguish the flames and to rescue the French prisoners made earlier in the day.

It was after six o'clock, but the fight was not over yet. On the north bank the cannon were silent, but in the town, at the end of every street, Frenchmen and Germans were firing into each other at close quarters, or fighting hand-to-hand with the bayonet. Several houses were on fire, and the struggle was becoming a fierce one, in which there was very little thought of quarter. At one point, as the French pushed into the courtyard of a house held by the Germans, an officer appeared at one of the windows, and, raising his hand, said something. All that the French heard was the word "*prisonnier*"; but they concluded, perhaps incorrectly, that he was asking to be allowed to surrender with his garrison.

The French captain ordered the "Cease fire," and entered the courtyard. The next moment he and several of his men fell under a volley from the windows. The whole may have been one of those unfortunate mistakes which occur in all wars. But the Frenchmen thought it was a piece of murderous treachery. Faggots soaked with tar were brought up, under a heavy fire; they were piled up against the door and walls of the house and ignited, and not a man of the German garrison came out of the house alive. It was Bazeilles on a smaller scale.

Nine German battalions held the town—*Landwehr* men from the eastern provinces, Poles, and Pomeranians—determined men, mostly about thirty years of age, coming of good fighting races, and veterans of the war of 1866. Outnumbered as they were, they made a dogged resistance. Towards seven o'clock four *Landwehr* battalions tried to retake the *château*. They actually got possession of the lower floor, but the French held out in the basement cellars and in the upper sto-

An Incident in the Battle of Villersexel

ries. There was a hard fight in corridors and on staircases—here with crossed bayonets, there with the rifle, firing through holes cut in floors and ceilings. The *château* at last took fire, and both parties had to abandon it. Colonel von Krane, who led the attack, narrowly escaped being cut off and burned to death.

By the light of the blazing building the Germans were driven back into the streets of the town. At ten they broke into the park again, only to be once more repulsed. Gradually the fight became confined to the streets near the bridge, where both sides fought behind barricades rapidly improvised, by the French to secure the ground they had won, by the Germans to maintain themselves in the streets and the little square near the bridge end.

For three hours, from ten till after one, this desperate street-fight went on by the light of blazing houses. In narrow lanes, in courtyards, inside the houses, men fought hand-to-hand. It was one of the hottest fights in the whole war. Strangely enough, both sides seemed to think only of pushing new forces directly into the narrow space where the battle was raging—the Germans by the stone bridge from the north bank, the French by the streets leading to the park. Neither party tried to push round beyond the town and enter it from other points; and outside the streets the troops not actually engaged listened to the din that rose from the little town, and watched the flames that shot up from the blazing chateau and the burning houses—flames in which many of the wounded were destroyed. One of the horrors of the fight was the smell of burning flesh in the crowded lanes.

It was between one and two in the morning of the 10th when the Germans at last let go their hold of the town and retired across the stone bridge. General Billot watched the fight from the ground he had held all day on the north side. The Marquis de Grammont stood beside him, in the light of the flames that still rose from the ruins of his home on the other side of the river. He offered the general to guide through the darkness a column which could fall on the rear of the Germans and cut off their retreat, but his proposal was rejected. It was felt at the moment that enough had been done. A victory had been won, and there was no disposition to run further risks in the hope of still greater results.

When the *château* was recaptured by the French about seven o'clock, M. de Serres, Gambetta's delegate, rode back to the point near Rougemont (more than five miles from Villersexel), to which the field-telegraph had been brought up, and thence, a little before 8 p.m., he telegraphed to the Government at Bordeaux:

> The battle ended at seven p.m. The night prevents us from estimating the importance of our victory. The general commanding-in-chief bivouacs in the centre of the battlefield, and the army has occupied all the positions assigned to it in the general orders for the march issued yesterday. Villersexel, the key of the position, was stormed to the cry of '*Vive la France! Vive la République!*'

The government telegraphed its congratulations to Bourbaki. He received them whilst the night battle was still going on. De Serres, in his eagerness to send the good news, had said that the battle ended at seven. It continued for something more than six hours after that.

The Prussian staff made a more serious mistake in its report. It declared that Werder had held his own "against the 18th and 20th corps and part of the 24th." But neither the 18th nor the 20th brought all its troops into action (though doubtless their being near the field influenced the result); and as for the "part of the 24th," it amounted to only four companies. It is not easy to say how many troops were actually engaged in the fight from first to last. Probably Werder had about 20,000 men in and near Villersexel, on both sides of the river, of which about 12,000 were seriously engaged. Bourbaki had about 50,000 in the 18th and 20th corps, and 20,000 more in the 24th on his extreme right.

But of these 20,000 not 300 were engaged, and of the 50,000 about half must have been in action at one time or another. In the fighting in the town and the park after sundown there were about 7,000 or 8,000 Germans against 9,000 French. Everywhere—except, perhaps, in Billot's fight against Von der Golz, where the opposing forces were about even—the advantage of numbers was on the side of the French; but they were mostly new levies, and they had to expel a veteran enemy from a very strong position. The mobiles and volunteers who fought their way through the streets of Villersexel were brave soldiers, and Bourbaki might well build high hopes upon this first battle in his campaign for the relief of Belfort.

Considering how much street-fighting there was in the evening and night, the losses were not heavy. The Germans admitted a loss of over six hundred men, the French about seven hundred. The Germans carried away some hundreds of French prisoners with them. Of the townspeople of Villersexel only one is known to have taken part in the fight, and he was a Polish refugee, Felix Romanowski, who had settled at Villersexel after fighting in the Polish insurrection of 1863. He shouldered a rifle on the morning of the 9th, and was unwounded at the end of the day. It is not unlikely that part of the time he was firing at his own fellow countrymen of the Polish provinces of Prussia.

To win a battle is one thing; to reap the full fruits of victory is another. Time was all-important to Bourbaki if his enterprise was to have any chance of success. Yet, instead of pressing Werder with all his available forces next day, and driving him northwards away from the roads leading to Belfort, he lost precious hours and days in hesitation, only to find, when at last he resumed his advance, that the Germans, largely reinforced, were ready once more to throw themselves across his path. The victory of Villersexel was almost the last flicker of hope for France. Héricourt, Montbéliard, and Pontarlier witnessed the collapse of the daring plan, the execution of which had been so well begun in the hard fighting through the short winter day and the long night at Villersexel.

ALSO FROM LEONAUR
AVAILABLE IN SOFTCOVER OR HARDCOVER WITH DUST JACKET

AT THEM WITH THE BAYONET by Donald F. Featherstone—The first Anglo-Sikh War 1845-1846.

STEPHEN CRANE'S BATTLES by Stephen Crane—Nine Decisive Battles Recounted by the Author of 'The Red Badge of Courage'.

THE GURKHA WAR by H. T. Prinsep—The Anglo-Nepalese Conflict in North East India 1814-1816.

FIRE & BLOOD by G. R. Gleig—The burning of Washington & the battle of New Orleans, 1814, through the eyes of a young British soldier.

SOUND ADVANCE! by Joseph Anderson—Experiences of an officer of HM 50th regiment in Australia, Burma & the Gwalior war.

THE CAMPAIGN OF THE INDUS by Thomas Holdsworth—Experiences of a British Officer of the 2nd (Queen's Royal) Regiment in the Campaign to Place Shah Shuja on the Throne of Afghanistan 1838 - 1840.

WITH THE MADRAS EUROPEAN REGIMENT IN BURMA by John Butler—The Experiences of an Officer of the Honourable East India Company's Army During the First Anglo-Burmese War 1824 - 1826.

IN ZULULAND WITH THE BRITISH ARMY by Charles L. Norris-Newman—The Anglo-Zulu war of 1879 through the first-hand experiences of a special correspondent.

BESIEGED IN LUCKNOW by Martin Richard Gubbins—The first Anglo-Sikh War 1845-1846.

A TIGER ON HORSEBACK by L. March Phillips—The Experiences of a Trooper & Officer of Rimington's Guides - The Tigers - during the Anglo-Boer war 1899 - 1902.

SEPOYS, SIEGE & STORM by Charles John Griffiths—The Experiences of a young officer of H.M.'s 61st Regiment at Ferozepore, Delhi ridge and at the fall of Delhi during the Indian mutiny 1857.

CAMPAIGNING IN ZULULAND by W. E. Montague—Experiences on campaign during the Zulu war of 1879 with the 94th Regiment.

THE STORY OF THE GUIDES by G.J. Younghusband—The Exploits of the Soldiers of the famous Indian Army Regiment from the northwest frontier 1847 - 1900.

AVAILABLE ONLINE AT **www.leonaur.com**
AND FROM ALL GOOD BOOK STORES

ALSO FROM LEONAUR
AVAILABLE IN SOFTCOVER OR HARDCOVER WITH DUST JACKET

ZULU: 1879 *by D.C.F. Moodie & the Leonaur Editors*—The Anglo-Zulu War of 1879 from contemporary sources: First Hand Accounts, Interviews, Dispatches, Official Documents & Newspaper Reports.

THE RED DRAGOON *by W.J. Adams*—With the 7th Dragoon Guards in the Cape of Good Hope against the Boers & the Kaffir tribes during the 'war of the axe' 1843-48'.

THE RECOLLECTIONS OF SKINNER OF SKINNER'S HORSE *by James Skinner*—James Skinner and his 'Yellow Boys' Irregular cavalry in the wars of India between the British, Mahratta, Rajput, Mogul, Sikh & Pindarree Forces.

A CAVALRY OFFICER DURING THE SEPOY REVOLT *by A. R. D. Mackenzie*—Experiences with the 3rd Bengal Light Cavalry, the Guides and Sikh Irregular Cavalry from the outbreak to Delhi and Lucknow.

A NORFOLK SOLDIER IN THE FIRST SIKH WAR *by J W Baldwin*—Experiences of a private of H.M. 9th Regiment of Foot in the battles for the Punjab, India 1845-6.

TOMMY ATKINS' WAR STORIES: 14 FIRST HAND ACCOUNTS—Fourteen first hand accounts from the ranks of the British Army during Queen Victoria's Empire.

THE WATERLOO LETTERS *by H. T. Siborne*—Accounts of the Battle by British Officers for its Foremost Historian.

NEY: GENERAL OF CAVALRY VOLUME 1—1769-1799 *by Antoine Bulos*—The Early Career of a Marshal of the First Empire.

NEY: MARSHAL OF FRANCE VOLUME 2—1799-1805 *by Antoine Bulos*—The Early Career of a Marshal of the First Empire.

AIDE-DE-CAMP TO NAPOLEON *by Philippe-Paul de Ségur*—For anyone interested in the Napoleonic Wars this book, written by one who was intimate with the strategies and machinations of the Emperor, will be essential reading.

TWILIGHT OF EMPIRE *by Sir Thomas Ussher & Sir George Cockburn*—Two accounts of Napoleon's Journeys in Exile to Elba and St. Helena: Narrative of Events by Sir Thomas Ussher & Napoleon's Last Voyage: Extract of a diary by Sir George Cockburn.

PRIVATE WHEELER *by William Wheeler*—The letters of a soldier of the 51st Light Infantry during the Peninsular War & at Waterloo.

AVAILABLE ONLINE AT **www.leonaur.com**
AND FROM ALL GOOD BOOK STORES

www.ingramcontent.com/pod-product-compliance
Lightning Source LLC
Chambersburg PA
CBHW031619160426
43196CB00006B/203